With Love, The Argentina Family

Memories of Tango and Kugel; *Mate* with Knishes

Mirta Ines Trupp

Table of Contents

Dedication

This narrative is presented with tremendous gratitude to my parents. It was due to their courage, coupled with love and devotion to each other and to their daughters, that they were able to leave The Argentina Family. It was the same impetus that gave their grandparents the courage to leave the *shtetls* of Russia. I hope my story serves as a testament of their journey from the *pogroms* of the Ukraine to the "New Jerusalem" in the Argentinean Pampas; from the cobble stone streets of Buenos Aires to where "the streets were paved in gold," *die goldene medina*: America.

As children, we might censure our parents for their actions, not understanding the underlying need that motivates their choices. It is not until we ourselves are parents that we realize the truth-*there are no guidebooks, no instructions.* We have snippets of superstitions passed on by our families, tidbits of tradition given to us by our culture. Most importantly, we have an overwhelming sense of love. It is with this emotion that we endeavor to set our children on their own journeys.

I dedicate this tale to my children and pray that wherever they go-*wherever the road leads them*-they go, with love.

Author's Note

The following story is based on my experiences, at times seen through rose-colored glasses, construed through ignorance, misunderstanding or simply the naiveté that shelters a young girl. My recounting of these events does not mean to represent anyone else's reality; they are reflections of my distinctive journey as an immigrant under considerably unique circumstances. Although countless of Argentine immigrants have come to the United States, many of them of mixed ethnicities, my story tells the tale of a multicultural girl who, because of her father's employment, divided her life in between her home country and her adopted country. The story of the whirlwind courtship that ensued could only have taken place under these circumstances.

I have attempted to share rich characters and unique scenarios some of which are by today's standards intrinsically innocent, but are no less real. I would like to thank my friends and family who not only offered their encouragement, but their *time.* Thank you for your opinions and suggestions. Events have been treated with a modest amount of artistic license, **names have been changed** in the attempt to provide a modicum of privacy; nonetheless the story is a proper accounting of my life as a Jewish, Russian, Argentine, American immigrant. ~ Mirta

Passport Entries

Date of Departure	Port	Date of Arrival	Port
Dec. 07, 1962	Argentina	Dec. 08, 1962	USA
April 03, 1969	Argentina	June 07, 1969	USA
Aug. 12, 1971	Argentina	Sept. 11, 1971	USA
March 18, 1972	Argentina	April 18, 1972	USA
July 05, 1973	Argentina	Aug. 02, 1973	USA
March 15, 1974	Argentina	April 13, 1974	USA
Sept. 06, 1974	Argentina	Sept. 28, 1974	USA
Dec. 26, 1976	Argentina	Jan. 21, 1977	USA
July 10,1978	Argentina	Aug. 04, 1978	USA
June 28, 1980	Argentina	Oct. 10, 1980	USA
July 12, 1981	Argentina	Aug. 21, 1981	USA
Sept. 11, 1981	Argentina	Illegible	USA
Dec. 20, 1981	Argentina	Jan. 06, 1982	USA
April 02, 1982	Argentina	April 10, 1982	USA
Aug. 05, 1982	Argentina	Aug. 08, 1982	USA
Oct. 07, 1982	Argentina	Oct. 21, 1982	USA
Nov. 25, 1982	Argentina	Nov. 29, 1982	USA
Dec. 24, 1982	Argentina	Jan. 06, 1983	USA

Disillusioned Dreams

For as long as I could remember, my mother, Carolina, cried about The Argentina Family. Although my father, Ruben, was thrilled to be finally living in the United States, Mami could not overcome her grief and feelings of isolation. You see, Papi had always dreamt of coming to the United States, but my mother had not.

My father was the orator of the family or more to the point; he was the *infamous* orator that everyone wished to avoid. For as many tales as he would like to impart, there were as many excuses to escape his lengthy discourses. During my adolescence, I admittedly was one of the great deserters, but as a child, when I was yet his princess and he, my knight in shining armor, Papi's stories were legendary and I was a captive audience. As I grew out of my rebellious stage and my father was seen once more in the frame of hero, rather than tyrant, his anecdotes painted scenarios that inspired curiosity and illuminated previously misunderstood situations. One such conversation was the topic of our immigration and the various circumstances that propelled his dream.

In the 1940's, Argentina was experiencing a roller coaster ride with Juan Peron. With his populist ideology, Peron was causing wild inflation and socioeconomic upheavals. He closed down newspapers and had political opposition members imprisoned and tortured. Under his rule, worker's unions grew and government programs increased, while the *peso* lost its value and inflation ascended to numbers never seen before. Although a world war had raged on for years, Argentina had maintained neutral; its government rejecting appeals to sever diplomatic ties with the Axis until 1945 when they conceded under pressure from the United States. However Argentina, considered having the most powerful militia in South America, never formally participated in any military action against Germany or Japan. At the age of 20, my father, Ruben was drafted into such an army, an army with dubious affiliations. His experiences there would form another chapter in the accounting of his exodus.

It was during boot camp that my father's background in track and field and penchant for acrobatic stunts caught the eye of his superiors. The slender, athletic man from Bahia Blanca was well suited for supplementary detail. Shortly after completing his basic training, Papi was informed that he had been chosen to serve in Peron's Guard of Honor, the *Granaderos*. Although they were mostly a ceremonial unit, it was considered a tremendous honor to be selected. At six feet, Papi was the shortest of the eleven other soldiers in the elite group. It was because of this national pride in the *Granaderos* that Sergeant Lomeli was outraged that the Jew, fresh off the train from the farmland, was allowed to join the others in the group; all proud and deserving Argentines.

The sergeant followed the men back into their barracks one afternoon after their daily drill. When he reached Sgt. Farinella, Lomeli voiced his concerns over the selection of Private Trupp. "I don't understand how this dirty Jew, this *poor excuse* for an Argentine soldier, could be allowed to participate in the *Granaderos*," Lomeli hissed. "This honor should be reserved for true Argentines and those faithful to our Church."

Sgt. Farinella pulled his colleague aside and out of earshot of the men. "Trupp's height, along with the fact that he is extremely agile and well suited for the rigorous maneuvers caught our attention," Farinella replied. "Didn't you see him catapult over a jeep the other day? He completed a summersault before landing! With all their drilling and parading, Trupp is a good choice for the *Granaderos*."

"But he is a *dirty* Jew!" Lomeli pushed Farinella aside and began walking away.

Papi couldn't help overhearing the outburst. The others in the barracks began to notice the commotion as well. He approached the sergeant and discretely said, "Sgt. Farinella, sir, if there is any question of my participation; I would willingly step aside for another candidate."

Unfortunately, Lomeli heard the comment and stormed back to where the two men were conversing. "You do not *deserve* to represent the Argentine army or to stand in honor alongside those who would protect *our* president. You are a lousy Jew and your mother is a filthy Jewish whore," the incensed sergeant spewed.

My father reached back and threw a punch before he even realized what he was doing. It was only when his fist collided with the sergeant's jaw, that Papi realized that he assaulted a superior officer. Lomeli had been taken by surprise and fell back with the impact. He slowly came to his feet and shouted for the military police. Farinella was not able to intercede on Papi's behalf when Lomeli ordered his soldier to a month in solitary confinement.

After only two days of sitting in the dark, damp cell, my father felt the strains of claustrophobic terror overwhelm him. He began pacing in the tiny quarters as he went over the events that led him to his current predicament. Working himself into a panic and suddenly unable to catch his breath, he fell into a fit of despair. He cried out to the guard for mercy, no longer able to bear his confinement. The guard couldn't help but hear the ruckus and reluctantly, sent a message to the soldier's superior officer. Farinella appeared shortly after and spoke to the guard in hushed tones. Papi heard his cell door open and saw his sergeant there.

"Trupp, get a hold of yourself!" the officer barked his disapproval. "You are to be a *Granadero*, for God's sake!"

My father explained that he was overwrought and feeling claustrophic. He listened while his sergeant roared his disapproval but heard his anger give way to understanding.

"You must pay the price for your actions," the officer replied firmly. "That being said, you know, I probably would have done the same thing. I cannot override Lomeli's orders; I will, however, instruct the guard to allow you to sit in the hallway during the day. He'll have to lock you up at night. Is that understood?" With the private's gratitude ringing in his ears, Sgt. Farinella left his orders with the guard; my father was allowed to remain in the hallway.

Papi leaned his head against the cool tiled wall and closed his eyes. He breathed deeply for the first time since his breakdown in the barracks. He thought of Lomeli and the other men who believed like him. My father, a Jew practically in name only, knew that anti-Semitism was part of life in Argentina. He had grown accustomed to the sneers and jokes. The fact that he knew almost nothing of his religion or its history was a bitter consequence of his grandparents trying desperately to assimilate with the Argentines. How ironic that they virtually gave up their culture and traditions and still, they were not accepted as true countrymen.

My father had had his fill of the dirty politics, governments being overthrown, and dictatorships being established. The country could not progress under these conditions and he knew that there was no future here for him. The claustrophobic panic of the jail cell was nothing compared to the feeling of impotence when he thought of his life ahead. Papi had always been a fan of American movies. With his eyes still closed, he pictured his favorite actors, Errol Flynn, John Wayne, Kirk Douglas. He recalled the various characters and their heroic struggles. Somehow, the good guy always won. Wasn't that the way in America? You work hard, you play by the rules and you are left alone to lead your life. He wasn't kidding himself; he knew America wasn't perfect, but one way or another; he'd have his shot at the American dream; the Argentine dream, the vision of his grandparents, was dead.

When he completed his time in the army, Papi returned to his family and informed them that he planned to sign up with the Merchant Marines and eventually immigrate to the United States of America. His brother Elias however managed to talk him out of it, convincing Papi that he would never survive the loneliness and innumerable hardships on his own. Elias promised his younger brother that if things didn't change in Argentina, they would make the trip together and begin a new life for their families in America. For years, they tried a variety of ventures, including running a store together selling plastics and household goods. On one infamous occasion, Peron's henchmen came asking for "voluntary" donations for Evita's social programs. The brothers knew there was no getting out of contributing; the question was *how much*? Apparently, the amount offered was not enough and later that evening, the store was vandalized. They were fortunate; the damage was purely monetary-others had not been so lucky. While the poor and ignorant hailed Evita's warped *Robin Hood* mentality, the middle-class suffered the reality. There was no true reform- no growth-no prosperity. The country's coffers were being raped while the poor were thrown scraps and taught to be beholden; Evita's programs paid with the blood and toil of the masses.

Almost ten years later, my parents met and as they made plans for their future, my father told my mother about his dream of immigrating to America. I suppose she never completely believed that he would put those plans into action. They married on July 9, 1960 and about two years later, I was born. My parents wanted to name me after a beloved grandmother and a long departed aunt, but *Marem Ides* was not acceptable in the country that demanded names be culturally identifiable and in sync with the national language. So my parents, following the tradition of most assimilated

Ashkenazi Jews, chose the first initials of my ancestors and named me the acceptable, Mirta Ines.

The situation in Argentina was becoming more and more unpredictable; the politics, the economy, and anti-Semitism weighed heavily on the minds of the Jewish community and population at large. The previous decades had been marked with constant military rebellions. The presidential palace, the Casa Rosada, had been bombed in 1955. Twenty civilians were arrested and murdered in 1956 during another attempted coup. Between 1960 and 1962, the year of my birth, the Trupp family, along with fellow Jewish Argentines, watched in horror and disbelief as new far-right parties came into play. One such group, the Tacuara Nationalist Movement was known as a *guerrilla* group and among other things, was extremely anti-Semitic.

The brothers had had enough and quickly began making their plans and getting their papers in order. They arranged to travel to Houston, Texas where several of their cousins had settled a few years before. Tío Elias and my father announced their plans to their parents one evening after dinner. Bobe Flora and Zeide Simon were not at all surprised. In fact, Bobe Flora simply said softly, "You go with love and God's blessings."

Misunderstandings

I was about eight months old when Papi and Tío Elias left Argentina. The men traveled ahead to arrange for housing and find jobs. Papi spoke "a little English" thanks to his preparations in the renowned British academy called Toil and Chat. He was aware that he had a limited vocabulary but much like his fellow Argentine expatriates, he was anxious to learn and expand his skills. Papi first realized that his skills needed honing when he and Tío Elias were seeking transportation from the international airport. He came across a young lady directing travelers and in his best British accent he said, "Excuse me, I do not mean to molest you, but..." Of course, he was translating from the Spanish word *molestar* meaning "to bother."

As soon as the young lady regained her composure, she was able to direct the two men to the nearest taxi stand. Tío Elias realized from the young lady's muffled laughter that Papi's question was not quite what it should have been. He elbowed his brother and mockingly declared, "You're such a smooth talker, just like *Car-ee Grran!*"(Cary Grant)

Papi was an artisan and had trained in the field of fine woodwork. He quickly found employment in those early days in Houston and was overjoyed that he was making a good salary, even if it meant working in an assembly line in a cabinetmaker's shop. Tío Elias also found work and together, the brothers began setting aside their money to bring their families to America. They made friends with a few of the tenants in their apartment building. The majority of their friends were Spanish speakers, either from Argentina, Cuba or Mexico, but their next-door neighbors were American. The two men, Bob and Steve, were also brothers and had just traveled across the country to find work in Texas. The New Yorkers were friendly and outgoing people; however Tío Elias and Papi struggled to understand their accents. Nevertheless, Papi and his brother didn't turn down the offered camaraderie; they were adamant about assimilating and didn't want to come across as crude foreigners.

Bob worked the graveyard shift and could be heard leaving for work every night around midnight. His heavy work boots going down the stairs announced his imminent departure and the roar of his 1955 Chevy completed the wake-up call. One night, Papi heard the boots sluggishly going down the stairs. A few minutes later, as he stretched and turned over in his bed, he heard footsteps coming up the stairs. Seconds later, he heard someone scrambling down again. He heard muted cursing as some sort of commotion unfolded. He woke up Tío Elias just as a loud knock was heard on their front door. Both men stumbled as they put on their pants; Papi hesitated before turning the knob and instead shouted, "Who's there? What's happening?"

Through the heavy partition, only every other word was understood as the muffled voice said, "It's Bob's ___ Can you help? B___ is dead! Can ______cable?"

Papi put his hands up to his face and cried, "*Hay Dios mío*! It's something about Bob. *Bob is dead*!" He turned to his brother and said, "They need help! They want us to cable their family!"

Tío Elias opened the door and saw Steve standing there with a toolbox. Steve was in his robe, looking a bit disheveled, but not alarmed. Tío Elias asked him to repeat what he had just said. Steve, realizing that the Spanish speakers hadn't understood, calmly repeated and emphasized each noun, "It's Bob's *car*. Can you help? The *battery* is dead. Can you lend us your jumper cables?"

After the sighs of relief and the hysterical laughter died down, the three men went down the stairs together, making so much noise and commotion that they woke up the entire building. By morning, everyone had heard about Bob's dead battery and Papi's translating skills. Someone suggested that Papi request a refund from Toil and Chat. Poor Papi! He was so embarrassed, but he used the experience as a great motivator. He was determined to improve his "broken English" and vowed that he and his family would be the best English speakers amongst The Argentina Family.

When finally there was enough money set aside, Tío Elias sent for his wife, Feli and children, Alicia and Daniel; Papi sent for his wife and infant daughter, *me*. Mami had been very nervous about getting on an airplane and begged Papi to set her mind at ease as soon as possible. Papi wrote several letters including the following labeled # 4:

Houston, September 22, 1962

My beloved Lina,

I'm responding again to your initial letter with regard to the air travel. Let me tell you that at first, it is very difficult, but I'm not referring to the aeroplane dispatching, but rather one's mental state, which is made up of the desolation one feels for having just departed and the anxiety one feels for having taking the first step on a wild adventure. All of this lasts just about five minutes due to the angelic stewardesses who tend to all the passengers in a heavenly manner. To help promote a relaxed environment, the stewardesses serve whiskey to the male passengers and another sort of liqueur to the ladies. In addition, they serve fine pastries and sweets; all this offered up with pleasant small talk to help distract the nervous first-timers.

I mentioned that it takes about five minutes for the anxieties to lessen, but in our case, it was actually only four minutes. There was a passenger speaking to her husband and in a rather loud voice said, "Oh dear! You'll never guess what I forgot to pack!" Her husband turned to look at her and responded, in a similar tone, "I know; the laxative suppositories." My love, you can only imagine the reaction, as it was just at that moment that people were getting to their most anxious point. That short conjugal interlude broke the curse of panic, which was violently brewing, as we all began laughing until our sides ached!

My darling let me tell you a little about our new home. It comes with all the modern conveniences. It has a gas stove; all you have to do is turn the knob and it lights itself. No more matches! (By the way, this is very common here). We have hot and cold running water throughout the house, a refrigerator and plenty of cabinets all over the place. There is an air conditioner and an air extractor, which came in very handy the other day when Elias burned our chicken stew. Our room has a double bed, two nightstands, a dresser and a huge closet, which is like an armoire built into the wall! Of course there is a bathroom with all the necessary appointments and all the floors have Plexiplast for easy maintenance. All of this for just $50.00 a month!

I am working in a cabinetry shop and making $1.25 an hour. I believe that I will soon be getting a raise, as they seem to be very happy with the quality of my work.

My dear, I have to end this now because Elias also wants to write a letter and if I continue writing, I will use up all the paper in this tablet and all the ink in the pen!

One last thing: I don't know how much you and the family are aware of what is going on in Buenos Aires - how much they are willing to tell the people - but let me tell you, so that there is no misunderstanding, <u>we here are quite alarmed</u>.

We hope that everything calms down very soon. I am grateful to know that you and Mirtita will soon be here with me...

With all my heart, Ruben

Grateful for their husbands letters but no less apprehensive about the air travel, the two provincial, grief-stricken women, left Argentina on December 7, 1962 accompanied by two children and an infant. Upon arriving in Texas, the women, who were fast becoming best friends, sisters and confidants, found themselves surrounded by a little colony of Argentine immigrants. Papi's aunt, Tía Sima, her husband Ignacio and their two sons, Jorge and Armando, Cousin Sam and several other cousins already lived in Houston. Their extended families and friends became our relatives. There were many others who had left Argentina that year and whether we were blood related or not, we were family. There was no confusion; no need to explain that so-and-so was a cousin, two times removed or that so-and-so was the great-aunt of so-and-so's cousin. The pain of leaving behind their loved ones, their culture, their identity, was their connection; it was the sinew that bound everyone together and made them cling to one and other for comfort.

California Dreaming

Papi adored his little family and wanted his young wife to be as enamored with this new country as he, but he felt her anguish. She missed The Argentina Family a great deal, although she was trying to be a supportive wife and a good mother. In his despair to prove he was right in coming to America, he followed through on some job opportunities and moved the family to Los Angeles. It was 1965 and California was booming. The job prospects, the promise of sunny weather and the need to keep the family together prompted a mass migration of Argentines out of bug-ridden, humid Houston to the Golden State. The family settled in the San Fernando Valley, a large area nestled in Los Angeles County. We all managed to live fairly close to one and other. Included in amongst the new Californians were Julio and Raquel Bernstein; Tia Feli's brother and his family.

My *primos hermanos* (first cousins) were Daniel and Alicia and their *primos hermanos* were the Bernstein kids, Fabian and Marcelo however; a sibling bond was created between the Bernsteins boys and the Trupp girls that rivaled any true blood link. No one ever considered correcting us when we said that *we* were cousins. When my little sister, Dani and Freddy Bernstein were born just a few days apart in July 1965, the family ties became that much stronger.

We adopted the Bernstein brothers' grandmother and were told to call her *bubbe* or as it is pronounced in Argentina, *bobe (bō-beh)*. With three boys to chase after, Bobe Freida welcomed the opportunity to have two devoted little granddaughters to dress up and coo over. The boys were very lucky to have their beloved bobe. It would be many years before Dani and I met our real grandparents.

Of course, there were other grand dames in the family. Together, they faced adversities, shouldering the burden of working, raising families and acclimating themselves to a strange, new environment. Coming from immigrant families themselves, they had been schooled not only to survive, but to flourish.

Tia Sima, the youngest of eleven infamous Kolinsky siblings, was raised by the legendary Bobe Maria; a woman with such a strong will that even the Tsar of Russia would have genuflected before her. The sisters were known to be hard-headed, stubborn and downright ruthless (especially while playing cards), but in truth, they *endured* - their homes sparkled, their children thrived, their families were nourished and nurtured even in the harshest of circumstances.

During this early, bittersweet period, all the women in *La Familia*, Mami, Tia Feli, Tia Sima, Bobe Freida and Tia Raquel showered us with love and guidance; they were *collectively* our mothers. The women secured the families together with a unique blend of silky-smooth thread and bands of steel. I sometimes wondered if those strong family ties would have been established if we all had stayed in Argentina. Certainly, the sense of desperation would not have been present.

La Familia had branched out and began to settle in the Valley. Each little branch seemed to connect to another lonely *paisano* (someone from your native country). They, in turn, became part of the newly constructed family. Whenever there was to be a gathering, Mami would say, "The family is coming." We never knew whom to expect, and more often than not, we would have fifty people happily crammed into a small two-bedroom apartment. Our gatherings were colossal and the noise we created was deafening with music, laughter and everyone talking over each other.

On special occasions, holidays or birthdays, Mami would make sure that we had a bouquet of flowers or a cake decorated with the words, "With Love, The Argentina Family." This was one way Mami included the beloved family members into our daily lives. Later, when it was time to make a toast, everyone would raise their glasses and exclaim, "*Para los presentes y los ausentes*!"(For those who are present and those who are absent) It was not unusual for some tears to be shed. Silently, everybody would be thinking about loved ones so far away; dreaming of the day they'd be together once more.

In the meantime, kids would be running in and out, under folding tables and between mix-matched chairs. The men would play dominos or *truco* (a traditional card game). They'd listen to *futbol* games on the radio and rant and rave until someone shouted "*Gol*!" With lethally-sharp toothpicks, they'd poke at their *picada* of pickles, cheese, and salami, drink effervescent combinations of seltzer and Cinzano and have fiery discussions regarding politics. The women, usually huddled in the kitchen, would discuss family issues, such as who was getting married, who was expecting a baby, which market had the freshest chicken, or more importantly, who was traveling to Argentina and could they bring back some *Hepatalgina*? (Medicinal drops for gastrointestinal ailments)

Everyone spoke at once; no one seemed to mind that others interrupted or raised their voices in order to be heard. There were groans and protests mixed in with shrieks of laughter. At some point, we'd all find a place to sit down so that we could finally eat. Delicious aromas would fill the small space. As children, we didn't realize that our comfort foods were a blend of cuisines, *Criollo*, (a combination of gaucho or indigenous fare influenced by the Spaniards) "Jewish" (actually foods typical of Eastern Europe) and Italian (due to the tremendous influence of the Italian immigration to Argentina). Each one couldn't be farther from the other culturally, but somehow the fusion of tastes and textures worked.

I noticed that the grown-ups would get very emotional and even angry at times when the subject turned to Argentina and it *always* turned to Argentina. One person would say, "*This* doesn't happen in Argentina" and of course, the next person would say, "*That* doesn't happen in America," splitting themselves into groups of pros and cons.

Years later, when I would reflect upon these conversations, I realized that those heated words were not necessarily against each other. They were internal debates, each person trying to justify the huge sacrifices made in order to seek out a better future. Still, as children, all we heard, *all we felt*, was the conflict. There, lurking in the background was the unspoken and remote possibility that we'd pick up and move back "home." Yet, where was home? To most of the young children, home *was* America and for those old enough to remember Argentina …well, the old adage of "You can't go back home" rang very true.

Being Thankful

Mami began her lifelong tradition of collecting things to send back to The Argentina Family. As soon as we outgrew a dress or grew tired of a toy, it was promptly packed away. My mother would always find someone in *La Familia* who was going home for a visit and who would be kind enough to take an extra suitcase full of goodies. Truth be told, sometimes we were not actually done playing with a particular toy when it would suddenly disappear. As she stored things away, my mother tried to explain that we should be thankful for our good fortune. Our cousins were poor and had a hard life. Although I was very young, I was aware that my parents not only sent clothes and toys to The Argentina Family, but provided financial assistance as well. It was obvious that without my parents help from America; The Argentina Family would have suffered further. Throughout the years, a question would gnaw at my young mind: if *we* returned to Argentina, as my mother often suggested, *who would help us*?

As a five year old, I was very comfortable in our little home and do not recall feeling deprived or God forbid, hungry. Mami and Papi made sure we had all we needed; plenty of good food, new party dresses for any occasion, toys, books and even a dilapidated, yet functioning, piano. We had settled in a cozy little apartment in Sherman Oaks with a park across the street and Chandler Elementary School just a few blocks away. Although at home we mainly spoke Spanish, Papi insisted that Mami learn to read, write and speak English. Because she grew up deep in the province of Entre Rios, she was only able to complete 7th grade however; Mami was smart and learned very quickly. Papi was very proud of how she excelled. I had started to learn English as well, but it was somehow easier for me and I always believed it was due to watching television. My favorite show was *Hobo Kelly*. I especially like the part when she would jump through her magical mirror and enter into new and exciting adventures. The charismatic hobo would travel to different countries and would talk about curious and diverse traditions. I think one of the reasons I loved that show was because Hobo Kelly made it acceptable to be different. I was quickly learning, even at that tender age, that we were different from the other families.

The apartment building on Hazeltine Avenue was filled with interesting people. It was two stories high and had an open courtyard at its center. Dani and I would ride our tricycles in the patio and Mami would mingle with the neighbors with her "broken English." Mrs. Lewis, who lived alone on the second floor, became somewhat of a mentor, taking Mami under her wing and teaching her many American customs. I loved spending time in Mrs. Lewis' apartment. She was like a grandmother or that slightly unconventional, favorite aunt. I realized years later that she was my "Auntie Mame," somewhat quirky and always on the verge of some discovery. One afternoon, Mrs. Lewis met Mami in the building's community laundry room. The two women were chatting about plans for the upcoming holidays. It seemed that Mrs. Lewis was in the mood for a Christmas party and asked if our family would attend.

"Mrs. Lewis, I am sorry, but we do not celebrate Christmas. We are *Yewish.*"

"I know Carolina, but it wouldn't be anything *religious.* It's just an excuse to get some friends together and have some fun. What about a New Year's Eve party?"

"No, Mrs. Lewis, we would not be able to go to that either. You see, in *Arr-hen-tina*, New Year's is a time for family, so we will be getting together with our little family here."

"Well, I guess I can understand. Say, what about having a holiday party-you know, but *not just for Christmas?* I will have my tree of course, and you can bring whatever it is you put out for your Chanukah and I'll ask my other friends to bring decorations from their homes too. It will be an international holiday extravaganza! We'll make it a potluck!"

Mami considered the idea for a moment and then posed another question.

"What is this…pod lack?"

"It's *pot luck* Carolina, and I suppose you might consider it an American custom. You invite people to your home and ask them to bring food to share. You see, it is a matter of *luck;* you might like what they bring or not."

"You invite people to your house and *ask them to bring the food?* Oh, this *must* be an American tradition. I never heard of such a thing in *Arr-hen-tina.* I would be embarrassed to ask people to bring food. They might think that we didn't have enough money or that I didn't know how to cook!"

"Oh no, Carolina, it is very common here. No one would think that! I've definitely decided to go ahead with my plans and send out my invitations for my first annual International Holiday Extravaganza. You will come, won't you?"

"I will speak with my husband, but I think, yes, we will come."

A week later the homemade invitation was hand delivered. Mrs. Lewis, being very crafty, had made a colorful invitation with Christmas trees and Chanukah menorahs, glitter and sparkles abounded. Mami had already spoken to Papi about the party and he reluctantly agreed to attend. I think Papi didn't care for Mrs. Lewis. She was a divorced woman, and although I didn't know what that meant at the time, I overheard Papi telling Mami that *esa mujer* (that woman) with her bleached platinum blond hair was too modern for his taste.

Looking at the invitation, Papi read the unfamiliar words. "What does this mean, *pot luck*?"

"Mrs. Lewis explained that when you have pot luck, everyone brings food in pots to share and if you are *lucky*, you will enjoy the food. See Ruben, I am learning new American traditions! You should be happy."

"Well, I think it is not in good taste to invite people and then ask them to bring their own food. That woman probably doesn't know how to cook! Maybe that is why she is divorced."

"Ruben! Don't be so *antipático*."

"I'm not being unsociable; I just don't like the idea of depending on luck for my dinner!"

"Don't worry Ruben. I will make good food and you can eat only my pot luck."

The evening of the party we all clambered up the stairs to Mrs. Lewis' apartment. Papi led the way carrying the largest pot full of *colita de cuadril*. Mami followed and carried another huge pot filled with *tallarines con tuco*. I carefully climbed the stairs balancing a platter of *latkes* and Daniela brought up the rear holding our only Chanukah decoration, a small brass menorah.

Mrs. Lewis, bedazzling in her holiday attire, greeted our family at the door. She shimmered from head to toe. One by one, we entered the apartment with our pots and platters as Mrs. Lewis sung out, "Everyone, the Trupps are here and it looks like they brought enough food to feed the troops!" The eclectic group of guests cheered and welcomed us with shouts of *Feliz Navidad*! *Trevlig Helg! Buone Feste*! Even our new friends, The Israelis, participated in the cheers with an enthusiastic *Chag Sameach*!

The Israelis lived on the second floor and across the patio. Mami had been thrilled to meet this family, not only because they were Jewish, but because they had Argentine in-laws! Dafna and Mami became best friends and all of Dafna's family suddenly became part of our family. It seemed that overnight, we added several new "aunts, uncles and cousins" to our mish-mash of relatives.

The potluck was a success, with various dishes representing countries from across the globe. Even Papi enjoyed himself, but later confided that he was thankful for his wife's cooking. What man would try his luck with someone else's pot of food, if he were lucky enough to have his wife's food on the table? It appeared that Mami enjoyed that compliment more than anything else at the first annual Holiday Extravaganza.

I had made a little friend of my own at Chandler Elementary School. I was something of a curious creature to Dodie Friedman, with my "funny name" and my poor English. Dodie was somewhat of a curious creature to *me* because she and her mother lived alone, with very little family nearby. Who had ever heard of such a thing? *No family*? We became very close and I was grateful for her friendship and acceptance. I was exceptionally aware that we were *new* Americans and it was important to me that we be *normal* like everyone else. I wanted to be like the families we saw on television, quiet and refined, with matching plates and enough seats for everyone-especially when there was a holiday, like Thanksgiving. The older cousins had brought Thanksgiving and all of its lore home from school and it had been *partially* assimilated. The problem was that many of foods traditionally accepted as appropriate for Thanksgiving simply were not part of the typical Argentine diet. Instead, Mami would make certain delicacies, like *ñoquis*, to mark the special occasion. All the aunts made their specialties; each one could not have been further from turkey with cranberry sauce or mashed potatoes and gravy.

When Dodie and I were in the first grade, the teacher informed us that we were going to have a Thanksgiving feast at school. Each student had to bring something from home to share. I was assigned a dessert. My heart sank when I saw

Mami prepare her famous *flan with dulce de leche*. I told her that I didn't think that was a Thanksgiving dessert, but she told me that was nonsense. Everybody loved her *flan* and she only made it for special occasions. Needless to say, Mami and I attended the Thanksgiving feast and when all the mothers displayed their desserts, ours stuck out like a sore thumb! There amid the pumpkin pies, apples pies and pecan pies was Mami's famous *flan with dulce de leche*. The teacher came to me and asked with feigned politeness, "Mirta, what is this?"(Actually, people usually called me Murda, Marta, Myrna, or even Meer-da but never *Mirta*)

"It's *flan* with *dulce de leche*, Miss Johnston," I answered meekly.

Miss Johnston turned to my mother and had the audacity to say, "How unusual! Is this what they serve in Argentina instead of pumpkin pie for Thanksgiving Mrs. Trupp?"

Mami was a little ashamed of her broken English, but she summoned up the courage to say, "Mees Johns-ton, we do not celebrate Tanksgivink in *Arr-hen-tina*."

Miss Johnston chuckled and said, "What do you mean, you don't celebrate Thanksgiving?"

I quickly remembered the story about the English pilgrims and the Indians and came to Mami's aid. "Miss

Johnston, the pilgrims came to North America *not South America.*"

Miss Johnston turned the color of bright cranberry sauce and mumbled something about getting more apple cider from the school cafeteria. Mami nodded her head and with a harrumph said, "*Gracias Mirtita!*"

The Going *Is* Great

Something happened in our little family that would change the Trupp's American adventure forever. Thanks to a friend's suggestion, Papi put away his hammer and nails and began a new line of work with Pan American Airlines. It was not a glamorous job, but the words *Pan American* transformed into something magical and glorious for us. The term was somehow personified and Pan Am became part savior and part family member. Why this adoration for an airline company? Papi said that the salary was extraordinary for a "simple workingman" and it allowed his family to live "like royalty." We, the royal family, could fly practically free of charge anywhere in the world. Of course, for Mami, the only other place in the world was…Argentina!

In April of 1969, Tía Lela was expecting her second child and Mami desperately wanted to be by her side. Thanks to Pan Am, Dani, Mami and I were able to travel for this special occasion. Arrangements were, seemingly, effortlessly made and before Dani and I learned the newest Pan Am jingle, we boarded our first 747 without truly comprehending what awaited us.

Mami's anxiety was palpable, Dani become sick to her stomach as soon as the plane took off, but I was fascinated by the sights, sounds and various personalities that accompanied us on our twenty-two hour voyage. Peering out the window, once the plane "reached its cruising altitude," I was mesmerized by the cloud formations; one in particular seemed to take on the shape of a medieval castle, with turrets and a massive gate. The plane appeared to glide through the opening, as if heavenly sentries opened the puffy, white gate and allowed us passage. With this fantasy unfolding in my mind's eye, accompanied by the hum of the powerful jet engines, I quickly fell sound asleep.

When I awoke, we had already begun our descent into Guatemala's international airport. We had to disembark and idle away a two-hour lay over. The stewardess opened the doors; the passengers scrambled down a metal staircase and scurried across the tarmac, stunned by the dense humidity and light rain. Once inside, Mami acclimated herself to her surroundings, checked in with the Pan Am agent and decided that we should stretch our legs by walking around a bit. The main corridor was haphazardly lined with various vendors selling food and indigenous crafts. Mami bought two handmade shawls from a woman fully clad in colorful, local attire. We could barely understand the lady, which I thought odd, but Mami explained that the woman spoke a mixture of Spanish and her native tongue. Dani and I both got a doll each. Mami bought a third doll for our cousin, Fabiana. The time quickly passed and once the paying passengers boarded, the remaining Stand-By travelers were allowed to embark as well. While it appeared to cause some anxiety to my mother, being the last to board only enhanced my experience of being a *special* Pan Am family member.

It was a relatively short trip to Panama and then a long stretch to Buenos Aires. I was easily contented with my books and the music being piped in and enjoyed through our Pan Am headphones. Dani did not fare as well but I thought to myself, we were not going to be faced with this ordeal very often. We should just "buck up" and soon it would be over. I had no idea my assessment was way off the mark. It was to be the first of many trips back to The Argentina Family. Although, we had heard over and over again about the massive extended family, we soon found out that Mami's only desire was to spend time with her sister, Adela, affectionately called Lela.

Tía Lela was very poor and lived in an antiquated apartment with her ailing husband, their children and her two younger brothers. In the dead of winter, the family lived without hot running water and was kept warm by small propane heaters (I was terrified of those portable heaters because I heard of a cousin that was badly burned when one exploded in her face). The family had a small kitchen that lead to a central uncovered courtyard or patio. To get to the bathroom, you had to go outside and cross the courtyard.

The toilet was rather archaic. You didn't push a lever to flush; you pulled on a chain dangling from a box that loomed from above. And there was another sort of toilet that didn't have a regular seat but had a tiny sort of shower that spouted water up into your face if you weren't careful. Mami said it was called a *bidet* and that all *civilized* nations should have them in their restrooms. The toilet paper was sleek and smooth, similar to what we used for our math problems in school. The teacher would have us fold the sheet into 16 neat and precise squares to accommodate our calculations. It was perfect for math class, but it didn't quite measure up in the bathroom.

Crossing the patio, you entered another set of rooms. The main living areas felt somewhat similar to a train as one room led to another. From the living room, you passed through a massive door and entered the children's room. The children's room led to Tía Lela's room. The paint on the walls was peeling from the humidity and it was always bitterly cold. Dani and I wore heavy sweaters *and* our jackets inside the apartment.

Fabiana and baby Lucas shared a small room. There was just enough space for a tiny bed, an even tinier crib and a small dresser. Fabi had a few toys scattered about and I had an immediate reaction seeing my old toys there. If I had ever felt a tinge of resentment for having to give up a Barbie doll or party dress, it was quickly erased when I saw how little my cousins truly had.

A spiral staircase jutted up from the middle of the patio. My bachelor uncles, Marcus and Alberto, shared a room perched on top of the landing. It was their retreat, a quiet corner away from nagging sisters and pesky children. The staircase kept us at bay; their privacy protected by our fear of climbing the rickety set of steps. Tío Beto was a quiet, timid sort of man, very much like my grandfather, Zeide Efraim. Tío Marcos was much younger than his sisters, outgoing and personable. He seemed full of life and music and I loved spending time with him. Tío Marcos played the guitar and liked to sing Argentine folk songs. He was the prankster of the family; he liked to tell off color jokes or better yet, sing songs that had double meanings. His eyes would twinkle and he'd crack a sly smile waiting for his audience to catch on. I wasn't supposed to be listening, but every once and a while, I *accidentally* overheard some tunes.

On another occasion when I wasn't *exactly* invited to participate in the conversation, I overheard the brothers talking to Mami about their work. They were eager to show off to their big sister and she seemed very impressed with their projects. She even suggested that they look into promoting the business in America. Since I wasn't in the room, I could only hear bits and pieces of their conversation.

I did manage to make out words such as artistry, sculpturing tools, porcelain, and ivory. It sounded like her brothers were artistic masters!

It was arranged that we would go visit Tío Beto and Tío Marcos at work the following day. I was excited to go on adventure. We had to take a short ride on a bus and then a terrifying ride on the subway. In our short stay in Buenos Aires, I came to learn to hate the subway. I was afraid of going underground, crowds of people rushing about, pushing you *in* when you wanted to go *out*. I was always fearful that Mami would get off the train and Dani and I would be stuck behind a massive wall of people.

We finally reached our destination. The building looked like a typical structure from the street. Old and dreary, the heavy door creaked when we pushed through. We went down a long hallway, Mami's shoes tapping all along the tile floor until we reached the laboratory. I asked Mami why it was called a laboratory. I had imagined an artist's studio, filled with paints and easels and all sorts of interesting materials. Since I was not given an answer, I figured I'd find out soon enough. Opening the door, we were immediately hit with a foul odor. I looked at Dani and plugged my nose. Surprisingly, she didn't look like she was going to lose her lunch; she always seemed to have a weak stomach. The odor was slightly familiar; it reminded me of the stench of burning plastic. Burning plastic? Like when my cousin, Marcelo tried to make Jiffy Pop popcorn and the plastic wrap burned on to the adjacent saucepan? No… I suddenly remembered...it was the same smell that came from Bernstein's Creepy Crawlers toy maker.

Tío Beto came out from the back room, wiping his hands on a cloth before reaching out to hug and kiss us. Dani and I followed Tío Beto and Mami to another room where I presumed we would finally see the beautiful works of art they had been describing. The odor followed us as we entered the laboratory. Tío Marcos was hunched over a table working very diligently on something, but I couldn't see. When he heard us come in, he jumped off his stool, blew out a Bunsen burner and came to greet us. As he moved away from the table, I got my first clear view of his project. There laid out along the table were dozens and dozens of…*what were they exactly?*

"Mami, what are those-*those things?*"

"They are teeth *mamita*, false teeth- dentures- like Bobe Carmen wears. Tío Beto and Tío Marcos are artists, *no?* They do beautiful work!"

"But they are huge! They look like King Kong's teeth! What kind of person has such a big mouth?"

Tío Beto answered, "Not a person, *mi amor*, a cow."

"What do you mean, a cow?"

"The dentures are for cows, *corazón*."

"Why? Who would spend money on fixing cows teeth?" I was trying to imagine a farmer walking over to his barn early in the morning with a stool, a toothbrush and a tube of Colgate.

Tío Beto laughed at my confusion but tried to explain the importance of keeping the cows healthy so that they would produce nutritious milk and tasty beef.

"Everyone knows that *Arr-hen-tina* makes the best beef in the world!" Mami added for good measure.

Tío Marcos continued to explain that the cows wore down their teeth quickly and without the false dentures; they wouldn't be able eat. If the cows wouldn't eat, they'd soon be worthless to the ranchers and dairy farmers. "So, do you want to see how we transform plastic and porcelain into gorgeous smiles for our bovine beauties?" my uncle asked with the familiar twinkle in his eye.

The image of the smiling cow on the milk carton back home flashed before my eyes and I thought I'll never be able to look at a glass of milk without thinking of those King Kong dentures!

After that eye-opening experience, the following days in Tía Lela's house were boring in comparison. We were like a family of hibernating bears, burrowing inside the tiny apartment. The sisters couldn't get enough of each other and our days revolved around their chats and of course, the new baby, who unfortunately was quite sickly. When per chance, we actually did venture out; I was overwhelmed with the sights and sounds of the city. The San Fernando Valley could not compare to the bustling metropolis of Buenos Aires. I noticed that my mother seemed to be in her element, soaking in the ambiance, the noise, the commotion. Swarms of people crowded the streets, businessmen in their fine suits carrying leather attaché cases, school kids in their *guardapolvos* (white lab coats) and *mochilas* (satchels) and housewives weaving in and out of small, grocery stores carrying their *bolsas de mandados* (weaved plastic bags for running errands).

What caught my eye the most were the nuns. I had never seen a *real* nun and here in the streets of Buenos Aires, they could be found at every turn. I had a strange fascination with these women ever since Papi took me to see the Sound of Music. Soon after, I was won over by the charm of The Flying Nun, The Signing Nun and even Mary Tyler Moore's nun in The Change of Habit. These women apparently spent their days helping people, playing with children and singing all day long. They even fell in love with lonely, heartsick captains and handsome doctors. *Who wouldn't want to be a nun?*

With all the naiveté of a young girl, I had once told my parents that I would seek the same career, so that I could sing and play and fall in love. I recalled that my mother turned several shades of gray and chocked on her *mate* before saying, "*Dios libre y me guarde*" (a fairly Catholic-leaning phrase meaning God free me and save me).

Papi laughed and laughed but finally managed to blurt out, "You can't get married if you become a nun, Mirtita."

Mami, regaining her composure, added for good measure, "You can't be a nun, Mirtita. You are *Yewish*."

Away from the hustle and bustle of the streets and sequestered again in the apartment, Dani and our little cousin Fabi got along and played together nicely. I was a little older and missed being with kids my own age. The black and white television set only offered three channels. Old episodes of imported cowboy shows or variety hours were hardly entertaining. Programs for children seemed limited to an Italian mouse named *Topo Gigio* and three famous Spanish clowns, *Gaby, Fofo and Miliki.* Spoiled by the modern and creative programming, not to mention the color TV we had at home; it felt like we were in the Stone Age.

Sometimes, we'd have company for afternoon tea or on occasion, some of the extended family would come dinner. Since Bobe Carmen came from an extensive family, there was no telling when one of her seven siblings might drop in. Mami was well acquainted with her relatives having lived with one or two of them throughout her youth. It usually was not under the best of circumstances and she was not always made welcome. One exception was when she was sent to live with Bobe Carmen's younger sister, Devora and her husband, Leon. Mami was accepted into the family fold as a welcomed daughter. She became the beloved older sister to the couple's little girls, Raquel and Silvia.

On several occasions, Tía Devora and her family would come to have dinner with us in that cold, damp apartment and soon enough, we'd all be sitting around the small dining room table; our appetites for good food and for good company satisfied for the moment.

Our first trip was emotionally intense and given the circumstances, Dani and I didn't meet the majority of The Argentina Family; that would have to wait for the next expedition. We were overwhelmed in every sense, emotionally, and physically. Papi had not been able to travel with us because he couldn't take so much time off of work. It was the first of many trips where we had to leave him behind and the feeling of abandoning him was acutely distressing. Dani and I were more than ready when it was finally time to go home.

Changes and *Changas*

Sometime during the school year, Dodie and I learned about the Girl Scouts. One of the troop leaders came to visit our classroom and told us about all the fun activities and learning opportunities. She brought a few girls from the troop and they performed the Girl Scouts pledge and showed us all the badges they earned. Instantly, I knew that I wanted to join. If I were a Girl Scout, then I would really be like all the American girls! The leader explained that we were actually too young to be Girl Scouts, but we could start as Brownies. She passed out brochures that contained membership information and the various costs for dues and uniforms. Dodie said that she'd ask her mother right after school. My thought was how was I going to explain this whole thing to my parents- meetings, dues, sleepovers, camp outs? I wasn't even allowed to sleep over Dodie's house! Papi didn't like sleepovers. He felt that they were unnecessary.

I told Mami all about the presentation and begged her to let me join. Of course, her answer was, "We have to ask your father." Asking Papi was never easy. Early on, I learned that I needed to formulate my questions *very carefully,* having all the details ready. It was like going before a judge! When I finally had the chance to speak to my father, I was very surprised by his response. He didn't mind the dues or the uniforms or even the camping. However, he wasn't sure about the Girl Scouts organization. In Argentina, the Boy Scouts kowtowed to the military and Catholic Church. Jewish boys never considered joining; Papi didn't know if they were *allowed* to join. What would the *bobes* and *zeides* say if Mirtita joined such a group?

I didn't understand why we had to worry about The Argentina Family just because I wanted to join the Brownies. I was too young to comprehend their trepidation of organizations, religious or otherwise. I begged and pleaded and Mami finally said, "Let me talk to Mrs. Freidman. She *is* Jewish after all. If Dodie is going to be a Brownie, maybe it's ok for Mirtita."

Mrs. Freidman, bless her heart, convinced my mother that the Girl Scouts had nothing to do with the Catholic Church and that the organization accepted everybody. Once Mami was assured that I wasn't going to be forced to go to mass, she convinced Papi to let me join. Soon, I was all decked out in my appropriately brown uniform and bothering all the neighbors in the building to buy cookies. Mami sent a picture of me in my uniform to The Argentina Family and explained that in America, everyone was welcomed to participate. I, of course, would end up collecting more colorful stamps on my passport than colorful badges for my Brownies sash, but my grandmothers wrote back praising the

Girl Scouts and our family for living in America, *die goldene medina.*

One thing Mami knew about was family. She and the other mothers were adamant about getting *La Familia* together every weekend. Sometimes we'd venture out to Griffith Park, Santa Monica Beach or Marina Del Rey. The family enjoyed outings to Santa Monica Beach because it had a grassy area where the adults could "enjoy the beach" without all that pesky sand getting into their *mate* (herbal tea) and *facturas* (pastries) and the kids could frolic in the water, as long as they could drag someone along to supervise. Likewise, the quiet marina was perfect for the families with small children and the adults appreciated the covered picnic areas and BBQ's. The men would spend the day preparing the *asado*; you could smell the garlic and parsley for the *chimichurri* all the way to the iconic Catalina Market. Any leftover oil, which had not been used in the *chimichurri* concoction, was used to slather on our pale white skin, so that we could have that fashionable Mar de Plata summer glow.

Although Papi's job at Pan Am was going very well, he began advertising his carpentry and handy-man skills. He and Mami had begun discussing the possibility of buying a house, so he eagerly set out to work on some *changas.* These side jobs were hard on us because it seemed we never got to see Papi anymore. He had begun working the swing shift at

Pan Am, which meant that by the time I got home from school, he was on his way to work. And when I got up in the morning, Papi was still sleeping. Soon, we figured out a plan to steal a few minutes together in the afternoons. Papi would pick me up from school and drive me home and we would have those ten minutes just to ourselves. I didn't have to share him with Mami or Dani or even Tommy or Lenny, the little boys Mami had begun caring for.

Papi needed a place to work on his *changas*, so he advertised again and found a neighbor who lived around the corner who was willing to rent out his garage. Papi set up a small cabinetry shop in the Jefferson's garage. On the weekends, I would walk over with his lunch or an afternoon snack and watch him work. He would allow me to stay and keep him company as long as I didn't touch any tools. I remember sitting on a stool in the corner, far away from the table saw and other sharp objects while he hammered away. We would listen to the radio, usually tuned on to a station playing Swing and Papi would sing along.

Mr. and Mrs. Jefferson eldest daughter, Laurie, was in my class at Chandler Elementary. Sometimes, she would invite me into their house and we would play, but I preferred to be in the garage. I like the sound of the saw and smell the wood shavings. Mostly, I just wanted to sit with my father.

One afternoon, Mrs. Jefferson came into the garage while Papi was hard at work and I sat doing my homework. While she was digging through some boxes, she called out to me. "Murda, why don't you came inside and do your homework with Laurie? Afterwards, if you like, I'll let you two girls help me with a new project."

Papi gave me the go-ahead, so I jumped off my stool and followed Mrs. Jefferson inside. Mrs. Jefferson was the craft queen. She knew every shape of sequin, every bauble and bead known to mankind. She had a cornucopia of glues and adhesives, along with bolts of velvets and rich colored fabrics shimmering with metallic threads. The dining room table was covered with projects and it was immediately obvious that the family was preparing for Christmas. Mrs. Jefferson said that this year's theme was "Currier and Ives." I shrugged my shoulders and said, "That's nice," having no idea what she meant.

Every year "for the Holidays," Mrs. Jefferson turned the living room into a Victorian dream. Family heirlooms and collected treasures replaced all the modern furniture and fixtures. The dining room was transformed into a gingerbread neighborhood and Mr. Jefferson laid out a train set that whistled around the winter wonderland. As they set up an enormous tree, Laurie asked if I'd like to help decorate. I hesitated, not knowing if my mother would approve. Laurie thought it was a funny request, but I called my mother to ask for permission. Mami said that it would be all right to help the Jeffersons decorate their tree. Ever so timidly, I accepted a handful of tinsel and copied Laurie as she placed some of the shiny stuff on the tree.

Mrs. Jefferson had purchased a strange looking record player in a second-hand store. She said it was an antique as she set the needle down on a rather large record. While Christmas music played softly in the background, we were served hot chocolate and gingerbread cookies. All the while, I was thinking, "What would The Argentina Family think about this? *What would the bobes say*?" When Papi finished working in the garage, he knocked on the door and called for me to come out. As we walked home, I told Papi about my afternoon.

"Do you think the *bobes* would mind that I was celebrating Christmas?"

"Were you celebrating Christmas? I thought you were eating cookies and decorating a tree!" Papi grinned at me. "Do you know what it means to celebrate Christmas?"

I shrugged my shoulders, "Well I guess not, but would it be *wrong* for me to celebrate?"

"Mirtita, I think that it would be wrong to celebrate something if you don't know what exactly you are celebrating. That's what I feel sometimes about our holidays. I don't feel right celebrating because I don't know the history behind them. In any case, singing songs and playing with glitter and paints doesn't make you a Christian, any more than eating a latke or playing with a dreidel would make Laurie a Jew."

"O.K., as long as you think it's all right and that the *bobes* wouldn't mind.

"Oh, I don't know about the *bobes*; that's another story!" he chuckled.

"Papi, be serious! Anyway, why don't you know about the holidays? Don't you have nice memories from when you were a little boy?"

"Now that you mention it, I have nice memories of going to temple on Saturday mornings with my father. Of course, I was very young then. My father told me that because we were *Kohanim*, it was our special duty to be present on Saturdays. The rabbi would call Zeide Simon up to the podium to read from the scrolls before anyone else had the honor. He had a beautiful voice; did you know that he wanted to be a *chazan,* a cantor, before they immigrated to Argentina?" Papi stopped for a moment and it seemed like his eyes were teary. "Look Mirtita, I don't know much about holidays and such, but I do know this; Christmas doesn't belong to us. We are Jewish and we have our own beliefs."

A few weeks passed by and it was time for Chanukah. The families were going to gather in our apartment for a little celebration. Dani and I, along with the Bernstein boys, begged our parents to let us decorate the house. Our parents had no objections as they had little experience with this particular holiday. Growing up in a Catholic nation, Mami and Papi had grown accustomed to their friends and neighbors celebrating a fairly solemn and religious Christmas. Chanukah was considered a minor holiday, even amongst the most devout in the Argentine Jewish community and because it came in the summer when everyone was on vacation, it was easy to overlook the event. The holiday, if acknowledged at all, was celebrated quietly by lighting the menorah and passing out chocolate *gelt* (coins) to the *kinder* (children). There were no extravagant gifts or festive decorations. Papi said that all that "hoopla" was an American custom, but the adults went along with our request because they wanted to add a little fun and sparkle to our festivities.

Papi made a large Star of David out of "a nice piece of wood" and he grimaced as I promptly covered it with white paint and glitter. Mami bought some Chanukah decorations at our local Thrifty's drugstore, a colorful cardboard "Happy Chanukah" sign and dreidels made out of honeycomb tissue paper. Tía Feli brought a bag full of plastic dreidels and chocolate coins wrapped in gold foil. Tía Sima made her famous sugar cookies in the shape of Jewish stars. Tía Raquel, always wanting to make things fun and creative, supplied the latest fad in American Judaism: the Chanukah Bush. The adults were not exactly convinced that the Chanukah Bush was acceptable, but since no one in the group could explain to their children what the holiday was actually about, they allowed the small, snow-white "non-Christmas" tree. To make it a little "more kosher," the accessories were all blue and white. These, of course, were deemed appropriate Jewish colors.

On the first night, under the shimmering Star of David, the family gathered around the kitchen table. Mami knew that the lead candle was called a *Shamash*; somehow the word sprung from deep within her memories. She lit the *Shamash* candle and then lit another solitary candle while we all watched. No one knew the three verses of the candle blessings, but we children had learned a Chanukah song in school, so we sang, "Oh dreidel, dreidel, dreidel, I made you out of clay…" Then with guilty pleasure, Dani and I and the Bernstein boys, opened the box of blue ornaments and tried to figure out how to hang them on the frosted bush. We wrapped a string of blue and white lights around the branches and tossed bunches of tinsel on for good measure. No one knew how to control the lights, which were frantically blinking on and off. It was not the quite the same effect of the Jefferson's majestic tree, but then again, what did we know about decorating a tree? When we were all done, we looked at each other and asked, "Now what?" Shrugging our shoulders, we turned to the adults for suggestions. Our mothers responded with the obvious, "Let's eat!"

With the typical amount of boisterous commotion and fan-fare, we all sat down to eat our fill. Mami and the aunts knew that it was important to eat fried or oily foods for the holiday, so we were presented with a mountain of *milanesas* (breaded veal cutlets), a huge platter of *latkes (*potato pancakes*)*, a variety of salads and a lovely *mayonesa (*Argentine style potato salad*)*, which Mami decorated with green olives in the shape of a *Magen David* (Star of David). For dessert, Mami made *buñuelos* from a recipe she had copied from her Doña Petrona cookbook. Even if the Betty Crocker of Argentina wasn't Jewish, she offered a wide variety of recipes which Mami managed to modify and apply to the holiday at hand. The deep-fried donuts with chunks of apples fit in nicely with the oily tradition. After dessert, we were each given a bag of *gelt* and a handful of colorful *dreidels.*

Our parents sat and watched us play and munch on our chocolates. I overheard several adults asking for a few drops of *Hepatalgina.* I don't think it was the oil-laden *latkes* or the *mayonesa* that caused the digestive upset. The adults didn't know the deeper meaning of Chanukah; their understanding of the menorah or the Maccabees was on a childish, fairy tale level at best. There was no comprehension of the cost to our

Chanukah heroes who refused to assimilate and yet, I came to believe, that it was the garish Chanukah Bush, glowing in the background like a neon light that made our parents feel uncomfortable. Changing holiday traditions was a risky business; the plug was pulled on this Chanukah experiment-never to see the light again.

Heartland Street & *Avenida San Martin*

Thanks to their hard work and dedication, my parents bought their first home on Heartland Street in the summer of 1970. It was a tremendous accomplishment for anyone, but for Papi, it was nothing short of a miracle. He proudly proclaimed that he was an immigrant and "a simple workingman" yet in a matter of a few years, they were able to move out of a cramped two-bedroom apartment into a lovely three-bedroom/one bathroom house with a large backyard. "Only in America!" he exclaimed.

Although I was excited about the move, the fact that we had to drive thirty minutes *on the freeway* to get there made it a little disconcerting. I had grown accustomed to my neighborhood and to our daily routine. Being so young, I had trouble discerning direction and distances; being thirty minutes away from friends and family was unsettling. That being said, I was eager to start the third grade in my new school. Shirley Avenue Elementary was catty corner from our little yellow house. Papi had insisted that the school be walking distance for his girls. I only had to pass five houses, cross the quiet street and I was in the school's playground. I felt safe knowing that my house was so close and Mami was just a minute away. The school was bordered by homes and from the playground; we could see the San Bernardino mountain range surrounding the Valley. There was one particular mountaintop that stood out from the rest. It had two predominant peaks that formed the capital letter *M*; seemingly stamped upon the skyline. I had also been able to see it from the park across the street of our apartment building, and so I dubbed it *my mountain*. It seemed that wherever I was in the San Fernando Valley, I could turn around and see my mountain. I found that very comforting, after all, I might have to move from Sherman Oaks to Reseda or even back to Argentina, but Mirta's Mountain certainly was not going anywhere.

One wintry day, Papi came home with some extraordinary news. Pan Am was offering their employees a transfer to the expanding airport in Miami, Florida. They would pay for the move and offered all sorts of incentives. Of course, for Mami the biggest incentive was being so much closer to Argentina. A trip from Los Angeles to Buenos Aires could take us about twenty-two hours with one to two layovers. If we lived in Miami, it was just a "short," direct eight-hour flight. Mami said that we'd be able to go for long weekends, just to pop in and say "*hola*!"

Dani and I heard Mami and Papi discussing the matter for days. We were terrified that they would decide to move us across the country. We had just settled into our new home and our new school. We even had a new puppy, a

German Shepard that we called Zorro; named for Papi's favorite dog he had growing up in Buratovich. We loved our cousins and our whole family that had been pieced together. If we moved to Miami, we'd be all alone and Mami would still be far away from The Argentina Family. Would eight-hours be close enough? Would it *ever* be close enough? Dani and I couldn't understand how they could even consider the possibility and when we were given the chance, we made our opinions known. Our parents were torn; the incentives to move were quite appealing however; they took our pleas into consideration and decided to stay in our little yellow house on Heartland Street.

Zorro unfortunately was not so lucky. Although Papi brought Zorro home based on his fond memories of the Shepard he had on the farm, he didn't take into consideration that he wasn't around much to take care of the puppy. Dani and I liked petting and playing with Zorro, but when it came time for feeding him or walking him or even worse, cleaning up after him, we left that all up to our father. The last straw came one afternoon while we were all outside playing with the dog. Certain body parts were becoming more and more apparent as Zorro became more and more excited. Being extremely naive, I asked my father, "What's happening to Zorro?"

Papi turned every color under the sun. He couldn't *or wouldn't* explain to his little girl about certain body parts. He turned to Mami for help, but she escaped into the kitchen hiding her blushing face. While in modern society, this episode would appear extraordinarily prudish; taking my parents' upbringing into consideration would later explain many of their actions, or in this case, their reactions. My mother was raised in the equivalent of a *shtetl* (small Eastern European village), right in the middle of Concordia, Entre Rios. Certain subjects were simply not discussed, which would explain why my mother thought she was bleeding to death when in fact she had simply begun menstruating. Prior to getting married at the age of 27, Mami's friends teased her incessantly saying that her groom would come to her swinging from the chandelier. On her wedding night, my mother looked suspiciously at the light fixture above the bed and called out to her new husband saying, "I don't think it will hold your weight, *querido*."

These revelations wouldn't be imparted until I was much, *much* older. In the meantime, I was not given any further explanation on my puppy's physical attributes. A week later, much to our dismay, Zorro found a new home, one presumably filled with little boys who knew about such things.

February 1971 brought Tía Lela, Fabi and Lucas to California. It took a lot of convincing on Mami's part, because Tía Lela was very afraid of traveling alone with two small kids. When they finally arrived, it was probably one of the happiest days in Mami's life. It was exciting for us too because this time, we were not the guests. We were the hosts! And because we were the hosts, we had the excuse of doing a lot of sightseeing. We went up and down the coast, to Malibu, to Disneyland, Knott's Berry Farm, Hollywood, all the great tourist attractions. Of course, it was all lost on Mami and Tía Lela. They would have been just as happy staying home, drinking *mate* and sitting around the kitchen table. It was during these gab fests, that Dani and I would get a touch of cabin fever. Bored with sitting at home, our little cousins getting on our nerves, it was inevitable that some whining and complaining would ensue. A few times, Mami and Tía Lela got so irritated with us that they shooed us out of the house with the backside of the broom.

The most memorable date of Tía Lela's trip was to be Wednesday, February 9th. At six o'clock in the morning, we were sound asleep, when suddenly we were awakened by a loud, rumbling noise. The ground began to shake and our little house was ruthlessly rocked back and forth. It was an earthquake, our first experience with the infamous California attraction. Papi jumped out of bed and started shouting for us to get up and to stand underneath the doorposts. It seemed to last forever, but finally the roar quieted down and the house stopped rocking. Needless to say, we were all petrified. Tía Lela, one usually prone to panic, actually made us laugh when she announced that she thought Papi had gotten up early to mow the lawn and was causing the ruckus. She said that she was about to go chase him with the broom but then she realized; even Papi's new lawnmower was not *that* powerful.

Tía Lela's epic visit finally came to an end. I hadn't known at the time, of course, but my aunt's trip was not merely a family visit. Recently widowed, she was contemplating moving to America to rebuild her life and reconnect with a beloved sister. There had been talk about Tío Marcos immigrating as well. Along with Argentina's continual economic decline, his health was rapidly deteriorating. He hoped that in America, he'd be able to find some relief, if not a cure for his unusual disease. It was not meant to be however; the siblings would remain separated due to a variety of factors. On a personal level, Lela and Marcos didn't have the fortitude to tear themselves away from The Argentina Family and on a colder, yet practical note; the time had passed when resident "Green cards" were handed out as if they were golden tickets. The families would not have been allowed to stay legally in America and without it being legal and above board; no one, including my parents could afford the risk.

It was also the beginning of another era for me. It was probably a week or so after the Sylmar earthquake, that Dodie, my friend from our old neighborhood, invited me to her house for a sleepover. Surprisingly enough, Papi allowed me to go. I hadn't seen Dodie since we moved away. We enjoyed our little reunion throughout the day and were allowed to stay up way past our bedtime. Finally, exhausted, we reluctantly went to sleep. Our rest was short lived, as sometime in the early morning hours we had an aftershock. Since the Sylmar earthquake was my first experience, I had no idea to expect another one so soon. And while this one was not anywhere near the 6.6 quake, it was still enough to rattle our nerves. I couldn't go back to sleep. Working myself into a panic, I began worrying about my family's safety. Who would take care of me and Dani if something happened to my parents? Would we live with our family here in California? Would they send us to live with The Argentina Family? Dodie's mother couldn't console me. She called my parents and Papi came to pick me up. This began a trend that would last for several years. I could not sleep over anyone's house after that. If my parents went out for the evening and left me with a sitter, I would will myself to stay awake until they returned. Even spending the night at the Bernstein's house was out of the question. I couldn't get rid of the anxiety of being abandoned, even when I was well cared for or surrounded by loved ones.

In the summer of 1971, Mami, Dani and I went back to Argentina. Taking the same route via Guatemala and Panama, I could have sworn that we passed through my mystical cloud castle. At nine years old, I had a curious and imaginative mind; I allowed myself to create fanciful scenarios all the way down past the equator and through the southern hemisphere. If I stared out the window long and hard enough, I could imagine gallant knights on white horses galloping along the side of the plane. I giggled at the thought of my celestial honor guard. The image made me think of angels and other heavenly beings. Where was heaven anyway? Did Jewish people believe in these things? The countless hours melted away as I entertained myself with these private thoughts, too intimate or too silly, to share.

In mid-August, we were freezing and miserable in Tía Lela's apartment on Avenida San Martin. This was still not the "big" trip to see The Argentina Family when Papi would be able to join us. This was mostly about getting the two sisters, Lina and Lela together. They had a lot of making up to do. As children in Entre Rios, they were torn apart because of Tía Lela's health and the family's poverty. Bobe Carmen had to constantly take the little girl for medical treatments to

Buenos Aires; so far away in physical terms, as well as monetary, it could have been on another continent. Mami had to stay behind with her father and little brother. Zeide Efraim would sometimes send the siblings to stay with relatives, as he could not take care of his children and the farm alone. My mother told us how lonely and homesick she became while staying with a particular aunt and uncle. Although they tried to be kind to their little guests, they were not used to children, as they had none of their own. She remembered timidly asking her aunt for a cube of sugar for her hot milk - it reminded her of home-but the aunt's stern response was, "We are too poor to waste sugar on spoiled children." Later, the sisters would be separated again when Mami was sent to live with family in Dominguez. Mami was treated as the poor relative, often cooking and cleaning to compensate for the roof over her head and the meager amount of food she was allotted. Their childhood was a difficult one and the siblings grew up constantly pining for one and other. When my mother married and moved to America, the sisters were once again, torn apart. Now, on these rare occasions when they were together, it was easy to comprehend why they couldn't get enough of each other.

Dani and I would stay in Tía Lela's kitchen for hours and listen to them talk. They'd sip their *mate*, eat freshly made *knishes* and we would quietly play in the corner, entertaining ourselves while trying to keep warm. Besides chatting in the kitchen with her sister, Mami loved getting her hair and nails done. She would go as often as possible and disregard the cost; apparently one American dollar was worth a *gazillion* of the Monopoly-like Argentine *peso.* Of course, Mami would bring Tía Lela and Dani and I would also come along for the day's primping and polishing.

Sometimes after a day in the s*alon de belleza*, Mami would be invited out for the evening. It was very rare, but upon occasion, Mami would go out to dinner with her brothers or cousins and we'd stay at home with Tía Lela and the children. I would suffer tremendous anxiety attacks and would will myself to stay awake until Mami returned. It was as if falling asleep meant surrendering control; I needed to be alert. I was not aware of earthquakes hitting Buenos Aires, but I had overheard the adults speaking of attacks. In July, a bomb had exploded outside a Jewish business, very close to where my grandparents lived. And just recently, there had been a report of another bomb exploding outside of the Hebraica club in Rosario. I knew that Rosario was far away, but the possibility of another attack provoked deep rooted fear. Quietly, I would take a mental inventory of everyone's whereabouts; Mami was out with the family, Dani and I were well taken care of by Tía Lela. And Papi…Papi was home alone.

Although he would continually reassure us that he was glad we could visit The Argentina Family, I was guilt stricken and suffered for his apparent loneliness. When it was finally time to go back home, Dani and I would play our Partridge Family record; singing evocative lyrics about flying home with a bizarre mixture of glee and subdued desperation.

It was mid-September before we boarded a plane and endured another twenty-two hour flight back home to Los Angeles. As soon as we landed, and even before the Fasten-Your-Seatbelt-sign was turned off, the restless passengers began gathering their belongings in preparation for a hurried and harried exit. Dani, Mami and I were ourselves anxious, but now accustomed to the routine; we knew that attempting to rush out would be useless. We sat patiently in our seats when suddenly we were met with a wonderful surprise. The stewardesses had opened the doors of the jet and Papi marched himself right in! The other passengers looked at us wondering why we were so special. There he was; dressed in his Pan Am uniform and holding three flower bouquets. After the hugs and kisses, Papi picked up our coats and bags and escorted us off the plane. We traipsed along right behind him, beaming as we held our bouquets and Pan Am souvenirs.

When we got home, he continued the welcome-home surprise. In the kitchen was a brand new table set; a round white Formica table surrounded by semi-circular swivel chairs made of yellow pleather. It was very modern and definitely very "Brady." It was the start of a tradition that he'd maintain with each of our trips. Upon on our return, we were always welcomed home with hugs and kisses, unexpected gifts, and unspoken, but undeniable relief.

When we settled back into our routine, Mami took me to see Dr. Pulido, my pediatrician. My parents had become very concerned about my anxiety attacks. After hearing the whole story, the earthquake, the failed sleepovers, the inability to sleep when left with a sitter, Dr. Pulido stated, "Mrs. Trupp, your daughter seems to suffer from a chronic sense of insecurity. What is she so afraid of? What do *you* think is causing this anxiety in your daughter's life?"

Lifelines

Papi had finally earned sufficient vacation time and so the next plan on the agenda was the long awaited family expedition back to Argentina. The trip was scheduled for March to coincide with our spring vacation; even so, Mami had to ask our teachers to allow us an extra two weeks off. The family was simply too large and spread out. We couldn't see everyone in just one week's time and after all, it had been ten years since we had all been together. I was shipped off with reading material and homework assignments to complete while "on vacation."

All the travel arrangements were made and I remember feeling so proud of my father. He always reminded us that he was a *simple workingman* but somehow, I didn't believe him. Papi took us to the airport when he bought the tickets and showed us where he worked. Everyone seemed to know him-the ticket agents; the handsome pilots, the sophisticated stewardesses-Dani and I were in awe. How could a *simple workingman* get us into the pilot's cockpit for a private tour? We even went into the Members Only club and Papi bought us each a "Shirley Temple" at the upscale bar. How many daughters of simple workingmen had official Pan Am travel bags packed with all sorts of goodies, such as Junior Clipper Crew wings, state of the art headsets and blankets with the words Pan American Airlines embroidered with golden thread?

My father proudly announced that the Trupp family would be traveling First Class. I didn't know what First Class meant, but he assured us that it was a very special. He didn't go into the details, such as explaining about upgrades or Stand-By policies. I somehow believed that the wonderful people at Pan Am appreciated my father so much that we were being treated to this luxury *just because.* I boldly declared that I aspired to be a stewardess when I grew up. I wanted to work for Pan Am and be part of that glamorous world. Papi became very serious and immediately told me, "Absolutely not, Mirtita. That's not the sort of job for a nice girl." And without further explanation, my plans for a career with Pan Am were grounded even before they had a chance to take off.

With the upcoming Argentina trip, the postman seemed to be delivering cartloads of mail, even more than our usual weekly correspondence. I often wondered what the he thought of us every time he delivered those blue and white-striped envelopes stamped "Via Aero." Mami and Tía Lela, being the most dedicated writers in *La Familia*, were keeping the postman busy. Papi called the letters *novelas* because Tía Lela reported on the comings and goings of each and every family member. He would often tease Mami saying that we even knew if someone was constipated, because Tía Lela wrote in such detail! Of course, we received letters from the *bobes* and various aunts and cousins. Family news went back and forth, along with birthday and holiday greetings, recipes and remedies for all sorts of ailments. Needless to say, each letter was an event at our house.

When the phone rang and we heard the voice on the other line say, "*Operadora Internacional*," we would shout out "Argentina! Argentina!" and our parents would come running. Calls from the Argentina Family were rare as very few people had phones in their homes. They'd have to bother a neighbor or walk down the street to a local pharmacy. Either way, they'd have to place the call with the operator and then wait until a line could be patched through; sometimes waiting for hours before being connected. Whether by phone or mail, these lines of communication were truly lifelines for our parents.

Although Dani and I spoke Spanish (Spanish actually being our first language), Papi wanted to make sure we knew how to read and write as well. He enjoyed the role of teacher and because he was always trying to improve his English skills, Papi asked me to be *his* teacher. I would come home from school and share my grammar lesson of the day. He would turn it around and teach the lesson to me in Spanish. Part of my tutoring included writing letters to my grandparents and other relatives. Papi took these lessons very seriously and impressed upon me the importance of maintaining the lines of communication. He would bring out a red marker so that he could make corrections to my "first drafts." Carefully avoiding that darn marker, I wrote many letters telling the family that we were very excited about our upcoming trip. When I wrote to a very important aunt, Papi took out his highlighter and circled the word *vos*, which means *you* in English.

"Mirtita, you have to show your aunt respect therefore; you must use the word *usted* when referring to this *tía*."

"I don't get it. The word *vos* and *usted* mean the same thing, right?"

"Yes, you are correct, but in Argentina, certain situations require the word *usted* to show that person deference."

"Yes, but *in America*," I said with a wide grin, "everyone is just plain *you*, because we are taught in school that we were all created equal!"

In another effort to maintain family ties, when the blockbuster film, *The Fiddler on the Roof* came out, it was decided that we'd all caravan "over the hill" to see the celebrated movie in style. The adults planned an evening of family fun in the city, first a movie debut, and then dinner at the famous Canter's Deli. In the elegant theater, Daniela and

I sat next to the Bernstein boys, cocooned by our parents and vast array of assorted aunts, uncles and older cousins. The adults laughed and cried; they clapped along with the gay music and sat silently in poignant reflection when the scenes turned solemn.

After the movie, the women wiped away their tears and sighed. The men slapped each other on the back and said, "Good movie, *eh*?" One of the cousins said that he was ready for a nice bowl of *borsht.* Papi announced he was in the mood for some herring and wondered if there would be vodka at the deli; it would be nice to toast the *bobes* and *zeides* before the meal.

Once finally seated in the restaurant, boisterously taking up a whole side of the restaurant, our parents lifted up their glasses and toasted, "*L'chaim*!" I asked my parents why they were so emotional. Mami explained, "This was more than just a movie, Mirtita. Of course, we laughed and cried with Tevye and his family. We celebrate their *simchas* and accompany them in their sorrows, because this was the story of our *bobes* and *zeides.* The characters could have been any one of our relatives; the paths that led them out of Russia were the same that led our families to Argentina, to Canada, and to America."

At that point, one of the uncles was so inspired that he grabbed an empty wine bottle, placed it on top of his head and began dancing and singing, "To life, to life, *L'chaim*!" We all laughed and clapped along, until the bottle fell and shattered into tiny pieces all across the floor. The waitress, who previously shouted out our orders for *varenekes*, brisket and farfel, now wailed, "Clean up at table 10! Another *groisser klotz* (big clumsy guy) playing Tevye!" The entire restaurant began laughing, and I wished I had something to pull over my *borsht*-colored face. Where was Yenta's *babushka* when I needed it?

What's the Difference?

Things were going well at Shirley Avenue Elementary. I was in the fourth grade and was a good student, excelling in reading, writing, geography and history (I'm purposefully omitting math). Mrs. Burger's lesson plan for the semester included public speaking. The assignment would take two weeks. During the first week, we had to stand in front of the room and tell our classmates what we were doing for our Spring break. The second week was a show-and-tell project. We had to bring in something unique, present it to the class and then participate in a question and answer session. I thought the first week was very interesting and after listening to everyone talk about camping and beach trips, I proudly said, "I'm going to visit The Argentina Family."

The teacher corrected me and said, "You mean you are going to visit *your family in Argentina*."

"Well, yes," I said, "but my mother calls them *The Argentina Family*, because that's how you say it in Spanish-*La Familia Argentina*. I'm going to have to speak Spanish because The Argentina Family doesn't speak English."

The teacher corrected me again and said, "Murda, you mean Portuguese, dear. Argentina is part of Brazil and they speak Portuguese."

I stared at my teacher in disbelief. How could a teacher make such a mistake? She must be testing me or testing the class for some kind of geography lesson. One student raised his hand and asked if there were kangaroos in Argentina.

"No, there aren't any kangaroos. It's Argentina, *not Australia*! Maybe you should catch the next Schoolhouse Rock. I think they have an episode on geography." Then turning my attention to the head of the class, I continued, "Mrs. Burger. Argentina is not part of Brazil. It is a completely different country. Can I show you?" I said as I pointed to the classroom's globe. "My father taught us all about the countries in South America. He brought home a map from Pan Am and we studied all the countries and memorized each capital. Argentina is definitely not part of Brazil and they speak Spanish, not Portuguese."

Mrs. Burger was not too pleased about being corrected in front of the whole class. She turned to the chalkboard and while erasing the morning's lesson, she murmured something about how lucky I was to experience such a different spring vacation. I recognized the emphasis on the word "different" and also realized that my story didn't seem to fit the mold. I didn't like the feeling of not fitting in with everyone else. My name was different; no one in my class was called Mirta. My parents were different; no one else's parents spoke English with a funny accent. My lunch was different; no one else brought *milanesa* sandwiches to school. My Spring Break story was certainly different. After all, who was going to go all the way down to a weird South American country nestled *in Brazil*?

The following week was show-and-tell. I tried to come up with something unique that would interest the teacher and the kids in class. As much as I wanted to be like everyone else, the teacher said *the most unique* presentation would get the highest grade. Being an overachiever, I wanted to earn the highest grade myself. I was certain that no one else drank *yerba mate* at home, so I decided to make my presentation all about the traditional Argentine herbal tea. On the day of the presentation, I packed up all my supplies, the loose green leaves, the intricately carved gourd, and Mami's prettiest silver straw with the gold-tip and placed them in a brown lunch sack.

As my turn was coming up, I asked the teacher if I could go to the restroom because I needed hot water for my presentation. She gave me permission and off I went to the girls' restroom. I took out all the items from the lunch sack and was letting the hot water run when suddenly 3 six-grade girls came in. I was always very intimidated by the older girls, so I tried not to call any attention to myself. That was easier said than done because one of them immediately noticed that I was unrolling a plastic baggie filled with a green leafy substance.

"Oh my God, I don't believe it!" she shouted. The other two girls came immediately to her side to see what was so exciting.

I looked at her curiously and asked, "*You* know about *mate*?" I thought maybe she recognized the tea and was surprised to see me preparing the drink.

"*Mah-tay*…I've never heard *that* term before. My brother calls it a different name and I've seen him rolling it up into small cigarettes." She turned to her friends and tossed her hair back, a-la-Marcia Brady, and said, "Girls, the little twerp brought marijuana to school!"

There was huge gasp followed by giggles. One of them turned and shouted as she ran out the door, "I'm going to the principal's office!"

I couldn't have been more confused! I didn't know what the fuss was all about and I certainly didn't know what marijuana was! Suddenly, the principal was in the girl's bathroom and demanding to see what I had in my hand. I showed him the tea and told him, "It is *yerba mate*. My mother has it every day."

He took the plastic baggie and the brown lunch sack and told me to follow him to his office. The six graders smugly returned to their classrooms bursting at the seams with this juicy piece of gossip. They were, after all, part of a drug bust at Shirley Avenue Elementary School.

The principal sent a message to Mrs. Burger and informed her that I was being detained in his office until my mother could come to school. He had called my mother and asked her to come to his office right away. It only took a few minutes for Mami to show up all in a panic. She was escorted into the principal's office and found me sitting quietly in a large leather chair. In front of me, laid out across the principal's desk, sat her *mate*, the metal straw and a plastic baggie filled with *yerba*.

"Mrs. Trupp, before I call the authorities, can you explain what these items are?" he said with his lips tightly pursed.

Mami gave me a baffled look and then turning to face the principal said, "This is *mate*. It is a tea we drink in *Arr-hen-tina*."

He looked at the both of us and saw the look of complete confusion and disbelief. For the first time, he actually opened the plastic baggie and took a long sniff.

"Mrs. Trupp, what is all this paraphernalia?" he said waiving his hand across his desk.

Mami didn't know what paraphernalia meant, but she saw that he was pointing at the long, silver straw and the gourd, so she explained, "We put the *yerba*, the herb tea, into this container. We call this container a *mate*. We add very hot water and a little sugar. We use a metal straw with a filtered tip to sip the tea. When we are finished, we add more water and pass it to the next person who wants to drink."

Mami said all this still shaking from the fright the phone call had given her. It didn't help matters to be standing in front of such an important man as the school principal who was threatening to call the authorities. She didn't think that *mate* was illegal in America. Would the authorities deport us for having *yerba mate*? She made a mental note to check her purse for our Green Cards, as soon as possible.

The principal asked Mami to sit down while he made a phone call. When he set down the receiver, he packed the three items into the brown lunch sack and said, "Murda, Mrs. Trupp, I have to apologize for all of this commotion. I admit that I am ignorant of Argentine customs, but this is 1972 and the world has gone completely mad. Our little elementary school, here in this quiet little town, has to run Duck and Cover drills thanks to a war that is raging over in Vietnam. We have to provide surveillance against rising gang activity. We are in the middle of a drug free for all. This product looks very similar to marijuana and I over reacted. Please accept my apologies."

He held out his hand. Mami shook the principal's hand, looked at me and shrugged. I was allowed to return to class and Mami went home. The principal explained everything to Mrs. Burger. Even though she accepted the principal's explanation, she still looked at me with a bit of disdain. In her eyes, I had caused trouble and I knew it was because I was just *different*.

The Big Trip

After much planning and packing *and* shopping for gifts for The Argentina Family, it was March and it was finally time to go! Tío Elias came to take us to the airport and made a comment about the amount of luggage. He was worried how it was all going to fit in his car. Papi muttered something like "Don't even mention it," as he doubled checked each bag that he tied with twine. I knew that it was a touchy subject because I had heard Mami and Papi arguing. Papi said that we were taking presents enough for the entire country. Mami just kept reminding him that if she took something for *this* person, she needed to take something for *that* person and after all, "*Son familia, Ruben*!"

My parents were beyond happy at the prospect of seeing The Argentina Family, especially Papi, as it had been ten years since he had last been there. This trip would indeed be very special. Dani and I knew that with Papi along, we were headed for quite an adventure. Mami had dressed us in matching purple jumpsuits. We felt grown up in our outfits. I was very eager to make the right impression and show everyone how much I had grown up. Certainly the big yellow smiley face embroidered on the front of the dress made us look very *hip*. We each had our special Pan Am traveling bags. Mami made sure that we packed extra underwear and some other necessities just in case. I, however, made sure that there was room for several books, and more importantly, room for my records. I brought along several of my favorite "LP's", especially my collection of *The Partridge Family*.

When we arrived at Ezeiza International Airport, the emotion was palpable. There was a man taking photographs of passengers as they walked into the building. It made me feel very important to have my picture taken. It was like a scene from one of those old movies I watched with Papi. A famous person would come out of the plane and hoards of photographers would come running to snap their picture as the celebrity waved to their adoring fans. We didn't have fans, but we did have people shouting and waving to us from the other side of the fence.

Going through Customs was always a very trying experience, but Papi seemed to manage it well enough. It was not the first time that I noticed my parents slipping some money quickly and quietly into the palm of an attendant or service person. I realized, very much like Dorothy in the *Wizard of Oz*, we were not in the San Fernando Valley anymore! I remember feeling my father's frustration of how things were done here, as he always seemed to mutter under his breath, "*Esto no pasa en los Estados Unidos*" (This does not happen in the USA). We finally cleared the Customs area and suddenly, there appeared to be five hundred people upon us. Everyone was crying and shouting. Strangers were hugging and kissing me. Dani and I were a bit overwhelmed and startled at our parents' reactions. Our luggage was distributed amongst those with cars; we were gathered up and taken to Mami's parents' house. Bobe Carmen and Zeide Efraim were waiting for us there, along with the *other* five hundred people who couldn't make it out to the airport.

My grandparents lived in an area known as El Once, the equivalent to New York's lower East side. It was a busy part of town, filled with apartments and shops and apparently, the entire Jewish population of Buenos Aires. Our grandparents' home was a tiny one-bedroom apartment on the first floor of a ten-story building. Their apartment, number 11, was at the end of a long hallway. People were lined up waiting for us as if we were royalty walking a processional. There were people on the staircase, leaning over to see what all the fuss was about and I heard one lady tell the others that it was Carmen's daughter from *Norte America.* This caused a loud and pronounced, "*Azoy*?" uttered in unison.

"Really?" one lady said as she sipped her *mate*. "I thought Lina and the girls were just here? They are back so soon?"

"They must be doing very well in *Norte America*!" another neighbor said as she spit three times over her shoulder. "*Kaynahoreh*!" (Yiddish saying to protect against the Evil Eye)

"*Yachnas! (*Gossips) Be quiet!" still another neighbor shouted out. "*I* heard tell that this time they came with Carmen's son-in-law, a real *macher* (a big shot) in Pan American Airlines! *Kaynahoreh*!"

I watched in horror as the three ladies all turned to spit three times over the shoulders, but didn't have time to comment *or* recoil as we finally reached the apartment. Once again, the crying and hugging began. My grandmother was a plump and chronically agitated lady who fluttered away as soon as she hugged us, unable to control her jittery state. My grandfather, a slender, usually calm man, wept as he hugged me and said, "Welcome back *cucale*." (Yiddish term of endearment)

There was food spread out over many tables in the small room. Amongst the *empanadas*, *mayonesa*, and *tartas de cebolla,* there was herring, *varenekes,* pickled tongue and a couple of bottles of vodka, just like in the old country. I had always thought that the "old country" meant Argentina. But with The Argentina Family, the "old country" meant Russia. The delicacies were meant to honor our arrival. There was a plate with something that resembled Jell-O, only it was brownish in color and speckled with bits of…could it be-*meat*? When I had a chance to ask my mother, she told me that it was a special Russian treat, called *holidetz*, made from chicken bones and fat.

The tiny apartment crammed with people was becoming a bit overwhelming. I was used to noisy family reunions, but this one, possibly because I was overtired from the trip, was quickly beginning to get on my nerves. Taking my plate, I went out to the tiniest of patios to get some fresh air. Not surprisingly, I found my father there as well. Papi didn't like cramped places either. I always remembered his story about being locked in the military jail cell. A family reunion in a miniature apartment wasn't exactly equal to martial punishment, but then again, maybe for Papi, it was.

"Hi Papi, want an *empanada*?" I asked handing him one off my plate.

"No thank you Mirtita, I'm full," he said patting his stomach with both hands. "How about that *holidetz;* did you try some?"

"It looks too slimy for my taste. Why is everyone still eating foods from the old country?

"Your grandparents were born in Russia-or there about. They were just little kids when they came to Argentina," Papi explained. "They were brought up speaking Yiddish and eating these comfort foods."

"*Little kids;* when exactly did they come here?

"I suppose it was in the early 1900's. Bobe Flora was born in 1903 and they were already here in 1906. I'm not sure about my father, but he was a young boy as well when his family immigrated. My father's side of the family first lived up north, in the province of Santa Fe before settling in another province, La Pampa. The town was called Bernasconi. That's where my parents met."

"That definitely was a long time ago. What about Mami's side of the family?"

"Your mother's family settled in Entre Rios. Your great-great grandfather was a teacher in the first Jewish school of Santa Isabel."

"Why did they come to Argentina?" I asked, not realizing that we were setting the foundation for our future hobby.

"They weren't the only ones Mirtita. Hundreds of thousands came to Argentina thanks to the Jewish Colonization Association. A man by the name of Baron Maurice Hirsh set up the organization to help the Jews escape."

"What were they running away from?"

"People were escaping horrifying attacks called *pogroms.* They were being attacked, murdered in the streets. Jews were imprisoned without cause; they were not allowed to study or work within their chosen trades. Their young sons were taken from them and forced into military service for years and years. Most of the boys never survived. The people had to escape and find a better life for their children."

"Why didn't they go to the United States? We have been reading about Ellis Island at school. America is called the great melting pot."

"Yes, you're right," Papi agreed. "Most of the immigrants found their way to the United States, but as America began to close her borders, Baron Hirsch and others tried to find another solution. Argentina was a young country, recently achieving their independence from Spain. It needed people to populate the land and so, it accepted these immigrants. They had to learn a new language and new skills. They had to acquire new social customs and get acclimated to the weather and food. For many, it was the beginning of assimilating to non-Jewish customs."

"What do you mean?"

"Well, slowly but surely, some men stopped wearing the traditional clothing of the religion. They wore clothes more in keeping with the style of the locals, even wearing the gaucho's *bombachas* when working in the fields or with the animals. Some shaved their beards and cut their hair. They kept kosher for as long as they could, but when faced with starving to death, they had to curtail their customs. Little by little, these courageous families began their new lives incorporating customs of their adopted countrymen, while maintaining as much as they could of their faith and heritage."

"Papi, I never knew all that. I should have asked you before."

"Mirtita, you are so young. There is plenty of time to ask questions and to learn about your family history. But now, I guess we better go back inside before your mother comes out here and accuses us both of being *antipáticos*," he said moving his eyebrows up and down like Groucho Marx.

The North Americans

We eventually made it over to Bobe Flora and Zeide Simon's apartment, also in the Jewish neighborhood of Corrientes and Pasteur. Bobe Flora would not be overshadowed by Bobe Carmen's reception. There was an exorbitant amount of food and an absurd amount of people to greet us. I was sure that the walls would burst at the seams. Amongst the guests were a few of Papi's old girl friends. I was shocked that they would come to visit, but *Rubencito's* return was a big deal in the neighborhood. Mami didn't seem to mind, she was just so happy about being in Argentina again.

Everywhere we went, it was announced, "*Allí vienen los Norte Americanos*" (Here come the North Americans). I would try to explain to anyone who would listen that we were not North Americans; we were just plain Americans. Papi tried to convince me to ignore the misnomer.

"Papi, but *we* are Americans! If they call us North Americans, that means we're also Canadians and Mexicans! *I* should know; you make us study the globe all the time!"

"Yes, Mirtita, but the people of Argentina live in South America and they feel they are Americans too."

"Well…I don't know about that. We live in The United States of America, right?"

"*Sí*, Mirtita," Papi said trying not to lose his patience.

"Well, you told me that this country is called *La Republica Argentina.* See? There's no mention of *America* in the name!"

"OK, Mirtita, but please, *try* not to argue with The Argentina Family."

Dani and I were placed in the limelight and asked to speak in English everywhere we went. Friends and family would exclaim with delight, "How well the little *Yanquis* (Yankee: a term of endearment, or a derogatory snub) speak the language!" I thought that was a funny thing to say and I told them so. Didn't a child in Argentina speak Spanish well? Of course, we spoke English well; we spoke it every day! Luckily, they laughed and agreed with me, because I wasn't supposed to argue…

People would ask about our home and where would we like to live, in Argentina or *Norte America.* It seemed to be on everyone's mind, because everywhere we went, someone would ask us the same question! We would always answer "America" and they would always smile and laugh and look at each other and say, "*Claro*!" (Of course) That led to the predictable discussion of which country was better and before you knew it, the grown-ups were in the same heated dispute I had grown to hate. But *I* wasn't supposed to argue…

We were tempted and enticed with all sorts of Argentine delicacies: *alfajores* (chocolate or powdered sugar cookies filled with *dulce de leche*-a caramel spread), *chocolate en rama* (strands of braided chocolate), *media lunas* and *sándwiches de miga*. While everything was delicious, I couldn't be swayed; I instinctively knew that they were trying to get me to admit a preference to all things Argentine. In defiance, albeit I was only ten-years-old, I challenged, "Aren't *media lunas* actually French croissants? Didn't we see *sándwiches de miga* in that old English movie the other day, Papi? You know, when those fancy people were having tea? They were called finger sandwiches, right?" Darn! I wasn't supposed to argue…

Inevitably, for some inexplicable reason, everybody would ask the little *Yanquis* to sing and Mami would make us put on a show. Dani and I had come up with choreography to our favorite Partridge Family tunes; we would perform in front of The Argentina Family and all the neighbors who wanted to see the *Norte Americanas*. We had been were received with great fan-fare. With Papi on the trip, we were exposed to most of the massive, extended family in a matter of a few weeks. Neither Dani nor I were ready to receive the amount of love that was showered upon us, nor did we know how to handle the superstar treatment that we received as the little *Yanquis*.

One afternoon, Zeide Simon took us to the park. It was such a special day that I would never forget it. I am sure that it was just as special for him. Zeide had many grandchildren by then, but we were *las nenas de Norte America* and therefore very dear to his heart. We carefully crossed one street after another, with Zeide holding our hands. We arrived at the park and we saw the most magnificent carousel. Zeide explained to the attendant that we were from *Norte America*. The attendant told him that he'd take good care of us. As we climbed onto the carousel, he began shouting at us as if we were deaf. He must have thought we'd understand him better if he spoke louder. He showed us a brass ring and told us to try to grab the ring off of its hook.

We were carefully perched on the beautifully carved wooden horses, holding the *churros* that Zeide bought us in one hand and holding on for dear life with the other as the carousel began to turn. We saw the other children reaching for the brass ring as they passed the attendant. Zeide kept telling us to reach for it, but it was not as easy as it seemed. I was afraid to lean over and the carousel seemed to be turning so fast. I think the attendant wanted to make a good impression on the *Norte Americanas*, so he let me win one round and Dani won the next. We each won a special treat and we triumphantly walked back to the apartment to show Bobe Flora, Mami and Papi.

The evenings were spent visiting family; apparently all of Buenos Aires was related to us one way or another. Mami and Tía Lela would spend the early hours huddled together in the small, damp kitchen sipping *mate*; crying, laughing and eating *pan* with *manteca* (bread and butter). Papi, repeating an old refrain, would exclaim that he was in the "Paris of South America" and would not remain sequestered in the kitchen with two emotional women. Venturing out alone, he'd splurge on shopping trips, buying all sorts of Argentine souvenirs, like intricate *gaucho* knives, belts and *boleadoras* (traditional hunting tool). He bought elaborate figurines carved out of bone, and decorative wall hangings made out of cowhides. I didn't know where he would put all these things when we got home. I wondered if Mami would approve, but I immediately caught myself. Of course, she would approve! They were all made in *Arr-hen-tina*!

There was a certain pride in the *porteños (*residents of the port city*)* that I could not understand. I didn't grasp the comparison between Buenos Aires and Washington D.C. Having never been to that great capital or anywhere else of importance, I didn't understand the relevance. Block after block, tall buildings took every inch of space. Imposing structures that housed famous museums, theaters or government entities looked ancient to my young eyes. I didn't like the dirty streets overflowing with frantic people and frenzied drivers. The buses were overflowing, so much so that sometimes, courageous passengers would simply cling onto the handrail outside of the bus and jump off at their stop. Even though we were in the Paris of South America, this "North American" missed her little yellow house on quiet Heartland Street.

Mas Al Sur (Further South)

Soon after, we were off on another adventure. Leaving the turmoil of Buenos Aires behind; we took a short plane ride further south to the agricultural, port city of Bahia Blanca to visit Papi's older sister. Tía Perla was married to Jacobo Felder and they had three grown children; Gisela who was married to Edgardo, Gaston, whom everyone said was the *playboy* of the family (I had no idea what that meant), and Monica, who would become like an older sister to me.

Charismatic and gallant, Gaston took great care to make us feel important and grown up. With his limited English vocabulary, mostly made up of Beatles lyrics and James Bond phrases, Gaston humbly declared that if he could speak English as well as his little cousins spoke Spanish; he would be very satisfied. It was, therefore, no surprise when asked who my favorite cousin was, I eagerly responded, "Gaston! He is my *mucho primo*!" This, loosely translated, was erroneously saying, "He is my *very* cousin!" I knew the moment the words came out of my mouth that it was incorrect, but there was no taking it back. Gaston felt the love with which the words were spoken and he took ownership of them. Exaggerating his English accent, he repeated the phrase, "Ee-hess, wee hour mu-chow pree-mouse." (Yes, we are *mucho primos*) Everyone shrieked with laughter at his silly antics and my grammar faux pas was forgotten. We would be *mucho primos* forever!

Bahia Blanca was a calm, farming town. I enjoyed the tranquility and was thankful to see that my aunt and uncle lived in a very comfortable, *heated* apartment. Tío Jacobo seemed to be much older than my other uncles were and always wore a rather gruff expression. Although he was kind to us, I was a little bit afraid of him. Not often at home, he kept himself occupied with his never-ending work. Papi told me that Tío Jacobo came to Argentina as a young, Polish immigrant. He left his family behind to make his fortune in South America. With a tremendous amount of dedication and ingenuity, Tío Jacobo had become a prosperous man and had many acres of rich farmland. I was very impressed and told Papi that I wished we could be so lucky.

"Tío Jacobo has had a very hard life. He struggled since the moment he arrived in the country with only pennies in his pocket and the good sense God gave him. And he has also had more than his share of tragedies…"

"What do you mean? What sort of tragedies?" I looked up at my father and saw his eyes had glazed over with tears.

"It's a long story Mirtita and you are too young to understand. *I* don't understand."

"I'm not too young; you can tell me."

"Well...you have studied a little bit about the Holocaust in school, right? You read The Diary of Anne Frank this year?"

"Yes, although we didn't talk about it at home too much. The story was very scary. I had a lot of questions about God and about being Jewish. Why don't we talk about these things? Kids ask me what Jews believe in. I don't know what to say. What *do* we believe Papi?

"Mirtita, I don't know what I believe or even what I am *supposed* to believe. I don't know if I believe in God."

I gasped, but found the courage to ask the question again, "But *why* don't you know?"

"My family's history is fairly sketchy...it seems that our ancestors were thought to be originally from Prussia. They must have wandered across the continent seeking a better life, probably living for a while in Poland, Lithuania and finally settling in the Russian Ukraine."

With a pout, I told my father that I thought he was going off on one of his tangents. Sometimes he would give us too much information and we'd be left trying to sift through to get to his message.

Papi told me to just listen; he would get to his point. "You see, after all that wandering around, they were accustomed to adapting to their surroundings, but the lifestyle created when my grandparents immigrated to Argentina was practically unrecognizable to what my forefathers had known. I don't know if it was out of fear or out of ignorance, or maybe it was the overwhelming desire to fit in with everyone else. I think that it was easier and maybe even, safer, *not* to follow the old customs. Sure, we spoke Yiddish and ate gefilte fish and matzah ball soup. We would get together for a holiday or a wedding and toast *L'chaim,* but to actually know and live the faith as our ancestors did; that became a thing of the past." Papi paused and looked down at me, finally realizing that he wasn't making any sense to his young daughter. "Look, I am proud to be a Jew and you should be too. Don't worry Mirtita. God willing, you will figure it out on your own one day."

"You said, *God willing.* I thought you didn't believe in God." I questioned mischievously.

Papi let out a stifled laugh. "I guess I am too mixed up to know what I believe!" He winked at me and gave me hug.

"What about Tío Jacobo? What didn't you want to tell me?"

"Well-you see…Tío Jacobo lost his entire family in the Holocaust; everyone except for a lone survivor; his young sister who was hidden away, just like Anne Frank. I can't bear to even think about it. I don't understand how God could allow such a thing to happen. Let's not talk about it anymore

Mirtita. We are here to have a good time, and that's exactly what we are going to do. Life is a blessing and you have to live it. Tío Jacobo is a wonderful example of just that.

It had been arranged to drive out to the *campo* for a traditional asado. It was fun packing up for the day and driving out to one of the farms my uncle owned. Dani and I were very eager to experience this traditional sort of Argentine day. When we finally arrived, three tall blond boys and a man wearing funny-looking pants were waiting for us at the gate. I asked my uncle about them. Tío Jacobo told us that he employed the man to take care of the farm. He explained that they were a German family and that those "funny-looking pants" were *bombachas*, the style that the *gauchos* wore. The farmer's wife came out to greet us. She wiped her hands on her apron, which was dusted with flour. She had made *empanadas* earlier and had just finished a batch of strudel. She wanted us to sample some traditional Argentine meat pastries along with her traditional German dessert. It seemed that everyone in Argentina was from somewhere else. Just like the United States, it was melting pot of immigrants.

While the grown-ups unloaded the trucks, Monica and Gaston introduced us to the farmer's sons. The boys were asked to show us around the farm and they happily agreed. The eldest one, Federico or Fredrik as his mother called him, was probably about eleven years old, but he was very tall for his age. Federico led the way, his two younger brothers, Dani and I practically running to follow his leggy stride. We walked for quite a bit and tried to have a conversation. I spoke Spanish well enough, but suddenly, I was overcome by a bout of shyness. It seemed that the boys were shy too, but they told us it was because we were *Yanquis* and they were not used to foreigners. To break the ice, we began by telling them we had never been on a farm and weren't used to seeing the animals.

"Where do you buy your food? Don't you have a farmer's market?" Federico asked. "Don't you see animals there?"

"My mother goes to a supermarket once a week," I explained. "She buys all the food we need at the store."

He was curious about the store. "What exactly is a supermarket and how does your mother manage to go only once a week?"

"The supermarket has all sorts of food in one place. We buy our breads, fruits and vegetables there, as well as milk and juice. Everything! The meat is packaged and frozen and probably can last forever!"

He smiled and asked me where did it all come from and I told him that I didn't know. Federico smiled again and walked us over to the barn and the corral. Dani and I happily petted the lambs and watched the goats and calves nursing. There even was a pony following his mother around. It was a scene out of picture book. All that was missing was Farmer John. The boys showed us how they milked the cows and even let us try our hand at it. They offered us a glass of milk, still warm from the cow's body. Dani and I, "Valley Girls" that we were, cringed. Continuing the tour, we walked past the chickens and pigpens and followed our charming guides to the next wooden structure. As we walked inside, Dani and I gasped in horror, for the small hut housed the hides and carcasses of various farm animals. Federico pompously said, "*This* is where the meat comes from." They laughed as we ran back to the farmhouse crying all the way.

By the time we reached the farmhouse, the *asado* was well under way. Tío Jacobo had prepared enough food for an army. There was plenty of meat to choose from and to our dismay; we realized that all the little animals we had played with earlier were represented on the gaucho's grill. Goats, chickens, lamb, calves…Dani and I became vegetarians for the duration of our vacation. Tío Jacobo was very proud of his meal and exclaimed, "This is real meat not like that plastic, frozen stuff you eat in America!" I took great offense to that statement and it would be a source of torment for many years to come. After the meal, one of the ranch hands began playing the guitar and another accompanied him on the *bandoneón*. The tables and chairs were moved to the sides and Edgardo led Gisela onto the makeshift dance floor. I was familiar with this music. The grown-ups always danced *tangos* or *milongas* when they were together. It was not happy music, I thought. No one smiled when they danced. It was almost mournful. I never understood why they loved it so, but it was always part of any family gathering and I guess it fit in with all the other drama surrounding the topic of Argentina.

After our visit in Bahia Blanca, we were to go even further south to visit Papi's younger sister, Tía Delia. That would lead us to my favorite place on earth, *Mayor Buratovich*. Small town, Bahia Blanca was practically a metropolis compared to rural Buratovich. Tía Delia and Tío Enrique lived "out in the country" with their four children, Marielita, Susanita, Miguelito and Arielita. It was common for children to be known by their diminutive name. Therefore, I was Mirtita, my sister was Danielita, and we would ever remain so for The Argentina Family.

The family had a small store, a *kiosco*, and their home, typical of most mom and pop businesses, was attached, right next-door. Tía Delia was a beautiful, sweet woman who adored her older brother. Tío Enrique and Papi had been friends practically their whole lives, serving in the army together. They were overjoyed to see us, especially because we had made the trip all the way down to *Burato*. The little town seemed to be in the middle of nowhere. Surrounded by acres and acres of farmland, it had four dirt roads and a town square smack in the center. From the park, you could walk to the church, the school or to the few little stores scattered here and there. Tío Enrique was more likely to have a customer pull up to his *kiosco* on a horse or in a *sulky* (a light weight cart), rather than a car. I loved the little town as soon as the train pulled into the frontier-style station.

Marielita and Susanita were 15 and 14 respectively. Miguelito was 13 years old and Arielita was the baby of the family at six years of age. Dani and I were very happy to spend time with this family. In Buenos Aires, all our cousins were either much older or much younger. Marielita and Susanita adopted us right away. We became their pets! They played with our hair, doing the famous *toca* style. They would make-us up as if we were "big girls" and then show us off to all their friends who thought we were so adorable.

We spent the majority of our time running back and forth between the house and the *kiosco*. The shop was filled with all sorts of goodies, but I didn't dare ask. I hadn't yet learned my uncle's mannerisms; I didn't realize his bark was worse than his bite until he began showering us with candy and *alfajores*. With a wicked grin he'd then growl, "Go on, and get out of my store!" We would run out the door laughing and munching away on our candy bars.

One afternoon my mother sent me on an errand; I came running into the kiosco shouting, "*Papi, Mami te quiere*!" Everyone laughed, as Papi answered, "Tell your mother, *Yo la quiero también*!"

I was trying to say, "Mami *wants* you!" but I mangled the translation and it came out as, "Mami *likes* you!" Papi answered in kind, "I like her too!" My embarrassment was only intensified by Tío Enrique's comments. He didn't approve of our language blunders. He thought Mami and Papi should only speak Spanish around us.

An old army buddy happened to have stopped in to greet the Yanquis and hear tales of *Norte America.* Ramon overheard the conversation and agreed with my uncle. His disdain for all things American was evident; his thinly veiled opinion of expatriates was piercing. My father, out of respect for an old friendship, tried to explain his position without causing further strain.

"Ramon, it is important for us to speak English and to get acclimated to the American culture. The girls speak Spanish and know about their Argentine traditions. Believe me, Lina does enough droning about Argentina *this* and Argentina *that.* The girls definitely know where they came from."

"Maybe so, but it wouldn't hurt if you'd stop waving the red, white and blue flag in their faces," the man snarled.

"Which flag would you prefer I wave? America is my country now; she has adopted me and I have adopted her. I may not be a rich man, but America allows me certain freedoms that I could never achieve here. I live in peace and that is probably the greatest gift a country could give her people."

Miguel took this opportunity to add his two cents into the pot. "When I'm old enough, I am getting out of this backwards town and am going to try my luck in America!"

Tío Enrique quickly retaliated with a great bellow, "Over my dead body!"

All this drama was beyond my comprehension. I didn't realize it at the time, but I came to believe that Tío Enrique's reaction was based on fear and regret. He feared losing his son to a place so far away from his reality that it might as well have been on the moon. However, in the moment when he blurted out his gut reaction, I was deeply hurt and my American pride was wounded.

That afternoon, Dani and I accompanied our cousins to their friend's home. With the "Mayberry" ambiance, we felt as if we could run into Opi Taylor as we strolled through the town square and down the few, short blocks. Arriving at our destination, we found the modest home full of noisy teens. Most of the kids were in the school choir; music was coming from all corners of the room. They performed a few songs and then of course, asked us to sing. For some reason, they wanted to hear our patriotic songs, so Dani and I belted out *You're a Grand Ol' Flag*, *God Bless America* and *This Land is Your Land* reminiscent of scenes from old Judy Garland movies. When the typical question followed and we were asked, "Where do you prefer to live?" I answered, "America *and* Buratovich!" Everyone cheered and shouted, "*Viva las Yanquis*!" It was pretty heady stuff for a 7 and 10 year old.

It was at this point that the group thought it would be fun to teach us a short Argentine poem to recite for our parents. I borrowed some paper and a pencil to write down the few lines that began...*En el cielo, las estrellas, En el campo, las espinas.* Off in the margins, I scribbled out a simple translation, although it didn't rhyme as it did in Spanish, it made it easier for us to memorize the lines.

In the sky, there are stars, in the field, there are thorns.
In the center of my heart, The Argentine Republic!

One of the boys asked if we thought our parents would like the verse. I laughed and assured him that anything to do with Argentina was sure to please my parents. The kids were impressed at my translating skills, seeing the English doodled off to the sides of my note. I was slightly bemused at their reaction; it had become second nature to me.

When the boys thought of another short song they wanted to teach us, Marielita and Susanita were not as eager. It was a political song, but the words had been changed.

"Julian, the girls shouldn't sing this, and besides," Marielita continued, "it's mean-spirited and who knows who might hear them. It could cause trouble."

"Why would it cause trouble? I want to hear it!" I exclaimed. And so the boys had me write out a little ditty that began, "Peron! Peron!"

As we walked home a short while later, I went through the events of the day. I thought of Tío Enrique and Miguel's outbursts. I thought about Marielita's warning about singing a silly political song. I remembered what Papi had said about America. It was not about striking it rich and becoming a millionaire. He was rich because he had peace of mind; he was rich because he felt free.

With all these thoughts rumbling about in my head, it occurred to that I was very proud to live in America, even though that meant I couldn't live with The Argentina Family that I had grown to love. In my ten-year-old mind, I began blaming Argentina for making my father feel it necessary to move away. *Argentina* had robbed us of The Argentina Family. In that moment, I knew that I could not recite that short patriotic poem; at least not as it had been taught. The words said, "In the center of my heart is The Argentine

Republic!" But that was not true! In the center of *my* heart was America!

I began thinking of how I could modify the poem to reflect my feelings. Dani had Marielita and the rest of the group occupied with some anecdote, so I walked the remaining blocks in silence. By changing a word or two, I could change the whole verse. All I had to do was find a word that rhymed with the Spanish "*Los Estados Unidos.*" Suddenly, I came up with the magic word and it was all thanks to a T.V. commercial-"The Frito Bandito."

After dinner, we all walked over to the café across the street from the plaza. The doors were wide open and the evening breeze flowed in between the colorful strips of plastic that created a makeshift screen door. We sat down occupying three tables in the small room. The kids enjoyed their *dulce de leche* ice cream while the adults sipped their wine. Miguel and friends said, "Let's hear from the little *Yanquis*!" The intimate crowd in the café began to cheer and so, "The Mirtita and Danielita Show" began once more.

Miguel held out a chair, which was meant to be a provisional stage, and gave me a hand up. He whispered, "Do the poem they taught you today." I smiled and said, "OK!" Taking a deep breath and looking straight at Papi, I began:

En el cielo, las estrellas, En el campo, los **bandidos.**

En el centro de mi pecho, **Los Estados Unidos***!*

There was a collective gasp in the crowd when they heard the changes in the verse. Then there was silence, but only for a second because they began cheering and applauding. I heard people saying, "Of course! She is right! Why would she feel otherwise?" "*Muy bien Yanqui*! *Otra*! *Otra*!"

They wanted more so I decided to sing the controversial song the boys taught me. Papi said he felt free as an American; being controversial didn't seem to stop anyone in America, and so I began: "*Peron, Peron! Que tonto sos! El general de…*" I wasn't allowed to finish. Papi jumped out of his chair, grabbed me about the waist and cupped his hand over my mouth before I finished calling the previous president foolish and his followers, stupid.

"*Basta*, Mirtita. You can't sing that here." And with that, the evening show was over.

The next morning, our cousins took us to their school. Again, we were made to feel like visiting celebrities. The students were dressed in their starched white lab coats. Argentine schools had strict uniform regulations and Daniela and I stuck out like sore thumbs. I wore striped blue pants with a red-fringed belt, a bright red crocheted top and a beaded choker. I loved that fringed belt most of all. It was something that Marcia Brady would have worn (I was definitely the product of the T.V. generation!)

It was a small school and all the grades, elementary through high school, gathered in the central courtyard first thing in the mornings. They sang the national anthem and stood at attention as the flag was raised, but that particular day the children only had eyes for the two strangers in their midst. I listened to the students singing, watched the blue and white flag wave about with the early morning breeze and felt very strange. Had it not been for a small twist of fate, Dani and I could have been students in this little country school. We might have walked to school each day with our cousins here in Mayor Buratovich. We might have grown up having birthdays, holidays with our grandparents, and not have to witness the melancholy on our parents' faces. There would not have been the need for cakes decorated with the words, "With Love, The Argentina Family" or toasts to "*Los presentes y los ausentes*," because we would have been together all along. There would have been no tormenting thoughts of picking up and leaving at a moment's notice, because Mami would have been happy in her surroundings. I found myself torn and confused. All my bravado from the previous night was gone.

Before too long, our final days in Argentina approached. We said our goodbyes to Tía Delia and Tío Enrique and then it was time to say goodbye to our cousins. They came with us to the station and even when we boarded, Marielita and I held hands through the windows of the massive old train, promising one and other that we would write every day. I cried out when the whistle blew and the train began to move. Marielita began walking faster to keep up, still holding on to me. Just like in those old movies I watched with my father, where couples refused to part until the very last moment; we gripped our hands together. When Marielita finally had to let go, I cried out the window, "*Te quiero prima,*" as Marielita frantically waved goodbye.

Dani, whimpering, sat clinging to my mother, as we experienced the most heart-wrenching event in our young lives. I turned my head and stared out the window as the train sped by acres of wheat and herds of cattle. With tears falling silently as the train tore us away from our family, I recalled how Dani and I reveled in the outpour of love we received from our adoring aunt and uncle, Tía Delia and Tío Enrique and the four children.

Gaston was waiting for us at the train station in Bahia Blanca. He drove us back to Tía Perla's apartment where we had lunch; Dani and I were only eating pasta, still traumatized from our trip to the farm. After lunch and a short *siesta*, we were taken to the airport, not much more than an airfield and small building, where we had to say our goodbyes again. Papi had a very hard time leaving his sisters. It was not easy to watch him as the tears began to well up in his eyes. About an hour later, we were back in Buenos Aires where the following days would be consumed with further tender partings.

Each day had become more and more painful as Mami and Tía Lela clung to one another. The weather was very much like everyone's mood, cold and wretched. I couldn't help thinking that back home it was spring. What were my friends doing? Even worse, and infinitely more profound, was the gnawing sensation in the pit of my stomach when I thought about The Argentina Family. Now that we had gotten to know everyone, we were being ripped away. I secretly thought it might have been better had we never met our family; never felt their love and the sense of belonging. It seemed to be a cruel joke. I desperately didn't want to leave The Argentina Family, but was equally desperate to *get back home.*

Quandaries

Although it was just a few weeks, it felt like we had been away for a lifetime. When we landed in LAX (Los Angeles - this young traveler had become used to airport lingo), I wanted to kiss the ground. I knew I was home when the airport staff politely greeted the passengers and directed us to our luggage and Customs. There was no clandestine interchange of money here. Things were done in a calm and orderly fashion, just the way Papi like it-just the way *I* like it. As we walked down the long passageway, I let my fingers glide across the multicolored tiled wall and soaked in the sense of familiarity, security and organization. On the freeway, I poked my head out the window and happily watched as the familiar landscape whizzed by. "My" mountain, the one shaped like a capital M, seemed to be welcoming me back home. Mami and Papi took us to Bob's Big Boy for dinner. Dani and I were thrilled, having put all thoughts of the farm behind us.

My father was ecstatic to be home; that was not unexpected. The surprise rather, came from my mother when even *she* commented on the ease of her daily routine. Paying bills by mail, going grocery shopping in one's own car, or the simple act of picking up the phone and hearing a dial tone was enough to have a positive affect my mother's downheartedness. That was not to say that Mami didn't feel the pangs for family.

My mother loved entertaining and being surrounded by loved ones. Mami was an excellent cook and feeding people was her greatest joy. The feeling was mutual; everyone she met recognized her generous spirit and kind heart and they reveled in her friendship. Although Papi liked having company over, he would have preferred smaller, more intimate groups. He also would complain that Mami over exerted herself, cooking sometimes for days. There was always more than enough food to feed our guests and all the neighbors as well. But where it caused Papi anxiety to act as a gracious host to twenty or more people at a dinner table, it was Mami's heaven.

Upon returning from our latest trip, Mami set about returning to her social schedule. The Israelis hadn't been to dinner for quite some time, so Mami invited her friends over for the following Friday night, eager to share the details of our Argentina excursion. Getting a head start on Thursday afternoon, Mami began preparing her festive meal. Although we weren't celebrating *Shabbat*, Mami decided to make fresh, homemade bread explaining that as a child, she used to help her *bobe* bake the *challos*.

"Bake *what?*"

"*Challah,* if I remember correctly or *challos* if there are more than two. I remember we used to make two for each family. I don't know why, but that was how Bobe taught us."

"This is fun; why don't we do this more often?" I added while getting flour all over the floor.

My mother shrugged her shoulders and sighed. She explained that life was different-we were all so busy, but she promised to make a challah when it was the season for *blintzes.*

"Is there a season for *blintzes* just like there is a special time to eat *matzah*?" I asked.

"*Si,* Mirtita. We are supposed to eat sweets and dairy food, usually in the month of May, sometimes in April I think. My *bobe* used to make sure we knew when it was *Shavous* because it was near her birthday." Mami said, smiling as she recalled the happy occasions. "Bobe always had wonderful stories to share, some were happy, many times they were sad, but I loved hearing about the old days when the family first arrived from Russia. They were very poor, but their little home sparkled from top to bottom. *Just because we were poor, didn't mean we couldn't keep a clean house*, she would always say. For Shabbat they would literally rake the floor, not sweep it you understand, because it was a dirt floor. They would white-wash the walls and scrub the grimy windows, made so by the merciless winds sweeping down the plains.

Afterwards, the table would be set with a clean white cloth brought from the old country and the family's candlesticks would be set at the center. The aroma of the freshly baked challah would fill the tiny little shack. Saturday nights, after the final Shabbat prayers were uttered, families from the surrounding farms - even the *peones* (the farm hands)-would come to share desserts and there would be music and dancing. The music of the *bandoneón* and *gaucho's* guitar mixed well with the freshly baked strudel and *lekach* (honey cake), as if it had always been that way. My *bobe* could recall many such evenings…funny, she could remember so many things from her childhood, yet she couldn't remember exactly when her birthday fell. I suppose she never became accustomed to the "Spanish" almanac; they followed the "Yiddish" calendar and so, she knew her birthday was sometime around *Shavous*!"

"What is *Shavous*?" I asked sneaking a few raisins that were meant for the challah.

"*Ay Mirtita*, so many questions! Why don't you pass me that little bowl with the egg wash and we will finish up here."

And suddenly, I was busy brushing the tops of the braided dough and so deeply captivated with the process that I didn't remember to ask any more questions to my mother's great relief.

Time flew by; we spent yet another summer in Argentina and returned home as the leaves began to change colors. Autumn brought crisp weather, new school supplies and also The Temple Dilemma. With the fall, came the High Holidays. Mami had invited the family to come to dinner for *Rosh ha Shanah* and we would be going to Tía Sima's house for *Yom Kippur*. The issue was not where we were going to eat. The Dilemma was about going to High Holiday services. Papi refused to go. He knew that it was very important to Mami and in most circumstances, he did try to please her, but he simply could not be made to attend services.

We didn't belong to a synagogue like others in the family. Because there were no boys in our household, my parents didn't budget for costly Temple memberships or Hebrew School classes. Others in the family had become temple members while the boys prepared for their Bar Mitzvahs, but since Dani and I would not be training for this rite of passage, there was no need for the extra expense. Since we were not temple members, Mami and Papi would have to pay for High Holiday seats or even worse, they would have to accept charitable donations from the synagogue and sit in the free seats in the back. Papi refused. His defiance stemmed from his frustration of not knowing the language or the "choreography" of the services; when to stand up, when to sit down, when to bow, when to cover his eyes. He would say that it wasn't necessary to spend all day in the Temple praying when you could speak to God in the comfort of your own home. It pained Mami deeply not to go to the synagogue as a family, but once Papi made up his mind, there was no changing it. Mami, Dani and I attended services on our own. Afterwards, we gathered at our house to celebrate Rosh ha Shanah with a family meal. As usual, there were too many people and not enough seats; the walls of the little house seemed to have to stretch to accommodate us all. The food was delicious, as Mami had been preparing for days: *kugel* and *knishes*, gefilte fish and chopped liver, *colitas de cuadril* (pot roasts), and *pollitos al horno* (roasted chicken). Mami had lovely floral centerpieces on each table; each bouquet carried its own little card, "*A Git Yur*, (Happy New Year) With Love, The Argentina Family." The candles were lit and glasses were raised to a hearty, "*L'chaim!*"

Days later, the same angst would take place when Papi would refuse to come with us for Yom Kippur services. Mami would always cry when she heard the *Kol Nidre*. I had no idea what the words meant, but there was no denying the emotions evoked by the cantor as he begun that particular prayer. I wished Papi would have joined us, stood alongside Mami and held her hand. I wished that we could have been together, the four of us, as I noted the other families gathered together in the sanctuary. I didn't understand the depth of his conflicts, his feeling like an outsider amongst the other worshipers or worse yet, his anger towards God. Soon enough, services concluded and once again, our families would gather in rooms too small to contain us and eat delicious foods and the adults would raise their glasses and say, "*L'Chaim*! *Para los presentes y los ausentes*."

Another season came and went and soon, friends at school were making plans for the winter break. My family was also making plans, but our plans were not about going "over the river and through the woods…" There would be no trips to the mountains to play in the snow. We were heading back to see The Argentina Family. This time, Papi would stay home and his girls would travel on their own.

Lines and Lineage

If we had been cold and miserable during our summer vacation, we were hot and miserable during our winter break; Buenos Aires in the summer was not fun. There were no air conditioned cars or air-conditioned homes-unlike the Bernstein or the Kaufman kids, no one had a pool. There was no escaping the heat or humidity, unless you left the city. We had the added pleasure of having to visit the Federal Building to get our passports validated.

The Federal Building itself looked like it had been standing for a hundred years. Dani and I had never seen such an old building in the San Fernando Valley. Walking past the soldiers at the front door, the first thing that hit us was the heat coming from within, and then there was the odor. These ancient buildings obviously were not equipped with modern ventilation systems. I thought for sure Dani would lose her lunch; she always seemed to have a delicate stomach; usually retching all the way from Los Angeles to Buenos Aires.

The building had several different floors and offered various services. We needed to validate our passports as citizens living abroad. Mami held my hand and I held on to Dani as we made our way through a throng of people. Although there were signs on the windows and arrows pointing to various rooms, there was complete chaos. People were trying to edge their way closer to the Information

Counter with no thought of forming a line and waiting to be served. *Even a grade school kid knew it was better to get into a line and wait your turn.* After an eternity, Mami was finally able to get someone to look at our documents. A slightly menacing man with a handlebar mustache and a three piece suit sat behind a massive, wooden desk at the Counter. He shuffled some papers around, took out several colorful stamps and proceeded to stamp away furiously on our papers.

"*Señora*," he said as he blew out a puff of cigarette smoke, "You must get new photographs and a notarized letter from your husband stating that you have permission to take his daughters out of the country. We should have your new documents ready for you in approximately three to four weeks."

Mami gasped and cried out, "But we are leaving in ten days! And my husband is in *Norte America*."

With a great sigh and with seemingly malicious pleasure, the man continued to stamp *CANCELADO* all over our documents. "*Señora*, I understand your predicament, but you must understand mine as well. How do I know that you are not kidnapping your daughters? We must have permission from the father." He stopped for a moment to extinguish his cigarette in an overflowing ashtray. "Furthermore, you have been out of the country for several years. One daughter is *Argentina* and one daughter is *Norte*

Americana. Your identification papers have expired, by the way. You should have had your documents revalidated and I see that you have not done your civil duty. You have not voted in several elections."

Mami regained some of her composure with this last insult. How dare he insinuate that she did not do her civic duty? "That is not true! We went to the Argentine consulate in Los Angeles. We spent hours in line with hundreds of other *Argentinos.* They processed our paperwork and told us that we had met with all the requirements."

"*Señora*, the current government does not recognize any arrangements that the prior administration established with the consulates in North America. Their stamps and signatures have no value here. So, you see, we have many documents to produce for you in very little time. It is impossible to complete all this in ten days *however*; that being said," he leaned in and motioned for Mami to come in a bit closer, "I can see you are desperate." Suggestively flipping through one of the passports, he closed it and laid it on the table. With one finger, he pushed it ever so slightly so that Mami could take hold of it. He looked at her from under his bushy eyebrows and said, "I might be able to do something to help a lady in your situation."

I looked at Mami and back at the sweaty man. I didn't like him and I wished my father were there. Mami picked up the document and fiddled with her purse for a moment. She slipped something in the passport and slid it across the table to the man who was now playing with his mustache.

"Your documents will be ready by tomorrow afternoon, *Señora*" he gave us a Snidely Whiplash smile and continued, "You will need to get new photographs up on the third floor and then bring them back to me."

Along with our necessary "Stand-By travelers" check-in at the Pan American office downtown, it took three trips back to the Federal Building to get our traveling papers in order. I lost count of how many times Mami had to slide some "encouragement" across a desk. Everyone we spoke to exclaimed that they were overworked and underpaid and were without the resources of modern, *Yanqui* technology. Mami surprised me when she said, "It doesn't take modern technology to form a line." When we finally had our paperwork in order, Mami exclaimed, "*Qué barbaridad*! Papi is right. This does not happen in America." You couldn't wipe the smile off my face for the rest of the day.

One lazy afternoon at Bobe Flora and Zeide Simon's apartment, Zeide offered to take us for a little stroll around the corner of Corrientes and Pasteur. We really didn't have the energy to get up off the couch, but Zeide offered us an ice cream cone and that was just the sort of convincing we needed. As we were leaving the small apartment complex,

Zeide waved to a neighbor in the shop next door. The neighbor's name was Faustino and with his white hair, big frame and overalls, he reminded me of the Coca-Cola Santa Claus. Faustino called out and invited us into his shop. The larger-than-life figure, perched on a small wicker stool, was weaving a basket. Dani and I watched with fascination as his wrinkled fingers braided the golden reeds into a beautiful piece of art. Zeide Simon introduced us to his friend and explained that we were his granddaughters from *Norte America.* Faustino didn't get up to give us a kiss hello, which is the traditional way of greeting a person in Argentina; rather he winked at us and invited us to sit down.

He called for his sister and we saw her come across a short outdoor corridor. The corridor was lined with hundreds of baskets and it led to another door. Zeide explained that Faustino and his sister, Sofia, lived in the apartment across the tiny patio. Sofia came to welcome us, but quickly returned to the kitchen crying about her burning *estofado* (stew). After a few minutes, Zeide Simon said it was time to go, but suddenly, I was not in a rush to get the ice cream cone. It was very welcoming in Faustino's shop. He invited me to stay and watch him work. Dani and Zeide walked to the ice cream store down the block and I settled down on a three-legged wicker stool that I imagined Faustino had made himself. He continued silently working, adding one reed and another, when suddenly; he peered up from under his bushy eyebrows and asked me what sort of stories I enjoyed.

"Stories, do you mean, what do I like to read?" I asked puzzled at his first question to me. Usually, the adults asked me about America or asked me to speak in English, as if I were a trained monkey on display.

"Yes, what sort of stories interest you?" He asked again.

"Well, I love to read about pioneers, not cowboys and Indians stories, but stories about pioneer families. I don't know why, but I like to read about kids my age living in other times. It seems like even though their life was difficult, things were so much simpler back then. Sometimes I wish I could have lived in those days."

"Why do you suppose that is?"

Again, I was surprised at his question. Although it was a simple question, I was surprised that he even cared. "I don't know," I replied with some hesitation. "Kids had to do exactly what they were told, but at least they knew what was expected of them every day. A girl knew *who* she was, *where* she was, and *why* she was doing *what* she was doing. My teacher says that it is important to know the five W's. Do you know what I mean…Who, What, When, Where, and Why? I suppose I like that. That leaves no room for guessing. There are no questions…" I suddenly became self-conscious about my outburst and stopped in mid-sentence.

"Well now, that *is* interesting view point. It is important to know one's self. What else do you like to read about?"

"Oh lots of things! I particularly like to read historical books. Actually, we were reading about Christopher Columbus again in school. I always thought that was an interesting story, so I'm glad we had a chance to learn more about him."

"Ah; good old *Cristobal Colon*. So tell me, what do you know about this man?"

"Well, everyone knows that in 1492, Columbus sailed the ocean blue!" I recited the childish verse, but since it didn't rhyme in Spanish, its charm was lost in the translation.

"I know a very interesting story about people who sailed over from Spain just about that time…maybe a little after. There was a family and they had a daughter, Sofia, who was just about your age. Ten, eleven, am I right?"

"Yes, eleven, that's right! What is the story about?"

"This is a story of a family that knew very well *who* they were and *where* they were and because of these things, they also knew *why* they had to run away. Would you like to hear about them?"

"Oh yes!" I exclaimed and settled back to rest against the cool tiles on the wall. I realized that he wasn't going to ask me to speak English or ask me to sing. He didn't ask me which country I liked best or if I would prefer to live in Argentina. He was just going to weave his basket and tell me a story.

The story was about a family that escaped something called the Inquisition in Spain. They were called *Marranos*, which was horrible word that actually meant pigs. I interrupted Faustino repeatedly and the dear old man never complained. He answered my questions and if he was surprised that I didn't know what he was talking about, he didn't let on. He patiently explained about how the Jews were forced to convert to Catholicism or face exile, torture or even death. He explained how many of the converts or *Conversos*, secretly tried to maintain their Jewish faith. Faustino told me that there were at least 500 known Marrano families in Argentina by the end of 16 century. Even though the Inquisition had begun in Spain, the Jewish families hiding behind their adopted religion were not safe in Argentina. They learned to live their lives outwardly being Catholic, but at home, they secretly kept their ancient traditions.

I was captivated and wanted to hear more. I tried not to interrupt because I knew that too soon, I would be called back home and the story would have to be put on hold. I couldn't resist however and asked Faustino to tell me more about their secret lives. He told me about the young girl, Sofia and her grandfather's special gift. When the girl's twelfth birthday came about, the grandfather took her for a long walk. They walked out of the small town and while standing alone in the middle of a vast field; the grandfather placed a locket around the girl's neck.

"Today is a special day, my precious one," her *abuelo* said. "There are many things I wish to tell you and maybe one day, I shall. However, for now, I want to give you this silver locket. We brought it with us from Spain, our homeland. Artisans from amongst our people made it especially for you. And you see? It has a tiny key. When you open the locket, you will find a lovely piece of red silk string."

"Why do I have to lock away the red string, *Abuelo*?" the girl asked.

"It is for good luck, *querida.* It will ward away the Evil Eye. But more importantly, I wanted to give you something that binds you to your people…One day, I will tell you about the ties that bind us all to a special past. I will tell you *who* you are and *what* you are. Until that time, my precious one, keep this string to remind you that you are loved, that you are special and that God is watching over you."

Faustino smiled at me as I wiped away the runaway tears. Looking across the store, I saw my grandfather, *my abuelo,* standing at the front door. It was dinnertime and I had to go home. I gave Faustino a kiss goodnight and asked if I could return the following day. With a chuckle, he replied, "Of course! I will be expecting you, my friend."

I was back in the shop right after breakfast the next day. Faustino picked up a new project and began weaving. I asked him to let me know if I became a nuisance, but secretly hoped that he would allow me to stay the whole afternoon. It was like spending the day with Papi while he worked in his cabinetry shop. Faustino assured me that I was welcome to stay. He told me that all the kids in the neighborhood liked to spend time with him in his shop and that he looked forward to sharing his stories. I asked him to tell me more about the family from Spain and their secrets. He began weaving another chapter as easily as he wove his new creation.

"Well you see, the grown-ups kept their secret so well that the children didn't even know what was truly going on. The adults feared that the truth would be revealed by accident, so they invented creative ways to maintain their culture and their traditions. Let me give you an example. Sofia's mama placed a statue of the Virgin by the door so that all the neighbors could see it when they walked by. Every time the mama walked in or out of the house, she would kiss the Virgin's foot. The neighbors saw this action and would comment on how pious the lady was.

"But Faustino, what was *the secret*?"

Faustino smiled at my impatience and continued, "Years later, when the mama passed away, the daughter returned to her parents' home. She began packing things away and when she went to move the statue of the Virgin, the little foot cracked open and something fell out."

"What was it?" I gasped. "Was it gold coins or jewels brought back from Spain?

"No, my little friend, something even more treasured, I would think. If I am not mistaken, your grandmother and grandfather have one on their doorpost. Do you know what I'm talking about?"

"Yes, I think I know. Bobe Flora always kisses the *mezuzah* that hangs on the doorpost when she comes in and out of the…Oh! The mother in the story hid the *mezuzah* in the statue of the Virgin! And nobody ever knew, not even her own daughter!"

"That's right. They had lived all those years in fear. The grandfather had long passed away-the papa and then the mama too. Sofia never knew that they were Jewish until all her loved ones were gone. She was a grown woman, a mother with her own children. Can you imagine her confusion? What was it that you said? Who, What, When, Where, and Why?

I didn't know whether to laugh or cry. Here I had been complaining about not knowing if I was American,

Russian or Argentine. Poor Sofia! What had her parents done? *What had they done*? They had saved her life! They did what they thought was best for her future. I suddenly thought about my parents. They had made some difficult decisions too. They had done what they thought was best. Faustino hadn't said a word. He kept his head low, his eyes on the basket. I squirmed in my little seat and said, "I think that was a beautiful story. A sad story, but it was a good one."

And with that, a wonderful friendship was forged. I looked forward to spending time in Faustino's shop as often as possible. Zeide Simon and Bobe Flora were more than a little jealous of how much I loved this old man. Zeide didn't know how to compete with the pied piper of the neighborhood and his wonderful stories. Bobe would tempt me with treats or spoonfuls of *dulce de leche* if I would just come back to her apartment. Mami didn't approve of spoonfuls of *dulce de leche* and even though it was the most delicious thing ever invented, I wouldn't give up an afternoon with Faustino for anything!

When our visit with The Argentina Family came to a close and it was time to return home, Faustino presented me with a beautiful basket, which he called a *Canasta de Moisés* (Moses' basket). The basket was a rich, golden color with an intricate pattern. Although the pattern was beautiful, the handles were what caught my eye. Faustino had taken reeds that had been dyed a deep shade of crimson red and woven them through the handles.

"*Mi amiguita*, this is a small token of my affection. I hope that you will remember to come visit me on your next trip. More importantly, just like Sofia, always remember that you are loved, you are special and that God is watching over you."

I hugged him tightly and unabashedly shed a few tears. Looking at the basket, with its bright red weave, I remembered Sofia and her red string. Was I misinterpreting the meaning of Faustino's gift? I gulped deeply and asked, "Faustino, tell me the truth. Did you make up the story? The family from Spain - *who were those people*? Who was Sofia?"

Faustino grinned. Throwing up his hands, he said, "Well, let me just say that the name Sofia runs in my family."

And with that, I was left to dwell on the question of his lineage until our next visit.

The Pied Piper of Pasteur

The question of Faustino's ancestry had caused me to question my own. The seeds of curiosity had long been sown and I, unlike the young girl in Faustino's story, was lucky enough to be able to ask *my abuelo.* I had a little time left before we needed to head out to Ezeiza International Airport, so I asked my grandfather to take me to my favorite plaza, the one with the beautiful carousel. Zeide Simon happily agreed to escort me and Dani to the plaza while the last minute packing efforts took place in the apartment. When we arrived, Dani took a turn on the carousel and I sat down on a park bench with my grandfather.

"Zeide, where were you born? When did you move here? Why did you come? What was your father's name? Where were the Trupps from?" I blurted out without any preamble or hint that my thoughts were going in that direction.

"Mirtita - so many questions! What has come over you?" He laughed. "I wouldn't know where to start."

"Can you tell me a story, just like Faustino?"

"Well, yes…I think I can match Faustino," he said, happy for the opportunity to compete for his granddaughter's attention. "Let me see now. I seem to recall a story about a man name Reuven…

Reuven ha Kohan had been fairly successful as the town's silversmith. His family, as well as many others in Traupis, had come to live in Lithuania decades ago after the mass migration from Prussia. Reuven's family was well known and respected, yet life was not always easy. Reuven was constantly worrying about his family's safety and stability. Now with the power struggles over between the neighboring nations, Catherine the Great was encouraging Jewish merchants and tradesmen to populate several provinces on equal terms with other "foreigners." In accordance to the decree proclaimed by Empress Catherine II, the Jews of Poland and Lithuania were welcome to come and settle in Russia proper. For weeks, the village families gathered nightly to discuss the prospects that the new policies offered. The men sought the rabbi's opinion, but they listened with greater interest to the men of commerce - they listened to Reuven. When Reuven's wife, Pese consented to her husband's fervent plea to trek across the continent, she wept on her mother's shoulder and held her close. "We will never see you again mama!" Pese cried. "Our children will grow without their bobe and zeide's love."

"*Sha, sha, my sheine.* Wherever you go, you go with our love and God's blessings." Pese's mother replied.

On a temperate day in the spring of 1772, ten families joined Reuven, Pese and their infant son, Chaim as they set out with all their worldly belongings. Wagons, practically buckling under the strain of the heavy cargo, crept along the dirt roads with hens cackling and oxen moaning along the way. After many miles, they reached a ferry landing. They were met by a detail of Russian soldiers. Reuven, who was able to speak a little Russian and even a few words in German, had been elected the leader of the group. He stepped ahead of the others and directed himself to the man in charge.

"Papers!" shouted the Russian sergeant. "Another group of wandering Jews, I suspect, eh?" he said to his colleagues.

Reuven carefully unfolded the leather satchel that carried his family's traveling papers. He motioned to the other men to bring their documents as well.

"Where are you all going?" he asked, not certain that the peasant understood the language.

"We have been given permission to travel to the area called Ukraine. We are going to settle there." Reuven answered in a clear and strong voice, yet one heavily laced with his Yiddish accent.

"Ah, so you are not such an ignorant Jew. You can understand me. Good! What is your name?" The sergeant bellowed to intimidate, but inwardly he was impressed with the Jew's knowledge of the mother tongue.

"I am known as Reuven ben Ysroel."

"No, no! That will not do. The new edict says that even you Jews must have official surnames."

"My family is Kohanim, descendants of the ancient priestly tribe." Reuven offered the explanation. "I have no official name other than Reuven ha Kohan."

The sergeant cursed. "That is no good either! What about the rest of your group? I suppose no one else has followed the policy. Did not your local authorities enforce the new law?"

"We have had no trouble with our local authorities and do not wish to have any with you sir. What do you suggest?" Reuven humbly implored.

The sergeant looked at the group in dismay. "I cannot allow you to continue with your papers such as they are. We have a scribe here who will make the necessary corrections to your documents. You will have to choose a Russian surname."

Reuven turned to his friends and explained the issue at hand. It seemed a relatively mild request. They had been apprehensive about encountering officials as they crossed the many rivers and borders. They had thought about bribes that they might have to pay. What harm was there in taking on a Russian name?

Reuven returned to the sergeant and in supplication said, "Sir, we are not educated in the Russian language. Could you not help us choose proper names?"

"What do you think? I have nothing better to do than stand here and think up names for all these families?" The sergeant scratched his wooly beard and adjusted his cap. "Where do you come from? I will give you all the same name."

"We are from the village known as Traupis."

"Very well, but Traupis is a Lithuanian name. The village is now on the Russian map as Troupy. You all will be known as Trupp."

Reuven shrugged his shoulders, turned to his fellow travelers and explained what the guard declared. He spelled out the name in Yiddish, T-R-U-P and repeated it for the Russian to make sure he got it right.

"No, you uneducated peasant; *Trup* means corpse! You must spell it with a *yer* at the end to make it a strong Russian name: Т-Р-У-П-Ъ." (T-R-U-P-P)

Reuven repeated the spelling and the men nodded their heads but immediately began discussing the letter *vav*. Was the vowel a *cholem malai* or was it used as a *shuruk*? This would obviously change the articulation of their new name. Reuven, dismayed at their ill-timed debate, asked the sergeant to disregard the conversation and with some embarrassment, explained that his traveling companions were discussing the pronunciation in Yiddish terms.

The sergeant, slightly astounded at his own patience, instructed the Jew that the Russian letter *У* indicated that the vowels should be pronounced as "troop" not "truck." He was beginning to think that it was easier to deal with uneducated peasants then learned Jews. The sergeant then waved over his scribe and instructed him to correct the travelers' papers. Finally, the task completed, the new Trupp families collected their children, and their wagons complete with oxen, geese and chickens and continued on with their journey. Pese, Reuven and Chaim, and the other families made their way to a village called Tartak in the Ukraine. On the first *Shabbos* in the new home, Pese lit her candles, made the blessing and remembered her mother's words, "You go with love and God's blessings."

"*Zeide*," I interrupted my grandfather with a slight sense of urgency. "That was a long *long* time ago! How can you be sure it is true? What about your family? What were your parents' names? Do you have a story about your mother and father?"

My grandfather shifted his weight on the park bench and glanced over to see Dani in the park's playground. He had been very satisfied with his story about Pese and Reuven, but if he wanted to surpass Faustino as the great storyteller, he obviously would need to continue spinning his tale.

Clearing his throat, Zeide Simon replied, "Well - you see - that is the way a good legend is told, Mirtita - a *bisel* of this and a *bisel* of that. There is truth in there you mark my words! Now…my parents were Yosef and Bersheibe. Let's pick up the story *not so long ago,* say about 1909," he winked and continued, "Bersheibe had said her final goodbyes to her family and friends. Tomorrow, she would follow her husband Yosef as they embarked on a great and perilous journey. They would trek through Western Europe and direct themselves to Hamburg. From that famous port, they'd cross a great ocean and God-willing, reach the shores of Argentina. Their children would have a chance to live in peace and prosperity. Gone were the days when Yosef and his family flourished in their trades. The years had been cruel to the community; those in power began a harsh reign against the Jews. People were trapped, restricted to an area known as the Pale of Settlement. Their businesses were crushed by taxes and harsh regulations. Violence against them was not only condoned, but also officially organized as brutal *pogroms* fell upon their communities time and again. Stories of emigration had been spreading from one shtetl to another.

Baron Hirsh, along with the Rothschild family and other prominent Jews of Europe took matters into their own hands and began the Jewish Colonization Association as they saw the dire consequences of the Russian Revolution unfold. With the aid and sanction of the Argentine government, the Jewish Colonization Association began the process of relocating the Jews of Eastern Europe to under populated, agricultural colonies of the South American *medina.* Provinces such as Santa Fe, Entre Rios and La Pampa desperately needed families to work the land. Baron Hirsh and the J.C.A. offered the Jewish immigrants a glimmer of hope. The soon-to-be *émigrés* began to think of it as the New Jerusalem.

When Bersheibe informed her parents of Yosef's decision to leave, her mother cried softly as her father placed his hands on her head and gave his blessing. As she left her parents' home for the last time, Bersheibe's mother cried out, "You are not alone. You go with our love and God's blessings!"

Zeide Simon, beaming proudly at me said, "And that, young lady, should tide you over until the next time. It is getting late and you, my little *Yanqui*, have a plane to catch!"

La Familia

We never knew exactly when Mami would decide to jump on a plane. She tried to keep to our school schedule, but on occasion, we had to be pulled out for an extra week or more. When we traveled, it was usually just the three of us as Papi was not able to get away. Dani and I missed him dreadfully.

When things were quiet and we were at home, our lives were relatively easy going. We had settled down in our tranquil, little neighborhood on Heartland Street. Dani and I walked down the block to school every day, Papi went to work at Pan Am and Mami stayed home, cooking, cleaning and writing long letters to Tía Lela. On the weekends, we were always with *la familia* for an *asado* or some other event. The million-dollar question was, "Are Fabian, Marcelo, and Freddy going?" If the Bernstein boys were not going, then the Trupp girls were not going…or so they said with all due respect and consideration for the authority figures! The Kaufman kids, Leandro, Gerardo, and Valeria, who were related to us through Papi's cousin Sam, joined our group as well. Sam and Mariel lived in a *very cool* house, a California ranch style house near the Hollywood hills. We all loved going to pool parties at the Kaufman, as well as trekking up "Sam's mountain" for his rendition of a traditional *gaucho's asado*, reminiscent of his days back on the farm.

Whether in someone's apartment, at the beach, on top of a mountain or in someone's back yard, these family gatherings would mean endless hours of eating and talking. While the menu was made up of various courses of Argentine fare, the conversation was completely uniform. The unvarying theme was the matter of our immigration. The debate was the same: Which country was better or even more to the point, *in which country were we better off?* It seemed that the adults had forgotten why they left the country in the first place. Argentina forever remained the Argentina of their youth. My parents, aunts, uncles-*everyone*-were trapped in a time warp where their *lunfardo* (slang) still existed and where accepted family traditions still played out as fifty years ago.

One evening, the debate got particularly heated. Papi's contribution seemed to add flame to the fire. "The United States affords us the freedom to live in peace and constancy. An immigrant, *a simple workingman*, can live like a king! Look at me: I have a stable and fair income and there is even a little money left over to help The Argentina family."

One of the uncles argued back, "That's all we do here in America. Work! Work! Work! Back home, we never worked these long hours. What about vacations, *eh*? In Buenos Aires, we always went away during the summer. When was your last vacation, *eh*?"

"I didn't come to this country to take two hour *siestas* in the middle of the day or three month vacations in the summer." Papi retaliated.

Just then, one of the aunts chimed in about religion. "As Jews in America, we can live without trepidation. Just last winter, we went to Anita's school for a concert. And would you believe it? There was a Chanukah menorah on display next to the Christmas tree!"

A few of the grown-ups bobbed their heads in agreement and the feisty aunt, feeling their support, continued. "You can wear a Star of David necklace out on the street. When was the last time someone warned you about your jewelry? *Eh*? Don't forget how we have been mistreated. Jews were not even allowed to bury their dead within the city limits, remember? Up until my great grandmother died in 1910, we were burying our people in the Dissident Section of *Chacarita*!"

"Yes, but we don't have any organizations here like we had back home." Another contributor piped in. "Where are the *Macabis* and the *Hacoajs*? The kids are bored. *We are bored*! Remember the great *asados* we would have en *el country*? What about the dances for the young kids? Where can our young people go to dance? You have to be 21 years old here! When I was a kid, I was going to dances by the time I was twelve!"

Tío Elias shot back, "If it is so good over there, why don't you go back? Go back to your daily practice of bribery and *pioladas (*thinking yourself smarter than others).

"We don't have to be *canchero*, a streetwise, smooth talking *porteño* just to get through our day to day routine." Papi added.

"You speak so negatively about the *porteño*, Ruben, but America is a dangerous place to raise our children," another family member said adding his two cents. "In Buenos Aires, our kids are running all over the city, jumping on subways and buses, visiting friends and family. The Argentina society provides an old-fashion sense of family and clean-cut social activities. Look around you. What do you see on the television, what do you hear on the news? Since we came here, we've seen nothing but trouble within the society, drugs, sex…they are all hippies! There is no sense of family; Americans are cold and unfeeling. Have you noticed when they are together; no one says hello *como la gente*! (Like civilized people) They walk in and say "Hi!" but there are no handshakes; there a no hugs or kisses. They *Yanquis* are making our children uncivil miscreants!"

Having enough, Papi shouted, "So, go already! *This* is a free country; you can leave whenever you want!"

As they ran out of real topics to debate, they resorted to the old standards: the food is better in *Arr-hen-tina*, the fashion sense is better in *Arr-hen-tina*, the people are better looking in *Arr-hen-tina*, the beaches are better in *Arr-hen-tina*, the soccer was better in *Arr-hen-tina*!

During these conversations, while the grownups were hurling their biting comments back and forth, the young kids, that is to say, the Bernstein boys and the Trupp girls, pretty much stuck together. Taking into consideration the chaos caused by *the adults* at such large gatherings, we were very well behaved kids. We didn't have cell phones or laptops, DVD's or other electronic devices, yet we found ways to have fun together. If we ever did do something slightly mischievous, there always was an aunt or uncle to reprimand us in the absence of our own parent. It was like having fifty parents at once. At any given moment, any one of them could feel it was their duty to come up from behind and say, *"Cuidado, eh?"* (Hey, watch your step).

On special occasions when the mothers didn't want to cook, the families liked to gather at a local pizzeria, Two Guys from Italy. The food was familiar and the ambiance was pleasant. One of the owners of the restaurant was actually Argentine, so we were made to feel right at home. The restaurant had a room in the back for parties and large groups. We definitely qualified for the large group classification. One by one, the families' cars would pull up to the restaurant parking lot and we would walk through the doors laughing and talking and causing a commotion. The kids already knew where to go, so we'd all run to the back room as if we were heading to an aunt's dining room. The adults would attempt to be a little more refined and would meander between the tables filled with "regular" patrons who stared at all of us thinking we were part of The Godfather's *familia.*"

As kids, we always noticed our families were a curiosity to others, but that was just a normal part of our lives. Although we had been raised in the United States, most of us were immigrants and shared the same issues of having Argentine parents. A simple trip to the supermarket could end up causing us enough traumas to last a lifetime. How do you recover from hearing your mother ask the butcher, "Excuse me, du ju haf *testiculos*?"

"I'm sorry ma'am? What did you say?"

"Balls-du ju haf any cow balls?

Argentines were known for eating great *asados;* the entire carcass was put to use. So, it wasn't such a surprise when the next thing our mothers would say would be, "How about brains?"

"Excuse me?" the startled butcher would reply.

Exasperated at not being understood, the question was repeated with a certain embarrassing attitude, "Du ju haf *any brains*?"

At this point, we'd be fidgeting and fussing with the shopping cart; Ding Dongs and Twinkies would fall from the shelves as we fumbled with the packages clumsily out of embarrassment.

When our friends would stay over for dinner, we'd have to explain the menu. One evening, against my better judgment, my parents invited Lorraine to stay for dinner; Lorraine, whose family seemingly came directly off of The Mayflower and *exuded* Americana. She accepted before I had a chance to warn her. So, I wasn't too surprised when Lorraine pointed at a platter of food and asked indecorously, "What is that?"

"That's *matambre*." I answered while restlessly playing with the silverware in an attempt to distract my guest.

"What does that mean?"

Shrugging my shoulders and trying to sound cavalier, I replied, "It means *hunger-killer*."

My innocent visitor, attempting a feeble joke said, "It sounds sinister. What's in it? How do you make it?"

"Well, you roll up eggs and garlic and parsley in some meat and then boil it. Sometimes, it's a little rubbery, but it's really not so bad."

"I'll try it, but do you have any ketchup?" Lorraine said, trying not to gulp too loudly.

"No, but you can put some *chimichurri* on it, if you like." I said, not really wanting to make eye contact with anyone around the table.

Papi then brought the rest of the meal in from the *parrilla* and set it proudly on the table. Lorraine couldn't help herself and asked again, "What's *that*?"

"Those are *chinchulín*," Papi replied pointing to the long, thin, entrails. "Those are *mollejas,* that is *entraña* and this is *morcilla*."

And with no further hesitation, he proceeded to serve the meat, not wanting his offering to get cold. I, of course, secretly wished we could have had ordered a pizza. That's when Mami proudly announced, "*Molleja*s are the throat glands in a baby cow," using a knife to point to her own neck, "Oh, and the butcher says that *morcilla* are called blood sausage."

Lorraine clutched her stomach and said that she wasn't very hungry after all. In fact, she had a stomachache and thought she better go home. Upon hearing the words "stomach ache," Mami said, "Can I give you a few drops of *Hepatalgina*?"

Souvenirs

The only male teacher at Shirley Avenue Elementary School was Mr. Thompson. The gruff looking man terrified me as I believed the horror stories that had been circulating around campus. Soon after school began, I realized the stories were unfounded and crotchety Mr. Thompson won me over. He had a soft spot for Choral music, in fact he was the music director for the school and he invited a few of us to join the school's chorus. That was the first time I participated in a chorus and I owe that dear man a debt of gratitude for opening that magical door.

Mr. Thompson's love of music spilled over into other subjects. He used music to teach us about art, science and math. Right before Halloween, he had us listen to a classical piece of music. It was called *Dance Macabre* by Saint-Saëns. He shut off the lights and asked us to close our eyes and just listen. Afterwards, we watched a movie where the musical instruments sprung into life in a ghoulish twist. Mr. Thompson gave each of us a conductor's baton as an early Halloween treat and instructed us to conduct the music in 2/4 time as the animated instruments danced across the screen.

The impact of the lesson; how we individually interpreted the music was so striking, that I couldn't get it out of my mind. Weeks later, I still was thinking about it when the Chanukah menorah replaced the Halloween pumpkins on our calendar at home. All I wanted for Chanukah was a recording of *Dance Macabre*. No one believed me and worse yet, no one knew what I was talking about. I would have made a bigger issue of it, but suddenly, as I realized that we were *not going* to Argentina for our winter break, I became preoccupied with making plans with my friends.

This was going to be the first time that I was actually at home during a school break and I had some catching up to do! For two glorious weeks, I was free! No school! No airports! No crying relatives! I wasn't quite sure what all the kids did during their winter break, but I was sure going to give it my best shot. A friend of mine invited me to join her in an after-school program. She was a Girl Scout and needed to earn a cooking badge. The program offered a baking class, so we signed up. Apparently so did twenty other girls. With so many girls, we had to take turns in the kitchen. On the third day, my name was finally on top of the list. As I turned from the counter to the oven, carefully balancing two cookies sheets, I saw Papi standing in the doorway. He was talking to my teacher. Dani came running up to me and said "Guess what?" She didn't have to say it, because I already guessed, but I asked her anyway.

"What?"

"Mami changed her mind. We are going to Argentina after all."

"When?"

"Tonight!"

And that was the end of baking for me. We arrived in Buenos Aires just in time for Chanukah. This was cause for another disappointment since Chanukah was barely acknowledged in Argentina. I was already grumpy about the trip; I didn't need another excuse. Mami realized that I was upset about missing out on our winter break and our Chanukah celebrations at home. She asked me what I wanted most for Chanukah and I reminded her that I had asked for the record by Saint-Saëns. Of course, she had forgotten all about it and figured that I had too. She offered me everything under the sun, but I would not have it.

We started going to one record shop after another. Tío Marcos and his new wife, Tía Flavia joined in and offered to take me on the hunt for the elusive recording We made a pretty odd looking team; a recently married couple, practically still on their honeymoon and a twelve year old American girl looking for a recording of a classical piece of music about dancing skeletons and devilish goblins. Finally, after dozens of shops, we found the record! I listened to it over and over again and tried to explain my teacher's lesson, but no one was actually interested and my ramblings of animation and syncopated rhythms came to an end. Surprisingly enough, the record itself did not come to some macabre ending. I think it was the first time that The Argentina Family *was glad* to see us go home.

A few months later, I graduated from elementary school. I said my goodbyes to Mr. Thompson, who had opened the world of music for me and to Mrs. Mitchell who had taught me the joys of reading. Mami made a cake and brought some flowers to the graduation ceremony. Written on the card, of course, was, "Congratulations! With Love, The Argentina Family."

I had a little blue keepsake book and made sure to fill it with signatures on graduation day. The teachers wrote "Best Wishes for continued success" and "A pleasure to have known you" (although they had never taken the time to learn how to pronounce my name). A few of my classmates wrote "C-U-in school" while others told me to have a "bitchin" summer. What was a *bitchin summer*? I wouldn't find out. I was heading back to Argentina.

The reasoning behind this particular trip was that one of my mother's cousins was getting married. Of course, that was the easiest way to explain the relationship, but in fact, the bride was my mother's cousin, once removed. Or rather, the bride was my third cousin. Did it make more sense to say that the bride's great-great grandmother was my great-great *great* grandmother? The fact of the matter was that a cousin was getting married and Mami didn't need any further enticement.

Immediately upon arriving, Mami arranged to meet with Bobe Carmen's *modista.* At long last, my mother was going to treat herself to a custom-made evening dress. Dani and I were also going to be outfitted for the family's gala event. I had been surprised that we skipped our usual shopping spree at Montgomery Wards or Sears prior to traveling, but Mami explained that we had just enough time to have our party dresses made especially for us- *Arr-hen-tina* style.

Bobe Carmen came to escort us to her friend's place of business. I was actually excited at the prospect of having a dress made especially for me. During the past school semester, I had read many historical novels and had become enthralled with all things Victorian. In fact, I had just completed reading a book on Florence Nightingale and recalled quite vividly a scene where she and her sister were fitted for evening gowns. The author had described in enchanting detail the various fabric options -the silks, velvets and brocades, the luxurious surroundings of the couturier's shop, and the lavish attention bestowed upon the young ladies. Needless to say, I was looking forward to the afternoon.

Walking along side my grandmother through the noisy, grimy side streets of El Once, I was overcome with suspicion. Surely, this was not the way to Bobe's *modista.*

"Bobe, are you sure we are going the right way?" I asked as we quickly crossed in the middle of the street. "Your friend's shop is around *here*?"

"Mirtita, I am sure that Bobe Carmen knows where she is going," Mami answered as horns blared and we narrowly escaped being hit by two irate taxi cab drivers. "What I'd like to know is if you are sure that Rivka will be able to do the work?"

"*Mamele shane*, don't worry about a thing! Rivka comes from a long line of dressmakers. Her grandmother worked for the nobility in the old country. You will be very pleased!"

I looked around and saw that we had entered what resembled a swap meet, an outdoors market of some sort. Bobe Carmen fluttered away and we quickly followed behind. A few turns this way and that, and she came to an abrupt halt in front of a large stall and said, "Here we are! Rivka, where are you?"

A short, but robust lady came out to greet us. "Carmen, is this your family? How nice! *How nice*!" The lady smoothed out her colorful skirt with one hand while the other went to fix her hair. "*Oy gevalt*! I must look like a fright and me, wearing my *babuska yet*! It's just so much easier to work without my hair getting into my eyes…well, you don't care about that. You are here to look at my fabrics, eh? So look- *look*! Anything you want, *anything*!" Rivka said, finally taking a breath.

I let me fingers glide over the bolts of material and tried not to show my disappointment. An outdoors market place with all sorts of vendors peddling their merchandise was not quite what I had imagined. With unusual aromas coming from neighboring stalls, and people hooting and howling promoting their wares, I tried to concentrate and looked for the fabric for my Victorian lady's dress. Rivka glanced over and saw me probing about.

"*Nu*? What do you like?"

"I was hoping to find something not so…I was hoping to find something fancier." I said feeling slightly guilty and not wanting to hurt anyone's feelings.

"Yes, I know exactly what you are looking for. *Motel*! Motel, bring me the lace that just came in. And the pattern books too…Mooooteel!" she squealed.

A tired, scrawny man came from behind a curtain carrying "the lace that just came in," with one hand and a *mate* in the other. It was an elegant lace and the perfect shade of eggshell blue. Now with renewed enthusiasm, I boldly told Rivka that I didn't need to look at her patterns. I already knew what sort of dress I wanted; the picture was etched in my mind's eye. I showed her how I wanted the sleeves to lay; I drew a picture of the square neckline and the empire waist. I wanted a satin ribbon to follow the lines of the high waist and tie demurely in the back.

"*Si, si, mamele shane*, anything you want, *anything*!" Rivka reassured. After Mami made her selections, Rivka guaranteed us that the rush orders would be done in time for the wedding. Bobe Carmen was thrilled to have taken part in the expedition but now; she was ready to head off. She was always in a hurry to get someplace else and so, in a blink of an eye, she was gone. Mami, of course, had plans for the rest of the day.

Dani and I found ourselves yet again sitting at afternoon tea with an elderly aunt and uncle. Mami had made it her mission in life to visit every relative from one end of the family tree to the other. While cloistered inside an apartment, which reeked of the strange combination of mothballs and matzah balls, Dani and I carefully sipped our tea and prayed that we would not have to use the dainty, hand embroidered napkins our great aunt had placed on our laps.

High tea might have been a tradition left behind by the British, but in The Argentina Family, the elders placed sugar cubes between their teeth and sipped tea from fine cut crystal glasses, as they did back home in Russia. They served *kamishbroit* and *mandelbroit* along with *masas finas*, elaborate,

European pastries filled with rich crèmes and chocolates. Although the elders spoke Spanish, the conversation was generously sprinkled with Yiddish, so much so that Dani and I couldn't keep up. Quickly becoming bored with the adults and experts at the art of quiet entertainment, we drifted off to a corner and amused ourselves until Mami said it was time to go.

The following day, Tío Beto and his wife, Tía Silvina took us sightseeing throughout the center of Buenos Aires. We spent the day jumping in and out of stuffy subway trains and crowded buses. They showed us the presidential palace and the famous obelisk standing in the middle of the "world's widest street"-Avenida 9 de Julio. Like tourist guides, they'd point out the British influences, the Italian styles and French architecture. Dani and I were too young to comprehend or even care about the buildings or their archaic histories, but we didn't complain for fear of returning to a stuffy apartment! Tío Beto and Tía Silvina were very anxious for us to take home a souvenir and we spent some time shopping on the famous, pedestrianized street; Calle Florida. I saw what I wanted in a shop's window and turning to Tía Silvina, I said, "I'd like a pancho, please."

Tía Silvina looked at me and then looked at Tío Beto. She patted me on the back and said, "Yes dear, in a minute" however; we kept walking down the street. Block after block, they would offer me this or that and I would politely refuse. Finally, they stopped at a sidewalk vendor and bought four hot dogs, one for each of us. "Mirtita, are you sure this is all we can get for you? Wouldn't you like to take home a souvenir? Tía Silvina asked.

I was very confused! I looked at both of them and repeated, "I would really like to have a pancho, please."

They looked at each other and Tío Beto said, "You have a *pancho* in your hand, *mi amor.*"

I looked at the hot dog in my hand and shook my head. I pointed at a store's window display and asked, "What is the word for this?"

Tío Beto began laughing and Tía Silvina explained. "We thought you were asking for a *pancho*! (Hot dog). We didn't realize that you wanted a *poncho!*"

We went straight into the store and I got my authentic llama-hair, fringed *poncho.* To top off the *criollo* experience, we rode back home in a horse drawn carriage, happily munching away on a delicious Argentine *panchos.*

The wedding day was quickly approaching and with no time to spare, on a blistery Tuesday afternoon, we went back to Rivka, the *modista* for our one and final fitting. Mami was thrilled with her dress and Dani, being quite young, was easily pleased. I, on the other hand, was practically in tears. Rivka brought out my dress and I knew instantly that it was a disaster. Before I had a chance to say one word, I was standing in the center of the room, completely undressed as Rivka, Bobe Carmen and Mami pulled and adjusted, zippered and pinned. I was pushed this way and that and finally was led in front of a mirror. Who was that little girl staring back at me? *I* was twelve years old. *I* was going to junior high school in the fall! Why was I wearing this little girl's dress? The sleeves were too puffy. I had asked for a square neckline, instead I got something that went practically all the way up to my chin. The empire waistline turned out to be a traditional A-line skirt and the simple, satin ribbon that demurely tied in the back was transformed into a sloppy clown's bow. It was all wrong.

"*Mirtitale*, you look like a princess! A *shane meidelach*. Rivka, it's perfect!" Bobe Carmen exclaimed.

Mami could see that I was about to burst into tears. In English, I quietly confessed my complaints, but my mother told me that there wasn't enough time to fix the dress. With our three gowns wrapped up, we left the *modista*'s stall and headed back to Tía Lela's house. I couldn't help but feel sorry for myself and pouted for the rest of the day and on through the next.

On Wednesday night, Mami began fussing with our luggage and pulling out shoes and accessories. I was confused since the wedding was not until Saturday. I stopped pouting long enough to ask her about it..

"The wedding is not for three more days, why are you getting things out now?"

"The wedding is tomorrow, Mirtita- well, the civil ceremony is tomorrow. We have to be ready to go early in the morning." Mami continued to explain that very often weddings in Argentina have two ceremonies. The first or formal ceremony is where the couple signs their marriage certificate at the Registrar's office. Since religious officiants don't have the authority to marry, the civil ceremony is mandatory. If the couple wants to have a party or a religious ceremony, they usually schedule the event for the weekend.

"So, you mean, they will be actually married tomorrow morning, but they have to wait until Saturday before they can go home together?" I asked.

Mami smiled and answered simply, "Yes."

The following morning, we went with several family members to the civil registry; everyone was very pleased to have the visiting *Norte Americanos* there for the occasion. Of course, the main event was Saturday night and it would take most of the day to get ready. I had reluctantly come to terms with my party dress and it didn't take too much cajoling for me to go along with the day's primping and pampering. I was glad that we had been occupied most of the day, what with the hours in the *salon de belleza*, followed by a leisurely lunch and then an afternoon siesta, the long hours of anticipation were whiled away. Even so, we were antsy by the time we finally left Tía Lela's house at nine o'clock that evening.

When we arrived at the *salon*, I realized that this wedding would be different from anything else we had experience back home. Accustomed to attending a wedding in a synagogue, where the elaborately decorated *chuppah* was set up and the seating was prearranged, the banquet hall atmosphere felt lacking. While it evident that a grand celebration would be taking place, the only thing that indicated a bride would soon be arriving was the white satin runner down the center of the room.

Crowds of people began milling about; I stood close by to my parents and held Dani's hand. Shortly after we arrived, people began to shout, "Quiet Down!" and "They're here!" Musicians began playing but I couldn't see where they were. Although it was beautiful, the melody was not the Wedding March or even the now popular, *Sunrise, Sunset.* Softy, a violin played the unfamiliar tune and the crowd began spontaneously parting. Mami pulled us to her side and we moved up to the front for a better view. The *chuppah* suddenly appeared as four young men walked in carrying four posts with a simple white canopy. When they stopped at the end of the runner, they held the posts high and the canopy unfolded revealing a Star of David embroidered on the top.

The rabbi and *chazan* walked in next and stood underneath the chuppah. I eagerly was waiting to see the bridal party; beautiful young ladies dressed in frilly matching dresses and handsome young men dressed in corresponding tuxedos. I was surprised to see then that the *cortejo* was made up mostly of relatives and all were dressed in their regular party clothes. Although the ladies sparkled in their gala eveningwear, they didn't match and there wasn't a frill, ruffle or flounce to be found. The bridegroom entered next and walked down the aisle, accompanied by his parents. Finally, the lovely bride appeared at the door with her mother and father on either arm. With everyone smiling at her, she glided passed us to meet and stand with her handsome groom. I couldn't help but think; one day I'd walk down the aisle to stand with my groom under a canopy. I blushed and then turned my attention to the ceremony, which had begun with the *chazan's* blessings. The prayers and vows were almost completely in Hebrew, which again was different from what we experienced at home. Not being able to understand the language made the ceremony seem longer than usual, but I knew we were finally done when I heard the stomp on the glass and the instantaneous "Mazal Tov!"

The canopy was dismantled; family and friends quickly surrounded the couple bestowing their good wishes, hugs and kisses. Immediately the atmosphere transformed and everyone was in party mode. While the photographer kept the couple busy, waiters appeared and presented enticing trays of canapés. We found our table and began partaking of the never-ending feast. When the first toast was offered, the bride's grandfather spoke in Yiddish and held up a small glass of vodka. With hearty "*L'chaim*" the adults joined the elderly zeide and drank to the young couple. The music started and we all jumped up to dance a *hora* (circular, folk-dance). The bride was lifted up in a chair and her groom followed. A handkerchief was thrown up to them; she and her new husband were swirled around the room as they each clung to a little corner of the white cloth.

We danced and ate throughout the night. It seemed as if the food was never ending, all sorts of dishes, pastas, chicken, beef, fish. If you didn't like one entrée, another quickly followed. The music was familiar now, the unique variety that seemingly only existed in our world. *La Cumparsita*, melancholy and tender, was followed by the jazzy *Bei Mir Bistu Shane*, which was followed by a Brazilian samba, which led to waltzing around the room to the tune of *Tum Balalaika*. Yes, this was now familiar territory.

The dessert tables were set up and the wedding cake was put on display. The top layer was decorated with silky ribbons, each ribbon had some sort of charm attached and hidden within the cake. I was told that the charms held unique messages, similar to fortune cookies. All the single women were called up to the center of room; I was encouraged to participate as well. Carefully pulling on the ribbons, we each found out our fate: *You will be rich. You will go on an exciting journey.* One of the girls shouted out with a loud "whoopee" when at the end of her ribbon, she found a golden ring. She would be the next to marry. I looked at the end of my ribbon: *You will meet a handsome stranger*; and I blushed. The charms were our souvenirs to take home and place under our pillows; they would entice happy dreams. By the time we finally clambered into the taxicab at five o'clock in the morning, I was more than happy to drift off into dreamland.

Friends and Foes

Fall finally arrived and along with the changes of colors and climate, came other new and exciting challenges. Back to School sales were in full swing. We recently returned from Argentina, and without any time to spare, Dani and I were anxious to get our new school clothes and supplies ready for the big day. Being a sixth grader and practically a teenager, I felt at ease at Shirley Avenue Elementary. Now, I was starting all over again at John A. Sutter Junior High School; being painfully shy, it was a daunting experience. Although many of the kids from my elementary school would be attending Sutter, we were all starting fresh and would be on the bottom of the totem pole. We were newbies; we were *scabs*. Scabs were tossed into trashcans.

The school was over a mile and half away, but even so, I was going to have to walk there every morning. Our daily routine had become hectic since Mami had recently started a part-time job and had to see Dani to school before going to work. Papi, who was working the graveyard shift, was already at Pan Am by the time I had to leave. I had made a new friend down the street and we decided to walk together to school, much to our parents delight. Leticia Galvan was the daughter of a Mexican immigrant, a single mother with three kids. Mrs. Galvan took in laundry and the house smelled like bleach however; Leticia's mother was very welcoming and I was made to feel at home. Mrs. Galvan had been worried that her daughter wouldn't make friends with "nice girls in the new neighborhood." After hearing a few stories about Leticia's escapades in their old neighborhood, I began to understand. They had lived in a tough area in the Valley called Pacoima. Mrs. Galvan tried to keep Leticia away from the older kids, but Leticia looked much older than her age and she fell in with the wrong crowd. Now that they moved to Heartland Street, Mrs. Galvan was sure that her *good little girl* would find other nice little girls to befriend.

Other than purchasing the usual Back-to-School supplies, I was very anxious to get a new "grown up" wardrobe. I was very aware that my skirts and dresses where not quite up to par, but Papi had a long held stance against blue jeans. Jeans were not for young ladies. He'd always thought the fit of the pant was too revealing and attracted unwanted attention. A young lady from a good family did not traipse around calling attention to her *tuches*…at least she didn't in Argentina in his day.

I was used to the seemingly infinite amount of rules and policies that controlled us. Mami and Papi had rules for every aspect of our lives, based on what they perceived as acceptable behavior for nice Jewish girls from Argentina. As a child, these restraints were at times comforting and at other times, stifling. Years later I would realize that even more so than "American" families, my parents *needed* to be controlling, to be overprotective. It must have felt as if tradition and cultural beliefs were slipping through their fingers faster than sand through a sieve. Sometimes, Papi would yield and convince Mami to loosen up a little. This time however, it was my mother who did the persuading so that finally, I could purchase the scandalous items. Leticia's mother took us both to buy our first pair of *Dittos* and *Chermin de Fer* jeans.

Leticia and I decided that we would do a practice walk to the school to see how long it would take us to walk there. We planned to get up early one day, dress for school, eat breakfast and head out. I wasn't yet thirteen years old, but I already was organizing and planning out schedules. It gave me the sense of control that I seemed to crave. The walk took us about a half an hour and on the way back, we stopped at the Dairy Queen for an ice cream.

During our little break, we talked about our families. Leticia told me that her father had left them a long time ago, but insisted that they were better off in his absence. Her father cursed and hollered at every one day and night, especially when he was drunk and Leticia said he was *always* drunk. I couldn't even imagine having a father like that. I had never seen my father drunk, or any of my uncles or cousins for that matter. There was always some wine on the table and we were even allowed to have some with a little 7-Up, but *no one* ever got drunk! Papi and Mami argued occasionally but they never cursed at each other. I began to realize how naïve I was of the realities of life. My parents had protected us so completely; I lived in a relatively quiet little world.

Leticia continued with her story; it seemed that she had to get it off her chest. When her father left, her grandfather came from Northern California to help his daughter and her three small children. Leticia said her grandfather was very old fashioned, a quiet, religious man. He set out new rules for the household, curtailing the hours that the children watched television and even making sure that they attended church. Sadly, he had recently passed away and Leticia crossed herself as she said, "May he rest in peace."

I told Leticia that my grandparents were all in Argentina and I didn't have an ordinary relationship with them, certainly nothing close to having daily contact. Sadly, my father's father, Zeide Simon was very ill and wasn't expected to live too much longer.

"The next world is a better place," Letty said empathetically. "You have to think that he will be happier there."

I shrugged my shoulders. "Well, I suppose so. I don't know too much about that."

"You don't know too much about Heaven?" she asked with a mouthful of mint chocolate chip ice cream.

"No, not exactly. We don't talk about it much at home."

"Well, as long as your grandfather has accepted Jesus as his savior, he will be alright and he will look after you when he is an angel."

"Letty, of course Zeide Simon hasn't *accepted* Jesus. He is not Catholic. We are Jewish."

Leticia almost chocked. "I didn't know you were a Jew. You speak Spanish and you don't look Jewish."

Feeling suddenly uncomfortable, I squirmed in my seat. "Well, we *are* Jewish," I said lifting my chin defiantly, "So what?"

"Well...if your grandfather... what did you call him- your *zay-deh*?" She finished her ice cream cone and said matter-of-factly, "If he doesn't accept Jesus before he dies, he is going to go to Hell for all eternity."

"Letty! That is not true! He is a good man. Why would he go to Hell?"

"You have to accept Jesus to get into Heaven, that's what we learned in Bible study. Don't they teach you that in Jew school?"

I swallowed my anger and wiped my mouth in frustration. I didn't know what to say. I didn't go to "Jew school." How was I supposed to respond to her when I didn't know what the Bible said about Jews, Heaven, or Jesus for that matter?

"Look Letty, all I know is Zeide Simon is a quiet, gentle man. He loves his children and his grandchildren and there is no way that *my* God or *your* God would send him to Hell for all eternity. And I don't want to talk about it anymore. Let's go home, ok?" And with that, we walked back home in silence until Leticia said, "I never met a Jew before."

John A. Sutter Junior High School was now in session. I had some great classes, thanks to my meeting with Mr. Howell, my counselor. One of my favorite classes was Power Reading. All we did was read silently for an hour. The faster you read the more books you could read. The more books you read, the higher your grade was at the end of the semester. What was not to love? But my favorite class was Junior Girls Glee Club.

Thanks to Mr. Thompson, I was ready for Mrs. Michaels' choral class. Mrs. Alberta Michaels became my idol. She was the epitome of femininity and American sophistication. Mrs. Michaels was very fashion forward. She had a striking collection of pastel designer suits. In fact, she had a powder blue suit to match her powder blue Cadillac with vanity plates that read, "ALBERTA." Her music class was led as if it was a finishing school for ladies. For example, in between learning our parts, we also learned that "young ladies never applied makeup whilst sitting in class or in mixed company."

Junior Girls Glee was a fairly large class of approximately thirty-five students. Mrs. Michaels could have managed us single handedly, having us wrapped around her dainty, manicured pinky finger, but she was assigned a student teacher, a young woman from the local university. The student teacher's name was Miss Danvers, which made me laugh out loud when the young lady was introduced to the class. I had just finished reading Rebecca in my Power Reading class and the insanely wicked housekeeper's name was Mrs. Danvers. I hoped that our Miss Danvers would prove to be slightly more accommodating.

The class was divided into three sections; Sopranos on one side, Second Sopranos in the middle and Altos on the opposite side. I sat in the Alto section and there is where I met Bonnie Shae Stewart. We became inseparable. She represented all the American qualities that I coveted and in her eyes, I was "exotic." She told me, some thirty years later, that she had always thought me intriguing and I inspired her to try new things. She said, "Who wants to drink skim milk when you can have Mocha Hazelnut Frappacino?"

Having given up trying to be "a typical American girl," I wore my *poncho* to school almost every day. It made me feel unique and I was experimenting with the concept.

Maybe it was not so bad; unfortunately, my Spanish teacher didn't particularly care for me, or my *unique* Argentine attributes. I took the class because it was required and Mr. Howell said, "It would be a cinch." It actually became a battle of sorts because the teacher wasn't a native speaker and my *Castellano* and her *Español* clashed.

"*Murda*, the word is *dinero*, not *plata*," she would say in her usual exasperated tone.

"I'm sorry Miss Griffin; I'm just used to saying *plata*, when I think about the word for money. I'll try to remember next time." I said wondering why the Spanish teacher couldn't pronounce my name correctly.

"*Murda*, the word for rain is pronounced iu-vee-ah, not ju-vee-ah. Class, do you see the word *lluvia?* When you have double "L's", it makes an "iu" sound."

I was just about to remind her that in Argentina, the two "L's" sound like a "J", when a wise guy in the back snickered, "I bet she says ju-vee-ah because she is a Jew! Who ever heard of Jews in South America anyway? She's too white to be Latina and too *Latina* to be *Jewish*!"

Miss Griffin overheard the comment and immediately sent the boy to the dean's office. She didn't make any further remarks that day, but for the rest of the semester, Miss Griffin seemed to have the need to prove that I was *not* a Latina. The same old, unsettling questions kept reappearing, whether I brought up the subject or it was thrown in my face. Was I Latina? Was I Russian? How long did I have to live in the United States before I could call myself an American?

Leticia had joined a group of girls that actually called themselves *The Latinas*. I wasn't exactly invited to join the group, but I tagged along out of curiosity. After all, I spoke Spanish and was born in a Latin American country. Most of these girls were born in California. I figured I had as much a right to belong as anyone else. I started hanging around the girls at nutrition break and lunch time. Bonnie of course, didn't come with me. She ate lunch with Paula and the others. *The Latinas* all wore gray pants, white T-shirts and big hoop earrings a-la-Selena. I wore my gaucho pants and llama-hair poncho.

They didn't like me and called me *huera* (white girl) but they tolerated me because of Leticia. I didn't understand half of what they said in Spanish and only later found out that they mostly spoke in slang or "street Spanish" and spouted *Viva la Raza* at every opportunity. I secretly thought, "Which *raza*?" Most of the girls were of Mexican descent. One girl was originally from El Salvador; another's parents were from Puerto Rico. While these girls were obviously included in the *raza*, the *huera* from Argentina was not.

When a few of the older girls began speaking about their *quinceañeras*, my curiosity was peaked. Their elaborate plans sounded quite different from what my family experienced. I knew that my older cousins in Argentina had celebrated their fifteenth birthday with festive dinners; they each received a commemorative piece of jewelry from our grandparents, some had parties with music and decorations. The whole affair sounded pretty similar to our sweet sixteen festivities here in America. But these girls were talking about renting banquet halls and buying Scarlett O'Hara hoop skirt dresses. Their friends all vied for a position in *el cortejo,* so that they could be ladies in waiting to the debutant.

When I mentioned that it sounded more like a wedding than a sweet sixteen, the girls sneered at me and questioned my Latin roots once more. They condescended to explain that the *quinceañera* typically wears a fancy white ball gown, very similar to a bride. She attends a special mass and is escorted to her gala event by her hand-picked entourage.. Leticia added that in her family, the *quinceañera* was given a doll, a parting gift from childhood. She frowned at me, silently insinuating that I *should know this stuff.*

At a loss, I blurted out the first thing that was familiar. "We are Jewish. We don't have mass."

This led to the typical accusation: "See, I told you she wasn't *Latina.*"

I was about to explain that Jewish girls had Bat Mitzvahs - that instead of mass, they had services in a temple and that some girls had lavish parties afterwards to celebrate, but since I wasn't going to have one myself, I didn't pursue that train of thought. I questioned my mother later that evening, but Mami couldn't offer much information on the subject. She had very few ties with the Catholic world; she didn't recall hearing about such traditions. I was left to reflect on the fact that *Arr-hen-tina* 15-year-olds, be they Jewish or Catholic, celebrated their special birthdays much differently than their counterparts throughout Latin America. In any event, it only took a few weeks before I realized that I didn't belong with *The Latinas* and returned to my own lunch group with Bonnie Leticia was angry with me and felt rejected. She began taunting me, calling me names; we stopped walking to school together.

Mr. Howell was the dean at Sutter and my counselor. He would walk around campus keeping his eye on all the activity and making sure things were under control. Many times, he'd stop and have a snack with us at nutrition or lunch. Bonnie and I, along with Paula and the other girls were pretty much already dubbed nerds, so eating lunch with the school dean didn't hurt our reputation. Mr. Howell, who could never seem to understand how I could be from Argentina *and* be Jewish, was fascinated by my heritage.

"I'm sorry *Murda*," Mr. Howell shook his head and continued, "I just never heard of Jewish people coming from South America."

Exaggerating my exasperation with him, I said, "It's not that we *came* from South America, we just ended up there. There are Jewish people all over the world Mr. Howell. My grandparents were Russian Jews…you know, like in the *Fiddler on the Roof*?"

"Oh yes, I saw that movie. It was fantastic! But does your family consider themselves Jewish, Russian or Argentine?"

"Mr. Howw-elllll!" I whined, "Do *you* consider yourself Methodist or American?" I said secretly hoping that his answer would help me with my own dilemma.

"Well, actually, we are Presbyterian, but I guess I get your point. So, you are Jews with Russian ancestry, born in a Latin American country, and are now are living in the San Fernando Valley?"

"Well, sort of…I guess. But we have applied for citizenship, so pretty soon I will be a J.A.P."

"What is that?" Mr. Howell cautiously asked.

"A Jewish American Princess!" I giggled.

And that was exactly what I was going to be. In a few weeks' time, Mami, Papi and I were going to be sworn in as American citizens. Papi had the date circled with his bright red marker and I, not wanting to be left behind, placed a sticker of an American flag on the calendar as well. I informed Mr. Howell that when we met with the judge, I was going to formally request to change my name. I had given it some thought and decided on the name Michelle, inspired of course by The Beatles. No one would mispronounce *Michelle*. I was planning on graduating junior high with straight A's and I didn't want Mr. Howell to announce me as "Murda Trup." My parents wouldn't recognize the name and I'd be lost among the other six hundred graduates. Mr. Howell promised me that he would write my name out phonetically and would make sure to pronounce it correctly, but I didn't believe him.

Our day in court arrived and my parents and I met with the immigration judge. We were alone in his office and after answering a few questions; I announced that I wanted my name to be Michelle Trupp. The judge looked at my parents who were slightly uncomfortable and disappointed in my decision. He suggested that I keep my name as a token of respect to my parents and family. He said that at the very least, it would always serve as an icebreaker when meeting new people. I thought of what Mr. Howell promised and what the judge had said and decided to stick with Mirta. Mami and Papi were happy and I knew that The Argentina Family would be proud.

With that important milestone behind us, the Trupp family, now proud American citizens, continued on with their daily lives. Papi continued to work at Pan Am. Mami began working at Litton Industries and Dani and I focused on school and our friends. Bonnie and I had become "bestest friends." We sang together in the Glee Club and joined B.B.G., much to our mothers' delight. B'nai Brith Girls was an international Jewish youth organization and all it was missing in Mami's eyes, were the Argentine Jewish boys! And speaking of Jewish boys, there had been a whirlwind of events that year, the traditional rite of passage for young men: The Bar Mitzvah.

I had been to a few Bar Mitzvah celebrations in the past, thanks to a seemingly unending line of male cousin, but between 1975 and 1976, it seemed I was in the Bar Mitzvah circuit. With the addition of my new girlfriends in B.B.G., I was also introduced to the *Bat* Mitzvah, an event that was not initially given the nod of approval in the traditional Argentine community. Week after week, we would drive to a different synagogue for so-and-so's Bar or Bat Mitzvah. If it was a family event, Papi would begrudgingly come along and "suffer through it," but if the honoree happened to be a school friend, I would be dropped off at the synagogue with a kiss and gentle push out the door.

Following several *Bat Mitzvot*, Judy, the *madricha* (teacher or leader) of our B.B.G. chapter, asked me if I was going to be a Bat Mitzvah. I giggled uncomfortably and replied, "Nope, but I should qualify for an honorary title! I've attended over a dozen events and they're all the same!"

"What do you mean, they are all the same?" Judy asked.

"Well, they are always on a Saturday morning. They sing the same songs and say the same prayers. They take out the scrolls and it sounds like they read the same thing. One week, I went to Debbie Fagan's Bat Mitzvah at Temple Beth Ami and missed going to Judy Lerner's Bat Mitzvah at Temple Bet Emet, because it was on the same day and the same time! As it turns out, I guess I didn't miss out, because they both read *the same part of the bible*!"

Judy looked at me as if she was looking at me for the first time and said, "*Mirda*, gee...I'm sorry...but I guess... I just assumed you knew..."

"Knew what?"

"I don't know where to start!" She exclaimed. "See, it is customary to call Bar and Bat Mitzvah kids to the *bimah* to read from the *Torah* (we don't call it the bible by the way) on Saturday mornings. The services are the same, whether or not there is a Bar or Bat Mitzvah that morning. It's not a *Bar Mitzvah* service. It's a *Shabbat* service. The reason that your friends were reading from the same portion is that *we all* read from the same portion, on any given Saturday-all around the world. When we begin the New Year, you know at *Rosh ha Shanah*; we begin reading from the Torah, just as if we were opening a book together, Chapter One-Page One. We keep reading it throughout the year, straight through-not skipping about. Whether you are in America, Israel or Argentina, we're a united community by basically reading from the same page. Isn't that cool?"

I wished the ground would have opened up and swallowed me whole. I was so embarrassed! Was there no end to what I didn't know? Thankfully, everyone I had met so far in B.B.G. was very friendly and welcoming. There was little religious activity however; my group seemed to be more geared towards social activities, camping trips, and charity events. Bonnie and I enjoyed the activities, as we enjoyed doing most things together.

Bonnie asked me to sleepovers at her house, but ever since the Sylmar earthquake, I had never been able to make it through the night at a friend's house (which was also why I never went on those B.B.G. camping trips). I was embarrassed to tell Bonnie but I finally had to explain my dilemma. After much coaxing, we planned a sleepover. Papi had mixed feelings over the arrangements. He wanted me to overcome my fears, of course, but he also wanted to get a good night's sleep. He'd have to be "on-call" throughout the night.

I had fun with Bonnie and her parents. We ate dinner, watched TV; put on our p.j.'s and got ready for bed. It didn't take too long before I started getting jittery. I felt the anxiety wash over me like a violent wave. I tossed and turned and finally had to wake up my friend. I was so ashamed, but Bonnie came up with an idea. We started singing. We sang all our favorite songs from the old movies we liked to watch and we sang harmonies we learned with Mrs. Michaels. Somehow, I calmed down and fell asleep. In the morning, my "bestest" friend and I were celebrating my first sleepover. Poor Papi was on pins and needles all night long, but he said it was a lesson well learned.

Another opportunity for lesson learning came on a typical afternoon at home; Dani and I were in the kitchen doing homework and Mami was drinking her *mate*. Dani was struggling with her vocabulary homework and asked, "What is the difference between Protect, Defend and Attack?"

I went into a long drawn out explanation, trying to sound like the competent Power Reader that I was. Mami stood leaning against the kitchen sink and took a long sip of her *mate*.

"I know Danielita- Protect!" she said bringing her arm across her chest and up to her shoulder-still holding the *mate*. "Defend," she said now crossing both her arms across her chest, making an X. "Attack!" she said forcefully while punching out her arm in front of her.

The *yerba* in the *mate* went flying across the kitchen floor. Dani and I were practically on the floor as well, doubled over and laughing at Mami's dynamic interpretation. "Well," Mami said, "at least now you know the *dif-er-rance*."

I shouldn't have laughed so hard. Soon after, I found myself in dire need of knowing the difference of defending and attacking. Leticia and her friends had connected with older kids in high school. They were a rough crowd. Leticia had taken up the habit of following me home from school-walking far enough behind so that I couldn't say she touched me, but close enough that I could hear her threats. She liked to say derogatory things about Jews or about show-off, "wanna-be" Latinas. I tried desperately not to pay attention to her, as Papi instructed me.

One day, in World History class, Miss Jenkins, was droning on about a particular Chinese dynasty. The students were growing restless as she gave up struggling with the pull down map and began passing out mimeographed copies. Leticia sat directly in front of me in one of those typical school chairs with the desktop attached. As the teacher was distracted, Leticia decided to have some fun with me. She turned around and whispered, "Better watch your back, you dirty Jew whore."

I don't know how it happened, but after weeks of her torment, I snapped. Without thinking, I slapped Leticia across the face so hard that she fell down and brought the chair/desk on top of her. The teacher gasped as the students cheered and urged me to continue, but I didn't move a muscle. I just hovered over Leticia lying on the floor. The next thing I knew, we were both sitting outside of the dean's office. Mr. Howell called me in first. He could not believe what Miss. Jenkins had informed him. I told him exactly what happened and what had been happening for months. I think he tried to hide a smirk as he imagined little *Murda Trup*, his straight-A student, in a fight with Leticia Galvan, a known gang member. I don't know what he did to Leticia, but I was suspended for three days. He apologized to me but he was bound by the regulations. Even though I was *defending* myself, I *attacked* first. From that day forward, Papi had to pick me up after school.

I had found it difficult to make friends outside of my little circle and even with my American friends; there were times when our bond seemed strained. Their lives were seemingly uncomplicated. They of course had their own teenage angst to deal with, but living with one foot in America and another in Argentina was a daunting task. I was also jealous of the fact that my cousins didn't go back to Argentina. In fact, most of *La Familia* never returned. Traveling to Argentina was not only physically exhausting: it was emotionally unsettling. My cousins were not burdened with these trips and in my eyes; they had time to become *real* Americans. While they played sports and went camping, learned to surf and ski, we were stuck in an elderly aunt's house drinking tea and having *sándwiches de miga.* While they explored the Grand Canyon and traveled to Hawaii, returning to school with a healthy glow, Dani and I were the strange kids that disappeared for the summer, only to return wearing llama hair *ponchos* and sporting winter's tell-tale pallor. Junior high school was tough enough for "regular" kids; the added pressure of being a foreigner with debatable ethnicity was harrowing.

When my three years at Sutter finally came to an end, I managed to leave on a good note. As I crossed the podium on graduation day, Mr. Howell kept his promise and announced my name clearly and succinctly: "Mirta Ines Trupp, member of the John A. Sutter's Honor's Society." I was so proud. I wished The Argentina Family could have heard it too.

Ascending

Junior high school was over and now I looked forward to a fresh start. I would get that fresh start in more ways than one. Mami and Papi sold our house on Heartland Street and we moved up the real estate scale into a brand new home. In keeping with the theme of upgrades and transformations, I looked to several teen magazines, such as 16 Magazine and Tiger Beat for ideas on how to reinvent myself so that I could move up the proverbial social ladder. I followed the trends and cut my hair in the new "Dorothy Hamill" style. I then proceeded to the next item on my "must haves" list for high school: Makeup. Papi didn't approve of make up for young ladies, but my cousin Alicia convinced Mami that I should be allowed a little make up at my age. Alicia bought me my first Maybelline mascara in the iconic pink and green tube, a set of Bonnie Bell eye shadows and a Yardley's "Pot o'Gloss." I was permitted to use a dab of Love's Baby Soft perfume and of course, my new shampoo, Gee Your Hair Smells Terrific.

Mrs. Michaels, our cherished teacher and mentor, had sent us on our way with a regal wave and a suggestion to sign up for choir at Chatsworth High School under the direction of Mr. Daniel Olafson. The problem was that I was supposed to go to Reseda High School. As luck would have it, the secretary at Chatsworth either couldn't read a map or heard my despair when I cried, "I have to go to Chatsworth with Bonnie Stewart or I will simply perish!" My paperwork was inexplicably approved. Together, Bonnie and I walked up the steps to our new school as Chatsworth Chancellors. We proceed with our plans and registered for classes, including Choir with Mr. Daniel Olafson. Mr. Olafson, soon to be known to us as Mr. O., determined that *even* if we did come with Mrs. Michaels' noble recommendations, we were not going to enter his mixed choir as incoming freshman. Bonnie and I entered Room K-78 for the first time as "Choralaires," the girls' chorus. Thankfully, Mami said that she would wait for the Holiday Concert before whisking us back to Argentina for the winter break. If I would have missed the concert, Mr. O. made it perfectly clear that I would drop a full grade and would not be considered for Choir or the competition group, Inspirations, the following year. There were no ifs, ands or buts about it. The performance came before everything else, including The Argentina Family.

Mr. O. treated his students as if they were his colleagues. He said that we needed him as much as he needed us - mutual respect and appreciation filled the music room. It was with this encouragement that I approached my teacher and basically reprimanded him on his choice of Chanukah music for the upcoming "Holiday Sounds" concert. I practically begged him to find us something other than the typical, childish melodies. He promised he'd look into the matter and I simply beamed at the man, nodding my approval. A few days later Mr. O. passed out new music to his Choralaires. The melody itself was fairly simple; the lyrics were anything but sugary sweet. Mr. O. suggested that I give the class a little background on the piece. I could have melted into my seat; I was so ashamed at my lack of knowledge. Mr. O., recognizing my discomfort, didn't linger and proceeded to lead us in the round. In unison the class began:

By the waters, the waters, of Babylon,

We sat down and wept, and wept for thee Zion…

While the left side of my brain was singing along, the right side was thinking: What does this have to do with Chanukah? *Babylon*? And why were they weeping?

Later that day, I heard one of the altos from Choir sight-reading through a new solo piece. She was also a Jewish girl and I couldn't help but wonder if she had mentioned something to Mr. O. about adding new selections. I listened with admiration as she practiced throughout our lunch break. The lyrics, while quite moving, were yet again, unfamiliar to me…*At the dawn, I seek Thee, refuge rock sublime…*

I wished I had heard the song before. When I auditioned for the youth group's production of *Fiddler of the Roof*, I performed a rousing rendition of *Have Yourself a Merry Little Christmas.* This new piece would have been infinitely more appropriate but still; I *did* get the part and made the *madrich* cry when I was called up to sing Hodel's solo.

Winter break began the day after Holiday Sounds and of course, we were headed back to Argentina for the two-week vacation. In the past, I would have dreaded the trip, since it meant suffering through the heat and humidity of Buenos Aires, but this time, on December 26, 1976, it was a little more enticing. Papi was even coming with us. My cousin, Monica from Bahia Blanca, not to be confused with Monica from Buenos Aires, was getting married on New Year's Eve. Even Tío Elias and Tía Feli came for the occasion. However, there was another reason for the trip. It was my 15th birthday. I was finally a *quinceañera* and The Argentina Family made me feel like a princess.

Because the family was so large and spread out, I had several small celebrations. Mami, who always jumped at the chance to buy us new clothes, happily purchased a new party dress, shoes and accessories for the special occasion. She even arranged for my hair and make-up to be done so that I could have a professional portrait taken. One night, as we were headed to one of the special dinners, my uncles, Marcos and Beto, presented me with two lovely bouquets of pink roses. When we reached the restaurant, Tío Marcos helped me out of the taxi. Arm in arm with my handsome uncles, we began crossing the street. Usually, in Buenos Aires, you have to run for your life as you cross a busy street, but suddenly, the cars stopped and let us pass. People were honking and waving their hands saying. "*Viva la Quinceañera*!" Tío Marcos winked at me and said, "See, you are very special here." Who wouldn't feel special with all the attention I was getting; gifts, parties, dinners and invitations to participate with the older cousins?

One afternoon, while lazing about in Tía Lela's apartment, my cousin Silvia stopped by and invited me to join her on an outing. Since I had bored watching an old episode of *Mission Impossible*, dubbed in Spanish of course, I was more than happy to tag along.

"Turn off the T.V. *primita;* get up and change your clothes!" She said as she reached into the closet and pulled out a blouse and a pair of pants.

"Where are we going exactly? Why do I have to change?" I groaned, but just for show, because I would have changed my clothes gladly just to get out and *do* something!

"We are going to meet Moishe and the gang at the *ken*. You can't go out looking like that! What would people say?"

I had forgotten; Buenos Aires was the Paris of South America. Everyone was very particular about his or her own outfit but they were more particular about *your* outfit. You couldn't just go out in a pair of jeans and T-shirt. You had to wear an *ensemble*.

"Wait…what's a *ken*?" I asked as I quickly changed behind the armoire's massive door.

"It's a place, a house to meet people and you know…just to socialize. It's a Hebrew word; I think it means a nest."

Silvia had a scruffy looking boyfriend who had just returned from Israel. He, along with a group of friends had made *aliyah* however; I didn't know what that meant. They *made aliyah*? Silvia had to explain that *aliyah* meant to ascend or to go up. The verb sounded just as funny in English as it did in Spanish. You could have *made* your bed, or you could have *made* a sandwich, but to *make aliyah* sounded peculiar, even with my cousin's explanation. No matter; I knew my education was lacking. I sensed my afternoon would prove to be slightly more enlightening than an old T.V. show; my mood was unguarded and receptive to the possibilities.

We took a bus and then walked several blocks, turning this way and that until finally arriving to our destination. If had thought that Tía Lela's apartment building was old, this house was practically prehistoric! We opened the front door and walked down a long passage way made up of an intricate mosaic of green and gold tiles. This house was similar to Tía Lela's, as you had to cross the patio to reach a series of rooms. Kids were spilling out through the open doors and Hebrew music was being played quite loudly on the Hi Fi. The walls seemed to be held up by dozens of posters all depicting various locations in Israel. I read the unfamiliar words: Masada - Jerusalem of Gold - The Kotel. Moishe came out to greet us and helped us find our way into a lounge area. People were all gathered around listening to a couple speak. Moishe said we had made it just in time.

"What's going on?" I asked Silvia.

She whispered back, so as not to interrupt the lecture, "They're visitors from Israel. They've come to talk to us about their experiences and to share information. Haven't you ever heard of the *Sochnut*?"

"Soch-*what*?" I giggled.

"The *Sochnut*. It's a Zionist organization. Lots of Argentine kids are making *aliyah*; students, young couples, even families. Israel is inviting her people to return."

"Why are so many young people leaving?"

"It's a political matter, as well as an emotional pull. On one hand, with all the military repression, we can hardly breathe, let alone plan for our future. The economy is getting worse every day; university students have no incentive to continue their studies. On the other hand, Israel needs us. We can be a part of history; rebuild and recreate a safe haven- *our homeland*."

"But hasn't it been safe here in Argentina? This is supposed to be *Paris of South America*-cultured and sophisticated. I mean, I know about the anti-Semitism and all, but…"

A young man standing nearby overheard our conversation and quickly positioned himself in between us; there was no mistaking his intent. Introductions were made and he immediately understood why I would have made such a statement. He looked at Silvia as if to say "May I?" and then he turned to me.

"Our great grandparents came here to escape the *pogroms* of Russia; they came to escape bigotry and ignorance. Unfortunately, it seems whenever there are problems, be they financial or political, the ignorant masses blame the Jews. It wasn't long after our families arrived that a series of riots and massacres took place in Buenos Aires. It was called *Semana Trágica* (Tragic Week); a week in January 1919 that began with strikes and picketing workers. One conflict after another began taking place; mobs went lose all over Buenos Aires destroying property, injuring-even *murdering* innocent people. The city was at a complete stand still, held hostage between the rioters and striking workers. The Argentine Patriotic League took advantage of the mayhem and specifically targeted the Jewish population of Buenos Aires; inciting *pogroms* and adding new victims to the ever growing list of dead and wounded."

"They ran through the streets in El Once, where our grandparents live, shouting "death to the *Rusos*," Silvia interjected.

The young man nodded and continued, "This League, which received military training and was supported by the Church, identified "*los Rusos*" with the Bolsheviks and blamed them for the current state of affairs with the unions. Jews here in Buenos Aires, *the Paris of South America*, were dragged from their homes, beaten, shot and killed."

"I had no idea…"

"Most people think about Nazis hiding out in Argentina, but the anti-Semitism goes way back. Ask your parents, ask your new friends. Argentine youth look ahead and face an unstable future; they look back and see a frightening history. Israel is inviting people to come home and help rebuild. I think we need to *at least* listen to what they have to offer."

Again, I realized how ignorant I was and how out of place I felt. For my fifteenth birthday, my cousins Monica and Rolando gave me a huge gold Star of David. I wanted to wear it as a testament but sadly; I didn't have a clue what it stood for or what being a Jew truly meant. I lived in a Peter Pan world, traipsing around in Never-Never Land. That point was made clear when, once again, my father's had *prehistoric* reaction to a most innocent event.

We were headed to Bahia Blanca for Monica and Martin's wedding. Instead of flying, we would travel overnight by train and arrive first thing in the morning. Although it was close to midnight, the train station was bustling with all sorts of interesting people; families, soldiers, and students returning home for the holidays. Papi and Mami were busy talking with Tío Elias and Tía Feli; and with Dani dozing off, I took the liberty to walk around a bit - just people watching. A young sailor walked by me and said, "*Que faroles nena*!"

Papi had seen the sailor from the corner of his eye and came quickly to my side. He asked me what the sailor said to me. I repeated what I heard, even though I didn't understand. Papi was very upset, but since the sailor was long gone, there was nothing to be done. I didn't say another word! When we got to Bahia the next day, I couldn't wait to tell Monica what had happened and ask her what *faroles* meant. She laughed and called my father "old-fashioned." *Faroles* are lanterns, Monica explained. The sailor had been flirting with me and was referring to my "bright blue eyes." My cousins assured me that I should be flattered. I was coming up in the world; I had received my first Argentine *piropo* (Something in between a wolf whistle and a compliment).

Monica and I had become very close. She was ten years my senior and I looked up to her like an older sister. I could talk to her about anything and she would gladly listen without judging. Being university students, Monica and Martin were constantly open to new ideas and philosophies. They delved into all kinds of metaphysical principles; always asking questions and meeting new and interesting people with similar inquisitive minds. It was during this time that Monica started talking to me about these different philosophies and paths to enlightenment. We seemed to be very much connected. I wanted to soak up everything she was imparting. My only issue with my beloved cousin was that she would drop subtle and sometimes, not-so-subtle, suggestions of the possibility of me moving to Bahia. The university had many American transfer students. She painted a pretty interesting picture for me. I could study in English, mix with the kids from the States and the Argentines, and have the social and family life that I craved. She knew what points to make because of my many prior complaints. Of course, the catch was that I would have to leave my family back home. *Leave the United States.* I knew I never could do it, but the idea was thought provoking. I had so much fun in Bahia and I loved being in Monica's beatnik world. When the subject would become too uncomfortable, I could tell her to "knock it off" and give as good as I received. Life in Argentina was **not** all that she made it up to be; I attributed her seemingly one-sided vision to her fierce patriotism, something with which I could relate. Through all the debates, we never had harsh words and we never parted with hurt feelings. I knew she wanted the best for me and I always felt free to speak my mind.

The next leg of this particular trip was to be by bus. We headed further south to Buratovich on an old bus with stubborn windows that wouldn't close and torn leather seats that poked our travel-worn behinds. The other passengers who boarded looked like they made the trip daily. Everyone looked hot and tired as they climbed in. I noticed a woman as she held out her money to the bus driver with one hand and tried to hold up a crying little girl with the other, while balancing several packages.

The woman glanced around the bus, saw there were no empty seats and proceeded to juggle her packages so that she could better hold up the toddler who was whining from exhaustion. I looked at Dani and she knew what I was thinking. How *enlightened* could we pretend to be if we didn't offer any help? I turned to the woman and suggested that she let her daughter sit with us. The little girl sat on my lap and in just a minute or so, closed her eyes and was asleep. With her tiny body sprawled across the both us, Dani and I swept away the pesky flies that came through the broken window.

The old bus went down the country dirt road and sunk into every nook and cranny. It felt like a ride in an amusement park. Up and down, up and down; thankfully, Dani didn't throw up! We soon arrived in Burato and the woman gathered up her daughter and her packages and thanked us repeatedly. She heard us speaking English the entire trip and although she wasn't sure why in heaven's name we would be on an old bus headed to Buratovich, she knew that we were *Yanquis* and she would have a story to tell when she got home that afternoon.

As usual we were received with great fanfare at Tia Delia's house. The girls were beautiful and I was in awe of their maturity. Miguel was as charming as ever and seemed to be in trouble all the time. One hot and muggy afternoon as we sat about the *kiosco* lazily eating up Tío Enrique's candy, Tía Delia suggested that Miguelito take us for a ride about town. Miguel probably shouldn't have used the particular tone, but being a teenage boy, bored, hot and miserable, he answered back, "Where do you suggest I take them in this lousy little town?" Tío Enrique came barreling out from the back room and I actually cringed. He bellowed something at poor Miguel; Dani and I jumped up and followed him out the store. They had an old beat up car that should have been in a junkyard, but we didn't care. Anywhere Miguel wanted to take us and by any means available, would have been fine by us. He drove around the four corners of the *pueblito.* We passed the park of course; it was the main attraction in the center of town. We passed the school and the church and several houses. We stopped by one house and picked up a few of Miguel's friends. Thankfully, his mood changed for the better. The friends asked us to sing something by The *Bee-At-Les.* A few minutes later, after we recovered from our giggling, we began singing *Yesterday* as Miguel drove down a dusty road. I realized that we were a little farther out of town. Looking around, I saw that we were in a cemetery. Miguel stopped the car on some old dry grass. We opened the doors to let the breeze flow a little bit. We sat there and sang Beatles songs with Miguel and his friends until it was time to go home.

Social Studies

Since their immigration in the 1960's, *los paisanos* (in my family, this means Jewish Argentines) founded a club that mimicked the beloved organization of their homeland- Hebraica. They began meeting in people's homes for *asados* and to celebrate holidays, but eventually, the group became so large, they decided to form an official club, elect a Board of Directors and rent a clubhouse. The social center was actually a loft in an old building located in the seedy part of Hollywood. Still, it was a place to go and the families looked forward to sharing a Kabbalat Shabbat, dances and picnics and most especially the New Year's Eve parties, which were mandatory no matter how old you were.

This assembly of rag-tag immigrants was desperately trying to assimilate into the American culture, but was just as desperately clinging to their Argentine identity. The complicated path was knotted with feelings of guilt for leaving their mother country, coupled with the stress to succeed - to prove that their suffering was not in vain. Added to the mixture, was their Argentine culture and their Jewish faith crying out not to be forgotten or given up. On any given occasion, a visit to a Hebraica event would offer the strange combinations of *tango* with *kugel* and *mate* with *knishes*. These settings would have made prime lab experiments for any up and coming sociologist who wanted to study ethnocentrisms… *We want to assimilate, but our Arr-hen-tina culture is superior. We want to fit in, but we don't want to let go of our past.*

Another reason the adults loved the club was the endless possibilities to make a *shidach*! (a love match) The women would sit together and study the possibilities of mixing this one's daughter with that one's son. Many were successful with their matches. Several of my cousins met and married their spouses through this method. I was not safe by any means. Even though my father was not too keen with the idea, my mother tried her best to point out some good candidates. One particularly humiliating memory haunted me for years and years. The dance floor had just been abandoned; the tango dancers retreated at the sounds of the Doobie Brothers. The two mothers got together and before I knew it, I was in the middle of the dance floor with poor Antonio Litvak, an innocent in the whole matter. Tony and I were stuck trying to dance to the un-danceable and interminable, "Without love, where would you be right now? Without loooove!"

Another opportunity for humiliation arose at the annual social event: the Purim ball. Year after year, there was the degrading beauty contest for the title of Queen Esther. *Year after year*, I begged to be excluded, but my mother always insisted that I participate. At one such event, Mami had her eye on *el muchachito* Aaron Aaronstein. He had just returned from a trip to Argentina and he was apparently a great catch! He was also crowned the King for this Purim's event. Mami thought that he would see me parading around in the Queen Esther contest and fall madly in love. Needless to say, I was not interested in *el muchachito* Aaron Aaronstein mainly because he looked like the teenage werewolf with his long hair, bushy beard and long overcoat.

The reigning Queen Esther always happened to be petite and slender and *always* "just happened" to be Sandra Filshtein. My thoughts flipped flopped from being humiliated at never being chosen to being outraged at the idea of a beauty contest. How *archaic* - a beauty contest? Worse yet, were the well-intentioned comments; comments that were supposed to soothe my hurt feelings:

"Well, you know, Sandra is more the *Arr-hen-tina* type, Mirtita. You are more like an American girl-*tan grandota*-tall and well, you know, robust…like a *Yanqui*."

Recovering from the sting of basically being called an Amazon woman, I retorted, "Aren't you always reminding me that I was born in Argentina and that I *am not* a *Yanqui*?"

"Oh, of course, yes, you are right!" the well-meaning socialite exclaimed.

"Of course, you are *Arr-hen-tina,* Mirtita. You are not like a *Yanqui*; you are *grandota* like your Bobe Flora. You take after the Kolinsky sisters!" said another Hebraica diva.

"So, I'm big-boned like the Kolinsky sisters? They are *Russian.* There isn't a drop of Argentine blood in any of us! And besides, you are missing the point. Queen Esther, believe it or not, was not *Arr-hen-tina.* She was Persian!"

It amazed me that in the span of one or two generations, these Eastern European Jews, went from *Feige*, *Chava*, and *Batya*, to Felicia, Juana and Beatriz and completely identified themselves as *Hispanas*; more to the point, *Argentinas.* They were most likely the product of generations of inbreeding amongst Jewish peasantry, and yet they felt the blood of *Martin Fierro*, the iconic symbol of Argentina, running through their veins. They knew more about the tradition of setting out their slippers for *Reyes* (the Three Wise Men) than they knew about the Purim tradition of *Mishloach Manot.* (Not that I had known anything about *Mishloach Manot.* I had only just learned about the baskets filled with treats while participating in a charity event with B.B.G.) There was no use arguing with them. Their image of Queen Esther was taken out of the latest edition of <u>*Gente*</u> magazine. Besides, who was I to argue? I was so confused about who or what I was that it took me over an hour to complete my DMV application thanks to one simple question…*what is your race*?

The ladies had given up trying "to make me feel better" and headed for the dessert tables to fill up on *hamantaschen* and *panqueques con dulce de leche.* In the long run I supposed, it was better not to have been crowned Queen Esther. I escaped having to dance with the werewolf and *that* was worth missing out on the fame and glory.

I didn't miss out on any fame or glory when at sixteen years old, my parents presented me with a 1968 Dodge Dart. Having my own car meant that I wouldn't have to take two buses to school in the morning and two buses back home in the afternoon! I had the freedom to come and go as I pleased…well, not really, but after informing my parents of where I was going and with whom and what time I was coming home, *I was free*! I picked up Bonnie every morning; she ate her breakfast and put on her make up while I drove us to school in the comfort of my pea green sedan. With the freedom of having my own transportation, my next objective was having a little spending money. I convinced Mami and Papi that getting a part-time job was the right thing to do. Bonnie and I set out to find a place that would hire the both of us. By some stroke of luck, we found work at the local Del Taco. Although my parents were proud of me and thought it was commendable that I wanted to pay for my little outings or shopping sprees, I was asked not to mention it to The Argentina Family. A young lady from a good Jewish family did not work in a fast food restaurant, or any restaurant for that matter. What would the *bobes* and zeides say? Serving food? That was practically a servant! Oh no, that was socially unacceptable! Hmm...wasn't Queen Esther a servant girl before she became queen?

In a very different sort of social experiment, the practice of adopting friends into *La Familia* and instantly generating new relatives continued to flourish in our enclave. Our families didn't simply meet new people and form acquaintances. If they were Argentine Jews, they were *familia.* And that was the way of it with the Fagan family. Luis and Natalia were friends with the Bernsteins. Their son, Brian had met my cousins Fabian and Marcelo through a variety of A.Z.A. and school events. Before too long, the Fagans were part of the fold and when they moved around the corner from our house, Brian and I practically became siblings.

One evening, my cousin, Fabian called to invite me and Brian to the movies. The boys were coming to our local neighborhood theater. Fabian also explained that Bobe Freida was coming along as the movie was rated R and they had convinced her to act as chaperone. Brian was not home, but I accepted the invitation because anytime with the Bernsteins was guaranteed to be fun. I didn't bother asking what movie we were going to see. I figured Bobe Freida was going with us- *how bad could the movie be?*

The boys wanted to see Black Christmas, a thriller about a sorority house. Fabian said that everyone was talking about it and that "it wasn't that bad." While we were in line, I turned to Bobe Freida and admitted to her that I didn't like horror movies. Bobe Freida told me to relax and not to worry. "After all, it is just make-believe," she said. If this wonderful old grandma wasn't afraid, then I certainly couldn't show any fear. *I had to grit my teeth all through the movie* and promised myself (again!) that I would never listen to another thing Fabian said. The movie was terrifying, but Bobe Freida *laughed* through the whole thing. I kept jumping out of my seat each time the villain attacked one of the unsuspecting girls. There was one scene in particular where a sorority sister was home alone and suddenly, there was a knock on the window. When the girl didn't get a reply to her "Who's there?" she pulled the curtains open only to find the hideous masked man waiting for her with an ax in hand. I nearly jumped through the roof. Fabian thought my terror was hysterical.

One afternoon, shortly after the movie disaster, I found myself at home alone. I was in the back of the house, in my room, listening to music. Suddenly, I heard some light tapping on my bedroom window. I ignored it the first time and even the second time, but by the third tap, I realized that I was not imagining it, nor was it a bird or a bug or anything else I had rationalized in my mind. The tap became a loud knock. I shouted, "Who's there?" but there was no reply. There was no way that I was going to pull the curtains apart! I thought of calling the police, but then there was a knock at the front door and then another knock.

I shouted again, "Who is it?" but when I didn't get a reply, I decided to call the Fagans who lived around the corner and ask for help. A few minutes later, the doorbell rang and I heard Luis Fagan telling me to open the door. I reached for the door with a trembling hand. As I opened the door, I saw Luis holding his son by his ear. He pulled him inside the house and demanded that Brian apologize. Brian confessed that Fabian told him about the movie and how it had terrified me. He thought that he'd conduct a little experiment, but never believed that I would have had such an extreme reaction. When Brian admitted that his study in my "socio-cultural" reaction went overboard, Luis began lecturing on the proper way to treat a young lady. While still holding on to his son's ear, Luis dragged Brian down the street and around the corner back to their house, where I presumed Mr. Fagan conducted his own brand of socio-cultural experiments.

Inspired

After attending several U.S.Y. social events and caving in to Paula Blumberg's persistent cajoling, I officially joined the national youth group program. Our chapter was a motley crew of Jewish teenage nerds led by a slightly older Jewish nerd-Mark Stein. Although I had intended to learn more about Judaism, I found that I was ashamed at my lack of knowledge. To hide the embarrassment, I had built up a wall of defiance. I questioned the need to curtail activities on Saturday afternoons, when we were all bored at home and would have welcomed some form of socializing. I wrote editorials to the synagogue's newsletter questioning the need for pricey membership fees and cost prohibitive High Holiday tickets.

After an event held at the temple, the youth group headed over to a favorite hangout. The ice cream parlor, with its 1910-ish atmosphere featured posters of Gibson Girls sharing shakes with their beaus and servers wearing pin-striped pants and straw hats. The parlor was famous for their ice cream, but they also happened to serve the best cheeseburgers and milkshakes in town. And therein lay the problem.

The group decided to grab some burgers and fries before calling it a night. We took up three large booths and made quite a ruckus. Menus were passed around, drink orders were blurted out to the waitress and it was exactly at that point, I got into trouble with Mark. I had asked for a vanilla milkshake, along with a cheeseburger. I didn't do it intentionally, but once put on the spot, I stuck to my guns.

"*Murda*, why don't you choose something else?" Mark asked politely.

"I don't want something else. I have a craving for a vanilla milkshake."

"OK, so have the fries and the milkshake."

"But I haven't eaten all day. I'm hungry and I want the cheeseburger too."

Exasperated, Mark leaned over and repeated his request, "Just have a burger and fries, like everyone else ok? Get a cola or something."

I wasn't going to give up so easily. I retaliated, "Mark, this restaurant doesn't keep a kosher kitchen and I know for a fact, that you and all the rest of the kids don't keep kosher. What is the big deal?"

"The thing is that we are out as a youth group. We might not keep kosher as individuals, but as a group, we should try to keep a Kosher-style. *You know* that means not mixing dairy with meat. Come on now, don't be obstinate."

But I was obstinate and because I was embarrassed, I became more obnoxious than necessary. I couldn't give in. "Sorry Mark, I don't understand "Kosher-style." Either you keep Kosher, or you don't. Show me in the bible where it says, "Thou shalt keep kosher…*style*."

At that point, one of the other kids decided he would take my side and changed his order to match mine. Mark was livid.

"You know *Murda*, when you are *really* inspired to learn, I'll be very happy to spur you on. In the meantime, you and Danny can go have your cheeseburgers and milkshakes in another booth. You guys are officially on your own for tonight."

Danny and I moved over to an adjacent booth and ate our meal in silence. I was steaming! But the anger and frustration were not actually geared towards Mark. I felt frustrated with myself, for the lack of maturity and for my lack of knowledge.

My mother encouraged me to continue participating in the youth group as well as the B'nai B'rith program. I met a boy at one of the socials. Josh was in the same AZA chapter as my cousin Fabian. The chapter, *Jonas*, was probably the most well known in the entire Valley. All the popular boys were in that group therefore; my status within my own group, *A Nashim,* was elevated due to my familial connections. I developed a crush on Josh although my friends didn't particularly care for him. Probably more than anything, I had a crush on the idea of him. We dated for a bit although Papi was not too keen on the idea of me having a "steady boyfriend." Of course Papi was not keen on the idea; this was the man that didn't allow me to read *The Archies* comics when I was twelve years old. He believed that nice little girls shouldn't be encouraged to read about boyfriend/girlfriend issues or sing suggestive songs. When Josh invited me to his prom, I had to carefully plan out how I was going to ask Papi for permission. There was no such thing as prom in Argentina. They didn't understand why it was such a big deal. The formal dress, the tuxedo, the corsage, and the dinner…it all sounded too official. And who was this Joe Schmoe anyway?

Papi was working the graveyard shift and we didn't see him most of the week. He'd usually call on his dinner break and would catch up with us by phone. I took my chance one night and asked him for permission to go to the dance. He asked me a million questions and the whole conversation literally took up his entire hour break. Mami and Diana were pacing back and forth in the kitchen waiting anxiously for Papi's reply. Finally, he agreed! Too bad the date with Josh turned out to be completely regrettable and not worth the cost of the fabulous dress, let alone the torment of the phone call.

Even under the hawkish glare of my father's eye, there were a few boys that came knocking at my door. More often than not, my mother had something to do with it. The network of Argentine *yentas* in the San Fernando Valley was constantly humming along. All it took was for one mother to place a call and before you knew it, dozens of matchmakers were looking through their little black books to find the perfect date for so-and-so.

There was Joel, who couldn't keep his hands to himself. When he brought me home, I ran past my parents who were practically waiting by the door. Heading straight for the bathroom, I proceeded to wash out my mouth with Listerine after having benefited from an unsolicited good night kiss from Mr. Octopus or was it Mr. Lizard?

There was gallant Miguel, who stood up when I entered the room and held my chair out for me (Big points for that!!) He was as charming as could be in front of the parents, a veritable Sir Galahad, but as soon as the folks were away, he turned into Conan the Barbarian. Since I was the *paragon of virtue*, that relationship didn't go far.

There was Gary, not an Argentine kid, but rather a somewhat annoying boy from school who sat behind me in Choir. Playing off of Ricardo Montalban's "luxurious Corinthian leather" commercial, Gary would constantly say, "Ah, luxurious Argentinean hair!" while messing up the hair that I got up at 5:00 a.m. to blow-dry straight. Nothing came out of that situation either.

Then there was David - David, who was every mother's dream. He was *un profesional* and that made him husband material - already out of school and making money. Tall and handsome, he had the manners of an English gentleman. When he came to the door to pick me up, he practically bowed in salutation. I was very shy but eager to impress this young man. Finally, a real adult! Not some nerdy high school kid. We went to dinner and later did some window-shopping. He kept his hands to himself, so much so, that he didn't even hold my hand as we walked through the streets of Westwood. (*No* points for him!) When we arrived back home, he escorted me to my door and very politely said goodnight. My mom was waiting up for me, of course. "So, did you have fun? Did he kiss you goodnight?"

"Yes, we had a very nice time and no, he didn't kiss me goodnight."

"Not even a little kiss on the cheek?"

"Nope-nothing-nada-zilch."

"*Que pavote*!" she said and turned around and went to her room muttering to herself.

I took pity on the poor guy…*his* mother probably warned him to be on his best behavior, act like a complete gentleman, and keep his hands to himself. I was, after all, a nice Jewish girl from a good *Arr-hen- tina* family.

This nice, Jewish, *Arr-hen-tina* girl, met and befriended a nice Anglo-Saxon, presumably Christian girl in sixth period, Creative Writing class. Lisa fit in the category of "Goody-Two-Shoes" as she was as straight laced as the Victorian corsets my novel heroines wore. I began noticing her strange behavior on Tuesday and Thursday afternoons. My normally calm, cool and collected friend would dash out of class and head out to the parking lot, trying to beat the mass exodus off campus. It was odd to see her rushing around, so I confronted her out of curiosity.

"You are always in such a rush to leave Mr. Potter's class. I think you have a new boyfriend and you don't want to tell me about him." I amiably teased.

Lisa actually blushed. "No, I don't have a boyfriend! I started going to a youth group after school. We talk a little and someone usually brings out a guitar. We usually order some pizzas and just, you know, hang out. It's fun. Do you want to come with me next time?"

"It does sounds like fun, but what sort of youth group is it?"

"It's from my church. Ben Stanley, our youth pastor, runs it."

"Your *church*- Lisa, I'm Jewish, remember?" My thoughts went straight back to junior high school and Leticia.

"*Mirda*, it's not about hell fire and brimstone. We just talk about living healthy lives and about being good people. We just hang out. Come with me and see for yourself."

The following Tuesday, I went along with Lisa to Pastor Ben's meeting. There was a group of twenty kids sitting around, talking and munching on snacks. Lisa introduced me to her friends; we picked up some pizza and iced tea and sat down next to a boy busily tuning his guitar. Pastor Ben came over to greet us and my stomach began to churn. Did anyone have any *Hepatalgina* handy?

"Hello Lisa. It's nice to see you again. Did you bring a friend today?"

"Yes, this is my friend. Mirda, this is Pastor Ben."

We shook hands and the young pastor smiled at me. He looked at little like a hippie with his long hair pulled back in a ponytail and his faded blue jeans.

"Mirda? *Mirda*?" He looked at me curiously. "What a nice name. What language is that?"

"It's actually: *Mirta*. It's Spanish. I was born in Argentina." I quickly swallowed a bite of pizza *and* the fact that I was Jewish and the granddaughter of Russian immigrants.

"Argentina? Well, that's interesting. I'm sure you have a very unique perspective of the Lord. Maybe you would care to share it with us later."

I shrugged my shoulders and smiled. *A unique perspective*, I'll say!

The group of kids had settled around the guitar player. Someone sat at the piano and began playing some familiar chords. Soon, we were all singing *Let It Be* and I began to relax. This wasn't bad at all, I thought. Nice, wholesome fun. Nothing wrong with that! *Right?* The next song was *Spirit in the Sky* followed by *Jesus is Alright With Me.* Grabbing another slice of pizza, I hurriedly engaged myself in the act of meticulous chewing rather than singing along.

I returned to the youth group on Thursday and accompanied Lisa several more times before Pastor Ben brought out a bible. He asked the kids to gather around and informed them they would be reading from the Old Testament that afternoon, the book of Isaiah to be exact. After a few verses, Pastor Ben turned to me and asked if I would like to take a turn reading. I read the unfamiliar passages and felt uneasy as all eyes were on me. When I was done, I passed the King James Bible back. He grinned and bowed his head as if to "Thank you." We read for a few more minutes and then Pastor Ben suggested that we could break into discussion groups. He walked over and asked me to help him take the empty pizza cartons into the kitchen.

"So, *Mirda* what did you think about Isaiah?"

"I thought it was interesting but I guess I'd need to read it again, you know, to sort of understand a little better."

"Was this the first time you have read Isaiah?"

I looked up and down, and grimaced before answering. "Well, yes, you could say that. I haven't had any sort of religious education."

"Lisa tells me you are Jewish."

"Yes, that's true. Is there a problem?" I said suddenly becoming defensive.

"No, absolutely not, I was just curious as to why you are participating with our little group."

"I like it here. I'm not worried about kids getting drunk or doing things that I'm not comfortable with. We have interesting discussions and I like all the singing. No one is judging me or asking me to do anything that I don't agree with."

"Well, I'm happy to hear that, but what about the religious part?"

"I guess when you talk about the Lord, I don't think about it in terms of Jesus. I just think about God. Besides, you mostly talk about the Golden Rule and about doing good works."

"What about when we talk about our savior or when I preach about sin? I believe that Judaism has different points of views. How do you reconcile what I preach with what your own religion teaches?"

"I-I guess, I don't know. I don't know what my religion says about those things. We don't talk about it much at home."

"*Mirda*, you know you are always welcome here but, you know I'm sort of a shepherd. If I see a lost lamb, I nudge it back on to the right road." He grinned and gave my shoulder a nudge. "I'd like to encourage you to get back on your own path, little lamb. Learn about your religion and ask questions, *ask a lot of questions*. Your ancestors fought hard to keep their faith and their traditions. They risked everything, moving from one place to another, so that future generations could have a chance to carry on. Talk to your elders and if they don't have the answers, find a rabbi or teen advisor."

I was at a loss for words, so I nodded my head in agreement and gave Pastor Ben a hug good-bye. When Lisa and I were driving home, I explained that I wouldn't be coming back.

"You know, Lisa, I think he did me a huge favor. He could have convinced me to stay and even try to win over a convert, but he inspired me to find out about my roots. I don't know much about anything, but one thing is for sure; I don't want to turn my back on my heritage. I just have to figure a few things out-don't worry!"

While I had this cultural *meshugas* rolling around in my head, at school my whole world revolved around Mr. O and Room K-78. Since starting in the music program with Choralaires, I yearned to be an "Inspiration." Mr. O hand-selected sixteen of his top musicians for this class. The elite group competed throughout the state and performed at a variety of venues, aside from the concerts held at school. When I made the cut my senior year, it was a dream come true. K-78 was practically my second home.

Mr. O was impressed with his Inspirations and while preparing for an important competition at Occidental College, he informed us of a monumental decision. We were going to perform Thompson's *Alleluia*, a piece so dear to him that he hadn't allowed another group perform or record it for several years. Mr. O continued with his surprise by reporting that *his* choral professor, Mr. Jim Neumann would be attending the competition as a special favor.

We had several other note-worthy pieces that tested our mettle with intricate harmonies and complicated rhythms. Learning to perform these baroque, sacred selections was intense work, but Mr. O treated us as professionals; we delivered because we worshipped the man. While practicing at home one evening, I noticed Mami and Papi looking at each other and I could have sworn that their expressions were slightly pained. Was I singing off key? What could make them flinch like that?

"Don't you like this music? Mr. O thinks we can handle these difficult pieces."

"Yes, Mirtita, I'm sure that Mr. *Auw* will be happy with the performance. But…"

"It's "Oh" ma…but *what?*"

"But…I am not sure what The Argentina Family would say." She blurted the words out quickly. "What would the *bobes* and *zeides* say if they heard you singing such words?"

"What words? I'm not even *thinking* about the words. It's all about the music!"

"Mirtita, *si*, the music is very beautiful, but you are a *Yewish* girl and you are singing about *Jesus*."

I shook my in disbelief. How could I explain…"Ma, something almost magical happens when we come together; the harmonies are so beautiful…it's like a painting. Mr. O can make us *feel* the colors that we are singing. Does that make any sense?" I didn't wait for a response as I could see that it did not make any sense.

"Mami, pretend we went on a vacation to Europe."(Not a chance…we always went to Argentina, but I was grasping at straws trying to think of a good analogy) "What if we took a tour of all the great museums and ancient buildings? Would you enjoy the great works of art any less because they were not Judaic? I don't believe you would, because you can see the beauty in everyone and everything. For me, it's all about the music. Please understand and be proud of our performance."

"Mirtita, we are always proud of you, *mamita.* You have to understand that in Argentina, things were very different for us. It is difficult to forget what it was like growing up in country where the constitution dictated the religion of choice; it is hard to forget the division between the religions and the mistrust amongst the people. Couldn't you sing *Yewish* songs?"

Finally the day arrived for our special event at Occidental College. We weren't nervous for the competition; we were ready to shine for Mr. O and dazzle his mentor. Song after song, we were right there-*in the moment.* The intensity with which we performed was almost palpable and then it was time for the *Alleluia.* The piece was sung *a Capella;* with no accompaniement, the room was completely silent - you could hear the proverbial pin drop. Mr. O raised his hands and on the downbeat, we began to sing softly, gently enveloping the audience in a pool of deep-blue velvety sound. Mr. O was not flailing his arms about as the intensity grew, but conducted us effectively with his eyes. We understood each nuance, each expression. My hands were clenched tightly against my body and I thought my fingernails would pierce the palms of my hands. Unconsciously, I leaned in toward Mr. O as our music soared and then suddenly, came to a tender resolution. With the final amen, the hall was silent for moment and then, we were rewarded with a clash of applause.

We were awarded the grand prize for the event. Mr. O was extremely proud, as were we, but mostly, we were eager to hear Mr. Neumann's feedback. Afterwards, we sat around the piano and listened to a tape playing back on a cassette player. Mr. Neumann had been whispering comments into a small microphone as we performed. He caught every fine distinction; he delighted in our "shading" and "tone." He said that we brought him great joy, a special treat for an old music teacher.

Later still, as we packed up and prepared for the long drive home, Mr. O approached me. Taking my elbow, he gently directed me to a quiet corner. "You know, *Mirda*, Mr. Neumann said something that made me chuckle a bit."

"What was that Mr. O?" I said, so pleased that he wanted to share something special with me.

"He said that everyone was completely focused and blending beautifully, but he noted one girl in particular; an alto, to be exact. Can you guess what he said?"

I gulped hard and replied, "No, Mr. O, what did he say?"

"Mr. Neumann wanted to know who the little alto was *singing with so much joy in her heart for our Lord and Savior*." Mr. O was almost giddy trying not to snicker and snort. "I asked him to point out the student and he pointed to you! I, of course, told him that that *particular* little alto was one of my Jewish students."

"Mr. O, I'm not sure what to say…" All I could think about was the *bobes* and *zeides* and The Argentina Family.

"*Mirda*, it's all right. I know you weren't singing praise to Jesus. It's the music that moves you. You're what the Inspirations are all about. Think about it…the *Alleluia* doesn't mention anything about Jesus or the Lord; in fact the entire piece is like a mantra, repeating the one word, right? Each person in the audience was touched, was *inspired,* to reflect on his or her own beliefs. The beauty of the music and the love with which it was sung allowed each individual to connect with God in their own way. That's a beautiful thing, my friend. And I'm thankful to you and to the rest of the group for sharing your music with us so beautifully this afternoon."

I gave Mr. O a tearful hug. I loved this man so much. He understood me and accepted me just as I was. I still had to learn who that was exactly.

Dayenu (Enough)

We were going to "have Passover" at Tía Feli and Tío Elias's house. Although my aunt and uncle lived in a comfortable home, when we all got together for a holiday or a special event, tables and chairs had to be set up all through the house; in the kitchen, in the dining room, in the living room and the den. Sometimes, extra-long folding tables would be set up with one end in the kitchen and the other end protruding through the sliding doors. Half of us would be sitting inside and the rest would be in the backyard.

This Passover was a little special because Tía Feli's father, Zeide Lázaro had come from Argentina. I had secretly been hoping to hear Zeide Lázaro recite some of the ancient prayers. I knew from the rest of the kids in B.B.G. and U.S.Y. that we had been missing out on what traditionally occurred at Passover meals. Apparently, while everyone else was gathering together to participate in a Seder, my family was simply gathering together to eat gefilte fish and matzah ball soup. I assumed that the Bernstein's grandfather would be able to take our celebration up a notch or two.

The mothers had prepared food for days. I had always realized that Passover was an important event, especially when Mami presented the beautiful flower centerpieces with cards reading, "*Gut Pesach*, With Love, The

Argentina Family." I guess I knew about Moses and the Red Sea, but it was mostly thanks to Charlton Heston and "The Ten Commandments."

Each of us received a little booklet that the mothers collected at their local markets, gifts of Maxwell House Coffee for their Jewish customers. I think our mothers tried to make the holidays more traditional; more in keeping with their childhood memories, but the fathers usually had very little patience. I couldn't recall a time when we actually recited more than a line or two from those little booklets.

Tía Feli lit the candles and placed them in the center of the main table alongside the beautiful centerpiece that Mami brought for the occasion. A fervent plea in Spanish blessing us all with peace, good health and a *Gut Pesach* (Good Passover) replaced the customary candle blessing in Hebrew that Maxwell House had printed out. I supposed that God would understand and forgive us for not following the booklet.

Mami helped Tía Feli bring out baskets of matzah and Zeide Lázaro poured a glass wine. I held my breath watching this elderly man steady his hand as he raised the crystal goblet. Zeide Lázaro began chanting the blessing for the wine as we all listened, "*Baruch atah Adonai, Eloheinu Melech ha Olam, Borei Peri Hagafen.*" As he began another verse, one of the uncles raised his glass and obnoxiously shouted "*L'Chaim*!

Let's eat!" Zeide Lázaro quietly sat down as the mothers jumped up to help Tía Feli with the first course.

Everyone started talking and passing plates back and forth. *Who wants fee-ish? Does anyone care about some chopped liver?* After the matzah ball soup, the meat platters came out and more matzah balls, but these were covered with *tuco*. I wondered if my friends were eating the traditional matzah balls *al pomodoro* at their Seders.

The house was full of laughter and delicious aromas. The adults sang the chorus portion of *Dayenu* and we all clapped along. It was, however, not quite the same Passover my friends were celebrating and as the chocolate covered matzah and the jellied candies were passed around, I had a suspicion that what we had just experienced was not *dayenu* (enough).

During spring break, I called Mark Stein, the youth group advisor, and asked him to meet me for lunch. He was happy to accept and suggested a New York-style delicatessen. *Pesach* was over and he was in the mood for a nice big Pastrami sandwich on rye. I was not too familiar with ordering in a deli. At home we ate a mish-mash of Argentine-Eastern European cuisine. I ordered a salami sandwich with extra tomatoes and mayonnaise on white bread. The waitress looked at me funny, as if to say, "Are you sure?" Mark looked perplexed as well, but he didn't say a word until she left.

"Ok, so what did you want to talk about?" He said as he munched on a crunchy pickle.

"First of all, I want to apologize for the scene I caused a while back at the ice cream parlor. I've been ashamed of myself ever since that night. I'm sorry if I put you on the spot."

"Cool. Apology accepted. What else you got?"

"I want to start learning about Judaism. You see, we never went to Hebrew school and my parents weren't really formally taught anything. My father never had a Bar Mitzvah."

"Your family *is* Jewish, right?"

"Yes, we are Jewish, but my parents were the children of poor immigrants. Between the language barriers and social issues, I think things got lost along the way.

"But you attend a Conservative synagogue?"

"Well, sort of. I participate in the youth group and my mom makes us attend High Holiday services. We aren't active members. Our families say that they are Conservative, but in my opinion, the only thing they are *conserving* are the food traditions, and just barely. I mean - we don't keep kosher or anything close to it. I think the adults lean towards the word "Conservative" because it reflects their other social values. You know? They are not exactly a modern group of people. As far as religious training, the boys have their Bar Mitzvahs and that's about it. You see? I really don't have a clue about anything. Could you help me? I don't have any money for temple or religious school and besides, I'm too old for religious school."

"*Murda*, you are never too old and don't even worry about money. I'll make up a list of some books you can start reading and when you're done, we can discuss them. OK? You know, you might want to think about becoming a Bat Mitzvah yourself. It's never too late and completely acceptable nowadays."

"Oh well… I don't know about having a Bat Mitzvah. I'll have to see about that, but I would enjoy discussing the books with you. Thank you for your offer to help." I took a sip of my cola and relaxed a little.

"OK, no problem." He took another big bite of a pickle and continued, "So salami and mayonnaise, huh?"

We laughed and I began to explain a little of the mish mash I had in my head.

World Travelers

After graduating from high school, I planned on setting out to Argentina with Dani. I had been thinking of postponing my first semester of college and asked my parents to allow me to stay in Argentina for about five or six months. They agreed to my plan and knew that The Argentina Family would watch every step I took and ward off every stranger. Dani, of course, would return at the end of the summer. Papi had made all the arrangements and we were flying First Class. He personally knew the crew that would be working our flight and told them to watch out for "his girls." When we boarded the 747, the stewardesses were well aware of the Trupp girls and made sure that we comfortable and well attended. We were, after all, part of the Pan Am family.

Meanwhile, The Argentina Family was preparing for our arrival. Even though we had been traveling for many years, this was the first time *las nenas* were traveling alone. Dani would be 15 in a month and would be celebrating her *quinceañera* in Argentina, just like I had a few years before. My cousin Monica and her husband, Rolando, were going to meet us at the airport and take us to Tía Lela's house.

When we arrived in Buenos Aires, we followed the other passengers to the Customs Area and prepared to present our luggage and documents. We had seen our parents go through the procedure; it did not cause us any anxiety to be on our own. Suddenly, we heard quite a commotion coming from behind the glass partition that separated the Customs Area from the Public Area. A guard was speaking to a frantic looking couple. He was shaking his head and waving his hands as if saying "No!" Dani and I stayed in line and tried to focus on the task at hand, but we couldn't help notice that the guards were beginning to look our way. A door opened and in came the frantic couple looking wildly around. The couple was Monica and Rolando! Their eyes met ours and they rushed to our side. After a hug and a kiss, they asked if we were all right. Dani and I looked at them curiously and said that we were perfectly fine.

As it was our turn in line, we handed over our passports, which held the expected monetary *contribution*. A few minutes later we were done and walking out to the public area. Monica and Rolando led the way but the guard at the door stopped us. He looked at Dani and me and then looked at our cousins and said, "These two are *las nenas*? I broke the rules and let you through so that you could help these two *little* girls?" Monica and Rolando broke out laughing and then the guard started laughing. Dani and I were not quite sure what had occurred, but it seemed that "Danielita and Mirtita" had grown up, at least at little bit.

It was on this trip that we met three more cousins, Andres, Gaston and Julian. We were told that they were cousins, several times removed, from our father's side but amongst the five of us, we could never figure out exactly how "removed" we were. Their maternal grandmother was our paternal grandfather's niece and so to make it easier, we just called each other cousins. It was all the same in The Argentina Family. We had never met the boys because they had grown up in a coastal city outside of Buenos Aires. Much to our delight, they were now living in the capital. Tía Lela had arranged an outing so that we could meet. The boys' father, Teo, came to pick us up and drove us to his home where the boys were waiting.

Dani and I were excited to meet the boys, especially because we were all of the same age. We entered the apartment and found the three boys lined up to greet us. Amalia, the mom, was there as well. We were introduced and the usual hugging and kissing took place. We were asked to take a seat in the formal living room. As we sat down, I noticed three books on the coffee table. I laughed and asked if those books were meant for us. Julian, the youngest, picked one up and said, "We were not sure how well you could speak Spanish, so we wanted to be prepared." They had three different Spanish/English dictionaries. Dani and I laughed and proceeded to thank them in our best *Castellano.*

That visit with the Reisenfeld's instigated a complete turnaround on how we felt about Buenos Aires. We began having the time of our lives. Since the Reisenfeld boys were our age and had made loads of friends in their short time in the city, we were invited to parties, dances, BBQ's and all sorts of events. Dani and I, the *Yanquis*, were the hit of every party and were bombarded with the usual questions, the most typical being, "Which country do you prefer?"

One thing that we noticed which caused us a little bit of surprise was that the Reisenfeld boys were rather isolated with regards to their friends. They went to Jewish schools, lived in a fairly Jewish neighborhood and only socialized with Jewish kids for the most part. When Dani and I asked them about this, they basically said that it had always been that way with the Jewish community in Argentina. Anti-Semitism was unrestrained and had been for many decades. It had become the norm for social groups to isolate themselves and to tolerate each other only out of necessity.

The Jewish community in Argentina was second only to the United States. They had been successful in leaving the wheat fields of the Pampas and the cattle breeding in Entre Rios to become, doctors, lawyers, teachers and business leaders in Buenos Aires. They built schools for their children to study both secular and religious programs. They built athletic clubs in the city to rival any of the better known, *Jews-need-not-apply* clubs. They built impressive country clubs where families met for "networking" and socializing, challenging the most popular clubs of the American "Borscht Belt." The Reisenfeld boys explained that it was easier for everyone to stay within their own culture and avoid conflicts. The boys repeated the mantra that had been repeated for centuries; stay with your own kind. Dani and I told them that we were unfamiliar with that sort of segregation to which the brothers responded, "We live with anti-Semitism on a daily basis."

They told us that just days ago, a bomb had destroyed their state-of-the-art school, an international distinguished O.R.T. academy. Another bomb had been dismantled by the police at the Bialik School on the very same day. They told us how seemingly good friends would unexplainably turn their backs on them and call them despicable names. They told us how their friend Max, who wanted to join the Naval Academy, was informed point blank that he would never become an officer because he was a Jew. They reminded us about Jacobo Timmerman and were shocked that we didn't know about Timmerman's arrest and torture a few years before.

"How could you not know about Jacobo Timmerman?" Andres exclaimed. "He is a famous journalist."

"I'm sorry Andres, but we rarely see news about Argentina back home, except maybe an article about Maradona and the World Cup. To tell the truth, people our age just aren't interested." I was embarrassed to admit it, but

I continued. "I'm not used to discussing world events, human rights or global politics with my friends. It's actually one of the things that I like so much about hanging out with your group of friends."

"We are *interested* because we have to be. Sometimes, it's a matter of life and death. We can't take things for granted here. We are interested because our futures *depend* on it," Andres explained, "and when you go back home, you should talk with your friends. Forget about Maradona and the World Cup! Tell them about Timmerman. Tell them about us."

On one occasion, Dani and I actually experienced the racism first hand while on our way to a dance sponsored by the Jewish community. As we arrived with the Reisenfeld boys, we were notified that a bomb had destroyed the dance hall. The kids were turned away by a group of fearful dance organizers and beleaguered policemen. We were warned to tuck away any *Magen David* jewelry and to disperse quickly. While no one was hurt, the hotel suffered quite a bit of damage. Our nerves were rattled and we shared an ominous feeling of being powerless.

Our cousins had put the frightening episode behind them and instructed us to do the same. Dani and I loved spending time with the Reisenfelds and so; we looked forward to new opportunities for diversions and distractions. Apart from sharing the typical likes and dislikes of most teenagers, the five of us had one very particular thing in common: Queen. It was the beginning of a long love affair with the rock band. We would sit for hours listening to records and the boys would ask us to translate the lyrics. That in turn, would lead to debates on the true meaning of the song…"Yes, but what were they trying to say *In the Year of 39?*"

One afternoon, while sitting listening to Queen, Gaston decided he was going to try to accompany Roger Taylor on the drums. Dani and I hadn't seen Gaston play the drums before, so we all gathered around him. Somehow I noticed that the cymbal was not screwed on tightly and as Gaston went to hit the metal disc, I instinctively put up my hand to shield Dani. In a blink of an eye, I knew that the disc was about to go flying off and Dani was standing right in its path. Instead of slicing her cheek, the sharp disc sliced the palm of my hand. I thought Julian was going to faint as the blood came gushing out. Since we were home alone, the boys scrambled to figure out what to do with me. I was at a loss. Where was the emergency room near Corrientes and Pringles? Gaston kept repeating "Oh my God, oh my God!" Andres took charge and wrapped my hand up in a clean towel. He led the five of downstairs and out of the building. One of the neighbors, a family friend, was a doctor. His specialty? *Urology.*

Andres rang the bell and waited for a response. He cursed when he looked at his wristwatch and saw that it was still *siesta* time. He banged on the door until finally the doctor answered. Looking slightly disheveled and with eyes half closed, the doctor opened the front door, took a puff of his cigarette and said, "*Que pasa pibe*?"(What's up kid) Andres grabbed my hand and shoved it in the doctor's face. He quickly explained what had happened, that we were visitors from America *and* that his mother was going to kill all of them for letting this happen while she was out grocery shopping.

The unkempt doctor moved aside and opened the door so that we could come in. He led us to the back of the house and through the patio where we entered a set of rooms - his clinic. He asked me to sit down and said that he'd take a look at my injury. I was still bleeding pretty heavily through the towel. Julian looked away. The doctor took another puff of his cigarette, removed the towel and exhaled right into my wound! I couldn't believe it! Surely this was not sanitary! He didn't even wash his hands. All I could think about was all those episodes of Medical Center, with gorgeous Dr. Joe Cannon. This doctor was not anything like Dr. Joe or my real doctor, for that matter.

He cleaned the wound, with the cigarette still dangling from his lips, and sprinkled some curative powder over it. I asked what the powder was for. With a raised eyebrow and a look of condescension, he explained that he used the powder on babies after he performed circumcisions; it helped with the bleeding. He wrapped my hand up and with a grumpy tone told us to go home. No charge. He was no Dr. Cannon, but besides a very small scar, I was going to be fine. The color came back to poor Julian's face. At least he didn't look like he was going to faint any more. Gaston kept apologizing. And Andres…Andres couldn't stop *laughing*. He said now I was really part of the Reisenfeld family. My flesh had been cut and had been dusted with "*bris* powder." I was kosher!

When Amalia Reisenfeld heard of our afternoon, she was furious and lectured all of us like a good mother hen. She felt responsible for us and made the boys promise to take better care of their cousins. Although generally thought to be a typical *yiddishe mame*, Amalia had reasons to be overprotective and a bit of an alarmist. Argentina was in the middle of what was called "The Dirty War."

For a period of approximately seven years, Argentines would live through an era of state sponsored violence. Led by the military juntas, the government was responsible for the illegal arrest, torture, rape, killing or "disappearance" of thousands of its citizens. Although the targets were primarily armed *guerrilla* groups, such as the Montoneros or the Guevarista People's Revolutionary Army, among the other victims were political activists, journalists, celebrities and university students. It was referred to a "systematized persecution of the Argentine citizenry" and its goal was to annihilate political subversion. Many would later say that Dirty War could be traced back to the bombing of the Plaza de Mayo in 1955, but many other people with long-term memories and righteous indignation, thought it went as far back as the riots of 1919.

Amalia was always shouting at the boys to remember "*Los documentos*!" Everyone was required to carry several forms of identification. Of course, Dani and I only had our American passports. We felt naively safe and protected; why wouldn't we? Mami was constantly stating that we were completely safe with family in Argentina. There was a sense of superiority on our part as well. We obnoxiously thought that as Americans, we would be respected and treated fairly.

With regard to Amalia and her sermon, she could have spared the boys the lecture about watching out for us. The boys had already become attached and were very protective. If we were with a group of people and suddenly a newcomer arrived, they guarded us just in case the guy had any funny ideas about hanging out with a *Yanqui*. *Yanquis*, both men and women, were known to be fast and loose and apparently they drank whiskey as if it were water.

One night we went out dancing with the gang. I was asked to dance by someone unknown to our little group. I could feel Andres staring at us as we walked onto the dance floor. The boy asked me my name and as I shouted over the music, he asked me where I was from because he could detect an accent. I told him that I was visiting from the United States.

He didn't believe me and pretending to laugh he said, "Ha, ha, ha. Try again. You are no *Yanqui*! What would you be doing here, dancing with me in this tacky nightclub, if you were some big-shot world traveler?"

I thought for a moment about explaining the whole Pan Am thing, but it was too complicated. We were dancing after all; the music drowning out any hope of a reasonable conversation. My partner took my silence as a sign of my confession. "See, I knew it. You are not from *Norte America, nena*. You are *Correntina*!"

Apparently, people who lived in the province of Corrientes had an accent that the *porteños* found unsophisticated. I finished the dance not being able to convince my partner that I was American. When I returned to my cousin, Eagle-Eye Andres asked what we had been talking about. I told him that the boy thought I was from Corrientes. He laughed so hard he doubled over and spit out his drink. People actually turned around to see what was causing such a commotion. Andres had half a mind to walk over to the boy and tell him that he "missed out-*big time*!" but not wanting to attract more attention, he just shared the laugh with our group. My new friends acknowledged that when they first met me, they had been taken aback. Meeting someone from another country, *from America* no less, was not an ordinary experience. Most people didn't travel back and forth across the continents even in this jet set day and age.

When we left the dance that evening, we all piled into a few tiny Fiats. A few of us had to sit on another's lap; one or two had their heads sticking out a window. Everyone lived fairly close by, so although we started out with several people crammed into the car, one by one the numbers dwindled as they were dropped off. Just as we pulled away from the curb after dropping off the last of the lap sitters, police lights flashed and both Fiats were signaled to pull over. The boy driving our car became slightly agitated but told the rest of us to relax. Andres *was not* relaxed and his expression did little to comfort me. I had seen the boys handle these situations before. I thought we could all pitch in and present the officer with a little enticement to let us off easy, but Andres told me quietly that this was definitely not one of those times.

One of the officers got out of the car, leaving two others seated in the vehicle. He instructed all of us to get out and line up against the apartment building. He demanded to see our identification papers. One by one, the kids pulled out their papers, but no one said a word. I could sense that my friends were clearly scared. It was close to five in the morning; predawn and we were on a quiet, deserted street. (No witnesses?)

When he got to me, his flashlight illuminated my American passport. He took the document and walked over to the patrol car. Andres looked at me and again, I was told to relax however; I noticed a lot of nervous grins in our little group. There was some discussion coming from the police car. Repeatedly, we could hear the words "American" and "Embassy." Suddenly, the door opened and another officer stepped out. The two officers approached me and shined their flashlights in my face.

"*Señorita* Mirta Ines Trupp. You are an American citizen?

"Yes sir, I am."

"I see by your passport that you are a frequent visitor. Are you enjoying your stay in Buenos Aires?

"Very much sir, thank you."

"As you are a world traveler, you must know it is dangerous to be out so late during these times."

"Yes sir. We are on our way home."

"Very good, we certainly would not want any trouble with the American Embassy. Enjoy the rest of your stay in

Argentina. As for the rest of you, I suggest that you be very careful. Do not make any further stops tonight. Do not speak to anyone on the streets…understood?"

The group replied, "Yes sir," in unison and we clamored back into our cars. Once inside, one of the boys said, "Thanks *Yanqui*! You saved us a long night in the police station!"

"Or worse," Andres said under his breath.

I smiled timidly and thought to myself, "It's so cool to be American!"

Part of the attraction of traveling was trying out our wings; Dani and I were enjoying our freedom in the city and the pseudo sense of celebrity we seemed to stimulate. Although we spoke Spanish very well, the accent was noticeable. We attracted all sorts of attention from family, friends and obviously, from complete strangers. Dani and I took full advantage of the extraordinary shopping opportunities. The stores lined up and down the fashionable areas of Buenos Aires were nothing like what we were used to in the San Fernando Valley. Back home, we'd drive to the mall and walk into one of many mega shops and start picking clothes haphazardly. It was all about self-service. Conversely, in Buenos Aires, we'd walk into a shop no bigger than our bedroom and begin the complicated task of explaining what it was that we were looking for. The salesperson would disappear to the back or pull something out of a drawer. They'd only take out one item at a time and if they considered you worth the trouble, they might let you duck into the broom closet to try things on.

There was also the issue with the money. Back home, there was no confusion; a dollar was a dollar, period. In Argentina, we were given large, colorful bills that resembled Monopoly currency and changed in monetary value from one minute to the next. There were "old pesos" and of course, there were "new pesos." I would pick up a pair of fabulous shoes and see it marked simultaneously at $100,000.000 *old pesos* or $100 *new pesos*. It didn't end with the different types of currency. There were more mathematical calculations to be done to figure out just how much those fabulous shoes cost in dollars. I left the math to Dani, who thankfully, was a whiz at it.

On one occasion, Dani and I decided to have some fun with the sales staff, especially the charming, handsome young men. It seemed a safe enough environment to try our flirting skills. We walked into the store and purposely began speaking in English. "Oh, look Mirta, they have Fiorucci jeans here." Dani purred mischievously.

"Cool. Let's see if they'll let us try them on." I answered just a tad louder than was necessary. The change in volume wasn't necessary; we had called attention to ourselves just be walking inside the store. There was something about us that screamed "*AMERICANAS*."

A salesman came up and said, "*Hola*." In an exaggerated accent, I said slowly and deliberately, "We'd like to try on a pair of jeans, but we don't know—*how do you say size Daniela*? Oh that's right - what *size* we were here in Argentina."

That immediately instigated a series of questions and then, *bam*! We had them eating out of the palms of our hands. They were bringing out all the jeans we wanted and showering us with compliments on how well we spoke *Castellano*. Every sweater or piece of jewelry we wanted to see was gladly retrieved and presented to us. We realized that they were trying to sell us half the store; they obviously wanted our money. They also wanted our phone numbers and asked us out for coffee, but that's where we drew the line. We were interested in trying out our wings, but we were not brave enough to actually fly off into the sunset with one of these charming *porteños*. We wrapped it up quickly, buying a couple of Fiorucci jeans and a few pair of bohemian earrings and then, off we went, back to the safe haven of our grandparents' house.

After showing off our purchases and spending a lovely afternoon with Bobe Carmen and Zeide Efraim, Dani and I said our goodbyes and headed back to Tía Lela's house.

We reassured our doting grandparents that we would be safe and off we went, confident in our skills to traverse the streets of Buenos Aires. Although back home in the San Fernando Valley, we were accustomed to our own vehicles; it was part of the adventure to hop in and out of public transportation. Some of the buses were privately owned and their drivers dressed them to the nines with the typical *fileteado porteño*, a flowery, ornate style of ornamentation. The massive windshields were framed with engraved mirrors, neon lights and sport banners. Even the tickets were multicolored, a different color depending on the fare and your destination.

We boarded the bus on the ever-busy Corrientes, forgetting the fact that we should have walked down the street, turned the corner and taken the #24 on Sarmiento. We told the driver *Avenida San Martin*, paid our fare and took our seats all the way in the back. We didn't think anything was wrong until we noticed that the bus had become unusually empty. Suddenly, the streets were not familiar and we had crossed an impressive bridge. Dani and I thought that the bus would eventually turn around and head in the "right" direction.

The driver announced "final stop" and as we hesitatingly got off the bus, I asked him where we were. He replied, "*Avenida San Martin, nena.*" And with that, he picked up his belongings and followed us off the bus.

"But, this is not where we are supposed to be!" I exclaimed.

"Well, sorry, this is where *I* am supposed to be." he said and pointed to an apartment building. "This is the end of the line. I live here."

"Where exactly is *here*?"

"Avellaneda." And with a curt *buenas noches*, he entered his building and shut the door leaving us *and* his #24 by the curb.

Dani and I looked up and down the street, having no idea where we found ourselves. There was a newspaper kiosk at the corner, so we decided to ask the man behind the stand how we could get back to El Once. He laughed and said, "You can't get there from here." An elderly woman overheard the conversation and came to our side. She grabbed my arm and asked me, "*Nenita*, were do you want to go?"

I explained what had happened; she then grabbed Dani by the arm and said, "Come with me." She took us around the corner and put us on another #24 bus. Explaining that we were *extranjeras* (travelers from abroad); she told him exactly where we needed to go and made sure that we had the correct fare. We thanked her and gratefully sat down directly behind the driver. By the time we got home to Tía Lela's house, she was in a panic. Poor Tía! She must have aged ten years in that one afternoon; we simply added the story to our travel diary as another Buenos Aires adventure.

Summer vacation flew by and Dani's days in Buenos Aires had come to an end. She was headed back home loaded up with stories to share and Fiorucci jeans to show off. I was uneasy to see Dani leave because as it turned out, she helped me through several nights of anxiety attacks during the trip. I hadn't completely outgrown my fears stemming from the Sylmar earthquake and it didn't help my uneasiness when I heard another bomb exploded in Buenos Aires, right outside of the Jerusalem Synagogue. But, Dani did return home and I was flying off alone to Bahia Blanca for an extended stay with Monica and the rest of the Felder clan.

My cousins were in the middle of a new discovery. They had met an interesting Brazilian man with a certain philosophy of life, energy and spirituality. He had come to Argentina to instruct like-minded people and when I arrived in Bahia, my relatives had just completed the two-part course. *El Curso* was all they could talk about. They were very excited about the program and wanted me to take the class as well. They introduced me to Paolo and the rest of their group of friends. It was all very *avant-garde*. I felt extraordinarily grown up and not a little proud that my cousin thought I was "open" enough to experiment with new ideas.

Paolo dubbed me the "Russian princess," insisting that I had been of noble birth in a past life. I laughed at him and told him that in The Argentina Family, *all* of the women were Russian princesses! Needless to say, we took an instant liking to each other. There was nothing secretive about *El Curso*, but it was hard to explain because there were so many facets to it. Some people might have thought it was some sort of a cult and that Paolo was idolized, but it all seemed harmless enough and I felt secure in my ability to challenge him if I thought necessary. More than challenging Paolo, I challenged myself with spiritual questions I was not capable of answering. I couldn't reconcile these new philosophies with the bits and pieces of religious principles I had amassed. How did God fit into these new age ideas? How could I make Judaism work with concepts of energy fields and beings from other dimensions? Was it possible to be even more confused than before? *El Curso* instigated more chaos than the intended tranquility.

I had been in Bahia for a few months when the old internal debates began to weigh on me. I loved this quiet town and enjoyed the sense of family I experienced. Tía Delia and family had moved from Buratovich and had opened a new *kiosco*. Daily, I would walk from their store to Tía Perla's apartment. Afterwards, I would have lunch with Monica and Martin and later, cross the town square to visit with Gisela and Edgardo in their quirky, clothing shop. Practically every night, I'd walk over to meet Marielita and Susanita for dinner and spend the rest of the evening with their gang of friends.

Since I was a child, I could remember the adults discussing the pros and cons of living in America. Now, here I was doing the same thing. Monica and Martin were providing me plenty of incentives to stay in Argentina. While the co-eds of Northridge were getting *stoned* at the frat house or getting plastered on the beach, I could be debating politics or dancing the nights away. I could be contemplating metaphysical phenomena or discussing the intricate musicality of John and Paul. Back home, I was a considered a nerd, an awkward girl, with a certain ethnic appearance. I felt that my family stuck out like a sore thumb; I was self-conscious and battled against a sense of inferiority when first meeting other "true Americans." In comparison, when in Argentina, I was infinitely more confidant, a by-product of years of being made to feel like a traveling celebrity. My thoughts were completely jumbled as emotions mixed with reason. One evening, as we were driving home, Monica popped in a cassette tape. The Beatles lyric matched the melancholy mood as they sang, "She's leaving home, bye-bye…"

The Best Laid Plans of...*Nice Young Ladies*

Since I skipped my first semester of college, I was a little out of the loop socially and definitely, scholastically. Although I was usually self-motivated and goal oriented, I was not certain about my career plan. In fact, I was somewhat apathetic about which path to undertake. My first choice of being a social worker was immediately and emphatically shot down, because "that was not a career for a woman." I would be subject to *unseemly human behavior*, not quite in keeping with a nice young lady. My parents were clueless about scholarships, colleges or career choices and since I was going to be married "soon" what was the point, really? I eventually settled into a Liberal Arts program and began preparing for a career as a teacher. My parents approved and I enjoyed the idea of being someone's "Mr. O."

Bonnie had moved away with her parents to Sacramento. Although I occasionally went out with Paula and remnants of the youth group, my social circle was fairly small. Memories of Buenos Aires with its whirlwind of activities plagued me, especially on long, boring weekends. Every now and then, "the gang" would go out dancing, but that usually was a hassle as we were all under twenty-one and there were limited places from which to choose. Although we had some money in our pockets and we all had cars, there always seemed to be a lack of ingenuity; we never had anything to do or places to go.

My little group was in a phase of shifting and drifting. Not only I had lost Bonnie but Brian had moved up to Santa Barbara to attend the beach town's university. Although not dreadfully far away, Brian went off to college and I was left without "my brother" around the corner. It wasn't too long after settling in that Brian invited me up to the beatnik, sea-side enclave; he was eager to show me his new home. He planned a whole day's worth of activities and even offered to drive down to get me. We agreed to meet on the following Saturday; I didn't even think of asking my parents for permission. The weekend arrived and I began gathering my belongings when Papi asked me what my plans were for the day. I explained that Brian was coming and we were heading up to Santa Barbara. When my father told me that it was out of the question, I couldn't believe my ears!

"Why can't I go?" I cried.

"Mirtita, it is not proper for you to spend the entire day alone with a young man. I don't want you to be alone in a man's apartment. What would people think?" Papi replied.

"We are talking about *Brian*, Natalia and Luis's son. He's practically *my brother*!"

"A young lady from a good family does not go gallivanting about all day *in another town* with a young man. I was a young man once and I know what I am saying."

"I am not going to be gallivanting around town with a stranger, Pa. This is *Brian Fagan.*" I repeated. "And if I wanted to do something with Brian, I wouldn't have to go all the way to Santa Barbara. We have been alone zillions of times!" I shouldn't have said that- I realized too late. This nice young lady's plans were summarily cancelled.

When Papi disallowed my plan of touring Europe with a group of coeds (no surprise there), Dani and I decided to return to Buenos Aires for our summer vacation. Of course, it was cold and wretched when we got off *our* Pan Am Boeing 747 on July 12, 1981, but as soon as we saw our cousins on the other side of the familiar glass partition, we were happy with our decision to spend the next six weeks with The Argentina Family. After a couple of days with Tía Lela and the grandparents, the Reisenfeld boys came to whisk us away. Andres told the kids at Templo Murillo that I had returned and much to my delight, they planned a variety of activities. With a little organizing, I planned out my days to visit with family and saved the nights for parties, dancing and *asados.*

On Friday nights, Andres and I met the group for Shabbat at Templo Murillo. Although it was known in the community as a Conservative temple, to my limited experience within the religious realm, it seemed quite Orthodox. The men sat separately on the first floor. The women sat upstairs in the *Ezrat Nashim*, the women's section. The services were entirely in Hebrew, not like services at home where they were held both in Hebrew and in English.

On one such Shabbat, sitting alone upstairs and isolated, I felt intimidated by the environment; I was at a complete loss. It didn't take long to see that although a few women were actively participating, the majority weren't following the prayers but preferred to gossip throughout the service. The men, praying on the floor below, were literally wrapped up in their own worlds. They had formed what I could only describe as personal cocoons, each one wrapped up in their *tallit* (prayer shawl).

I whispered to the woman sitting next to me, "What are the men doing?"

She looked at me as if I was a creature from another planet and replied, "They are *davening*, of course."

"*Davening*, what does that mean?"

"*Oy*, what a *goyish kop*! (gentile's brain) They are praying, what else could they be doing?" she replied and quickly turned back to her friend.

My limited understanding of the different forms of Judaism cultivated judgment and defiance. I felt bereft and personally excluded, but I never followed through- I never thought to delve deeper and seek valid answers or at least, thought provoking responses.

After services, the congregation shared an *Oneg*, a chance to mingle with friends and family while enjoying desserts and pastries. Andres and I met up with the others in the social hall. We had made plans ahead of time so we were prepared for an evening of fun. I teased them shamelessly about the "kosher-ness" of going dancing following a two-hour Shabbat service, but they just laughed and off we went.

They were a great bunch of people, mostly college students. The girls were all extremely pretty and extraordinarily bright. Other than their individual studies, they were interested in fashion, movie stars and, not surprisingly, politics. The boys were just as charming and intellectual. Ariel was in the army, just finishing up his service. Gabriel, an engineering student, didn't always show up, but he attended occasionally and was well received. The *madrich* or leader of the youth group, Edgardo, was only about two years older than the rest of us. It didn't take long before I realized that he had his eyes on me. I was a *Yanqui* and I supposed it would be pretty cool to have a *Yanqui* girlfriend. After all, everyone knew how *Yanqui* women were. They were fast and loose and drank whisky, just like *Shon Wine* (John Wayne). Andres wasn't sure if he liked the idea of the *madrich* hitting on his cousin, but it was all very innocent and since we were always all together, the opportunity for anything too scandalous never came up.

On Friday, July 25, 1981, Shabbat services had come to an end and the girls and I walked downstairs to meet up with the boys. Once again, our plans included stopping in at a new dance club. The entire youth group had shown up for the occasion, even Gabriel was there. Somehow we all managed to squeeze into one miniature Fiat, two sardine-can Citroens and a decrepit Peugeot that the guys were able to finagle. Edgardo was trying to be very charming and asked me to join him in his own personal car. I went along, but I had brother and sister Patricia and Carlos, join us. We stopped for pizza at our usual hangout, El Imperio, on Canning and Corrientes and later, headed out to the club. By the time we got there, it was jammed packed. In a blink of an eye, even though we had spent hours and hours dancing, it was five o'clock in the morning and time to go home. We had been invited to spend the day at Ada's *quinta*, her family's country house for an *asado*.

We'd planned to meet up again at seven o'clock in front of El Imperio. Edgardo offered to drive me home after Andres mentioned that he wanted to take his girl home first. Finding myself suddenly alone with Edgardo, I became very nervous. What did nice young ladies do in this situation? I tried to make idle conversation, but his thinking was more romantically inclined. When we finally arrived at the Reisenfelds, he stopped the car and leaned over to kiss me. I was so nervous I had the shakes! In the instant that it took him to scoot over to my side, I thought to myself, *Don't be such a goody-two-shoes. Let him kiss you!* And so I did. But, rather than feeling like Doris Day in the arms of Rock Hudson, I felt absolutely no attraction. There were no fireworks, not even a spark. I couldn't even tell if *he* had felt some fireworks. Actually, I think he was so wrapped up in the idea of kissing a *Yanqui* that it didn't matter! I quickly and awkwardly left his car and walked into the Reisenfeld's apartment building. Knowing that the elevator was out of order again, I hurried up the stairs to the apartment. I was very careful not to wake up the family. Andres arrived shortly after, which was a good thing, since we had to change and head back out right away.

I dressed casually for the occasion because we were going to be *en el country*. I washed my face, scrubbing off all my makeup and changed out of my party clothes. Andres lent me his green polyester Adidas tracksuit. A quick cup of coffee and we were out the door! By 7:00 a.m., we were all gathered in front of the pizza place we had left just hours before. Edgardo was already there and in complete *madrich* mode, barking out orders about who was traveling with whom and which route was the most logical to take.

Everyone was surprised when a tiny Fiat pulled up and Gabriel stepped out. He had even brought a friend. The guys in the group were immediately a little leery of the newcomer. They were protective of the girls, mostly made up of sisters or cousins or lifetime friends. This new guy was completely unknown and therefore not to be trusted.

Gabriel introduced us to his friend. Marcelo lived close by in Almagro and they had gone to the O.R.T. academy together. The others in the group hesitated before begrudgingly welcoming him. I, on the other hand, was head over heels for this guy as soon as he stepped out of the car. I noticed that Flavia was already trying to wheedle a ride with Gabriel and Marcelo in the toy-like car, but luckily it was so small, that there was no room for my competition! We all piled into our designated cars per Edgardo's instructions and headed off to Ada's parents *quinta*. The summer house was a little over an hour away but the time was spent singing and laughing and passing gum and snacks back and forth between cars. When we arrived, we were all introduced to Ada's parents and made ourselves at home.

I took off on a little expedition around the family compound, looking at the horses in the corral and petting the dogs that were tied up to a massive old oak tree. Marcelo came up to me and suggested we take a little walk. We ended up walking outside of the compound and down the dirt road, which lead into the small town. It was strange how easily we fell into conversation; we didn't notice that quite a bit of time had passed since we left the group. Marcelo asked me about my life back home. He wanted to know what I did for fun; what kind of social life I led. I gave him a short synopsis and tried not to sound too pathetic, but it was hard to compare what I had back home to what they were used to in Buenos Aires. He asked if I had a boyfriend and I blushed when I told him no. I told him about Edgardo; how awkward I felt when we were alone together and the fiasco of a kiss we shared and Marcelo laughed. I supposed our conversation reminded him of something, because he suddenly started singing a song about a young girl who was falling in love. By the time we finished our walk, I knew that Marcelo was Jewish, did not eat fish, did not smoke and had a fabulous tenor voice. I made a mental note to thank Gabriel for bringing his friend to the party.

Upon our return, we were met with some sour faces. Edgardo was furious because the *Yanqui* seemed to be playing the field. Andres was upset because I hadn't told anyone that I was going for a walk. Flavia was green with envy, convinced that I had snared the new guy. I hadn't planned on staying away from the group for so long, but I thought everyone was over reacting and candidly told them so. The rest of the afternoon was spent eating *asado* and singing around the fire until dusk. When Marcelo reached for the guitar, I leaned in a little closer and waited to hear what he'd play. He began strumming a familiar tune; I knew the chords but couldn't quite place the song. A7 to D and back again, down, down up, up…it finally clicked and I began singing the popular Supertramp melody. Surprised, Marcelo looked up and nodded his approval. Following my lead, we performed the whole song through. When the kids applauded, he confessed that he had never heard the song before. The others said it was kismet and we all laughed, but it *was* a bit odd to be so in sync with a complete stranger.

Right before it was time to go, Marcelo went around to the guys in the group and asked them for my phone number. No one was willing to give him any information and in fact, Ricardo told him that I was leaving the following day for Brazil, for Bahia to be exact, and wouldn't be back for weeks. Ariel, who had overheard the conversation, approached Marcelo and told him that I wasn't going to Bahia in Brazil, but just to Bahia Blanca and would be back the following week. Ariel explained that I was staying with Andres and gave him the Reisenfeld's phone number. Why he didn't ask me, I was never told, but that was how Marcelo of Almagro got my phone number.

Upon arriving in Bahia Blanca, all I could talk about was this guy, Marcelo. I was adamant about not coming across as a wild *Yanqui*, so I drove my cousins crazy with questions about "acceptable flirting behavior" in Argentina. He didn't even ask me for my phone number. I certainly wasn't going to ask around for his! Monica, Mariel and Susana laughed at my concerns and told me to just be myself. My *mucho primo* Gaston pretended to be jealous of my crush and asked, *who did this guy think he was* getting me all flustered. The problem was that at 19 years old, I was shy and awkward, too naïve for American standards *or* Argentine standards for that matter. For most girls my age, this was a run of the mill flirting opportunity, but my parents had raised me with practically Victorian sensibilities. This was a brave new world for me.

We spent the night at Gisela and Edgardo's apartment. Dani, Gisela and I planned to get up at an ungodly hour to watch the wedding of the century; Prince Charles was marrying Lady Diana. It seemed the whole world was obsessed with the royal couple. Gisela had set up the coffee table with all sorts of treats, *sándwiches de miga* and scones with homemade jam. We sat in our pajamas and watched the entire spectacle while sipping British tea and Argentine *mate*. It was quintessential girls' time and I was over the moon with delight sharing the experience with my cousin, but in the back of my mind, I was anxious to get back to Buenos Aires. I couldn't stop daydreaming about the boy from Almagro. I was nervous about *not seeing* him again when I returned to Buenos Aires and nervous about *seeing* him when I returned to Buenos Aires! After all, what was the point of making plans? I had to return home in a couple of weeks and that would be the end of that.

First Impressions

Dani and I arrived in the capital with all the savvy of experienced travelers. Like Ezeiza International Airport, arriving at Aeroparque, the airport used for domestic flights, was second hand to us. While most of the kids in the San Fernando Valley were trying to figure out how to "get over the hill" to roam the bohemian shops in Westwood, we were experienced travelers; two cosmopolitan girls hailing a taxi and circumnavigating the streets of Buenos Aires. We were headed for the Reisenfeld's apartment; Amalia and the boys were eagerly awaiting our return. After lunch, Dani and I decided to go shopping for last minute souvenirs in Santa Fe, a swanky part of town. We were gone for a few hours and upon our return, Amalia shouted out from the kitchen that I had received a phone call. My heart almost stopped! I hadn't mentioned Marcelo's name to anyone because I knew that the Reisenfeld boys would jump at the chance to tease me. Looking at Daniela sheepishly, I called out to Amalia and said, "Who was it?"

"It was a young man from Templo Murillo. I forgot his name…." her voice faded off.

Temple Murillo? Oh no…"Was it Edgardo?" I asked while my heart sank.

"No, no," Amalia popped her head out from behind the kitchen door and wiped her hands on her apron. "It was a young man named Marcelo. He said he called back after he got off work."

Dani and the boys started howling and whistling as my face turned every color under the sun and I said, "Oh, that's nice."

I tried to act nonchalant, but I jumped every time the phone rang. The hours seemed to drag on but finally at nine o'clock, Marcelo called. There was no privacy to be had as the only phone was in the dining room and we were all seated around the dinner table. I told him that I was very happy that he called but was surprised that he found me since he hadn't asked me for my phone number. When Marcelo told me how Ariel felt sorry for him and gave him the Reisenfeld's number, I vowed to give Ariel a great big hug! Marcelo asked if he could take me out after services on Friday night. He had to work, but he'd be able to pick me up from temple by the time services were over. I knew that I was blushing and that the entire family was watching me, but I smiled and agreed to meet him on Friday at Templo Murillo.

I must have changed clothes ten times that Friday night. Nothing seemed to fit right, nothing seemed to give me the extra boost of confidence that I so desperately needed. I finally gave up and came out the living room where Andres was patiently waiting for me. He said I looked great, handed my coat and told me to hurry up. As we walked to the temple,

Andres asked me if I was excited about going out with Marcelo. I told him that I was nervous about the date. I wasn't sure what he was expecting of me and I was a little afraid that the *Yanqui* reputation was going to get me into trouble. He laughed at me and assured me that Marcelo probably realized what sort of girl I was, having spent the afternoon with me at Ada's *quinta*.

I was fidgety throughout the Shabbat service. The girls teased me and threatened to tell the rabbi that I wasn't paying attention to his sermon. If I had a faster wit, I would have made a comment on their shocking behavior week after week up in the *Ezrat Nashim*, but since I always thought of something clever to say two hours *after* the fact, I just shifted uncomfortably in my chair and said in English under my breath, "At least *I* have a date tonight."

After services, the group met outside to decide how they were going to spend the rest of their evening. Siblings, Patricia and Carlos were sitting in their car. I decided to sit with them while I waited for Marcelo. It was a typical sardine-can automobile, otherwise known as a Citroen. Since we were talking about cars, I told them that I had a Toyota Corolla back home. Carlos asked me if I knew how to drive a stick shift and when I told him that I didn't, he invited me up to the driver's seat for a quick lesson. The three of us, laughing hysterically, maneuvered ourselves around the tiny car so that

I ended up behind the wheel, Carlos was sitting next to me and Patricia was in the back. Carlos started explaining about the different gears and we had our heads together as I looked down to the clutch. Suddenly, the door flew open and I felt someone reach in and tug on my arm. I looked up and it was Marcelo! My first reaction was to smile and say hello, but the look on his face was too alarming.

"What is the matter with you? Are you ok?" I asked.

"What is the matter with *me*? What do you mean?" I'm practically running down the street, hurrying to meet you and you are in some car with some guy doing who knows what!"

I slowly got out of the car and saw the rest of the group staring at us. Carlos and Patricia also got out of the car and joined the others. I adjusted my coat and took a minute to think to myself, *is he kidding*?

"Look Marcelo," I said calmly even though I was ready to throw something at him, "We finished Shabbat services and I was just waiting here with my friends. This isn't "some guy." This is Carlos and I've known him for a while now, *much longer than I have known you*."

Taking a deep breath, I continued, "As far as *doing who knows what*, Carlos was just showing me how to drive a stick shift. His sister Patricia was sitting in the back seat. I wasn't "doing" anything for you to get so excited about!" I glared at him and added, "Do you have anything you'd like to say?"

Everyone was staring at us and I was humiliated. I was just about ready to go home with Andres, when Marcelo apologized and said that he over reacted. He asked if I still wanted to go for some coffee with him and I think I heard all the girls gasped when I answered yes.

Andres, acting like an overprotective brother, came over to kiss me goodbye and whispered in my ear, "Are you sure you want to go with this creature?"

I kissed him on his cheek and whispered back, "I'll be fine."

Marcelo and I started down the street with dozens of eyes on us. I heard them laughing as we turned the corner, certain that we were the butt of some joke Edgardo most likely blurted out.

Marcelo turned to me and apologized again. "I'm sorry I overreacted, but when I saw you in the car, I thought you were with Edgardo. I remembered you said that you were uncomfortable with him, and I just blew up. Can we start this date over?" And then, with a devilish sparkle in his eye and more *savoir faire* than any San Fernando Valley boy had ever shown, he said, "Take my hand, so that you won't get lost."

With that soliloquy, the boy from Almagro went from Neanderthal to my very own, "Mr. Darcy." That was our first date, August 5, 1981 and I was hooked. We ended up seeing each other every night for the next two weeks. He had school during the day and he worked at night, but afterwards, he'd always come to pick me up. We talked for hours on end, revealing ideas and goals, comparing experiences, likes and dislikes.

One evening, he came to Bobe Flora's house for dinner with a new Long-Play record he promised to share with me. Long after the meal was over and the table was cleared, we sat in the kitchen talking until dawn, listening to *Baker's Street* and sharing stories. Marcelo told me about his childhood, the schools he attended and his religious background. His family considered themselves Conservative but except for a few variances, including the fact that his parents were very well read, his family and mine shared similar traditions. I confessed my lack of knowledge and once again, my obstinate defiance reared its ugly head. He saw right through me and noted that it was *because* of my lack of knowledge that I felt so isolated. Hesitantly, I informed him that a friend invited me to join a Reform congregation and I waited anxiously for his reply - I didn't have to wait too long.

"We have heard about the Reform movement. A lot of people don't accept it; they go so far as to call it a form of Christianity." Marcelo offered.

Startled, I almost shouted, "Why would they think that?"

"It's too modern. Too much is left up to the individual. It's almost like saying: I'm a Reform Jew, so I don't have to do anything."

"My friend told me that it's *harder* to be a Reform Jew *because* it is up to you. You have to be more knowledgeable so that you can make informed decisions. What's the point of doing things out of rote, if you don't know why you are doing it and if it doesn't help you feel spiritually connected to God." I argued.

"You should come to Templo Bet El and ask our American rabbi, Marshall Meyer. Do you know him?"

"No, sorry I don't. Should I know him?" I questioned.

"He is extremely famous around here; or maybe, I should say *infamous*."

I was intrigued-an infamous rabbi? "Why? What has he done wrong?"

"Oh, it's not that he has done something wrong. He is just not your typical rabbi, I guess. Some people think he is too modern. There aren't many choices for Jews in Argentina. It sounds like you have many options in America, Orthodox, Conservative, and Reform. We pretty much have Orthodoxy here. People pick and choose what they want to do or not do, but the rabbis are very traditional."

"Hmm…people *pick and choose* what they want to do, huh?"

"OK, smart-aleck, do you want to hear about Marshall, or not?" Marcelo sneered at me playfully.

I giggled and waved my hand as if to say, "Continue."

"Ok, so this American rabbi came to Argentina in the 60's. He was at the Congregación Israelita here in Buenos Aires. All of the sudden, people were attending Friday night services like crazy! His personality is very charismatic and what he was preaching was very controversial. He became so popular that he founded a rabbinical school for Conservative rabbis."

"So what is so controversial?" I asked sipping my umpteenth cup of coffee.

"A school for Conservative Judaism-that was practically revolutionary. Like I said, there were no options here. Marshall founded a new congregation, Bet El, where I work right now. He's quite an activist too. He says that as a religious people, we have to speak out against the violations of human rights. A lot of the leaders in the Jewish community are afraid to act, afraid for their lives and for the lives of their congregants. Marshall denounced several important military leaders, accusing the government of torture and persecutions and telling the congregation not to let the *desaparecidos* simply disappear without decrying the injustice and inhumanity of the government's actions."

We kept talking throughout the night, not all of it was so heady. I also found out that he loved the music of *Hen-e-sis* and *Dee-ap Pool-pull*. It took me several minutes to realize that he was saying Genesis and Deep Purple and we laughed until our sides were aching. Bobe Flora woke up to find us sitting on the kitchen floor drinking coffee. She just smiled and said, "What will the neighbors say?" Marcelo sheepishly got up, kissed both of us goodbye and went home.

Since it was still very early in the morning, my grandmother began shuffling back to her bedroom and suggested that I try to get some rest before the hustle and bustle of the day began. Although my body agreed that it was time to sleep, my mind took over and I began to feel the stirrings of panic. I hadn't had an attack it quite some time. I tried to talk myself out of it, as I lay in my bed. I told myself that I was overtired and emotionally spent. After tossing and turning for a few seconds, there was no denying that I was heading for a full blown anxiety attack and the only way I knew how to calm myself down was with human contact. I needed desperately not be alone. Dreading having to disturb my poor grandmother, but feeling my throat begin to constrict, I quickly walked to her bedroom door and knocked. Without waiting for a reply, I let myself in and saw Bobe Flora sit up.

"*Que pasa* Mirtita?"

Bobe Flora knew about my panic attacks but I still felt ashamed to admit my weakness. "I can't sleep Bobe." I somehow was able to unclench my teeth and get the words out of my mouth.

"Come here *cucale* and sleep with me," she said as she pulled back the covers on my grandfather's side of the bed. "I know exactly how you feel."

"You do? I didn't know you suffered from panic attacks."

"This is not a panic attack, my *sheine*. This is a reaction from being separated from Marcelito. I feel the same way sometimes when I think about your zeide. Your zeide was my *b'sheirt*, my soul mate. My first impression is that you just might have found your *b'sheirt*. I wouldn't be surprised if that was the problem all along. Your parents told me that you suffered from separation anxiety after the earthquake. Maybe it wasn't about being separated from your parents. *Maybe* it was your *neshama*, your soul, awakening to the fact that you were not complete."

"But Bobe, Marcelo and I just met! We really don't know anything about each other. It's too soon."

"*Querida*, you are thinking with your head and not your heart. Your soul is trying to tell you something. I think you just might have solved your little problem and I would be willing to bet that this is the last time you have one of these episodes. You have found your *media naranja* (literally, half orange); you are not incomplete any more. Try to lie down and rest now."

I closed my eyes and began to feel myself relaxing as my grandmother stroked my hair. Could she be right or was it all the ravings of a superstitious, lonely old woman? I wasn't able to debate the question any longer as finally, my body surrendered to peaceful sleep.

On my final Friday night, we went to Templo Murillo for services. The group was amazed that Marcelo and I were still seeing each other and that we apparently had become "an item." The girls cornered me and asked me about our relationship. I told them that while we had become attached very quickly, it was obviously going to end as I was going home in a few days and we would be thousands miles away from each other.

Before we knew it, it was time for me to go home. I had said my goodbyes to The Argentina Family, grandparents, aunts, uncles and cousins. The kids from Templo Murillo came to the Reisenfeld's house. We would all drive in a caravan to the airport, but Marcelo was going to meet me there. The emotion and stress level was palpable. It felt like a bad scene from an old movie. The kids tried to lighten up the moment, but I could barely speak for fear of crying.

I had been in this airport countless times. I had said goodbye over and over again, but this time it was different. Before, I had known that the separation was temporary, that I could hop back on a plane and be back in my grandmother's kitchen or my cousin's living room in a blink of an eye. This time was different because it felt permanent. I had my little romantic fling and now it had come to an end.

They announced our Pan Am flight and the hugging and kissing began. I said goodbye to everyone until there was no one else but Marcelo. He looked like he wasn't breathing. In fact, he looked like he was going to burst. He held out his arms and we embraced. Everyone started to clap and whistle, trying to make us laugh, but we just started crying, both of us…*hysterically*. I turned away from him and into Amalia's arms. She had been like a mother to me and I *needed* a mother at that moment. Somehow, as if sleepwalking, I got myself together and without looking back, walked away and onto the escalator. When I settled in my seat, I started crying again. What had I done?

And So It Begins

Mami and Papi were waiting for us when we arrived in LAX the next day. I had told them about Marcelo throughout several phone calls, but they had no idea that things had gotten so intense. Feeling miserable and sorry for myself, I didn't want to talk about *him* or the trip. Because the beginning of the fall semester was just a few weeks away, I forced myself to focus on a few menial tasks, but I refused to go out otherwise or meet up with my friends. Mami of course noticed my odd behavior and offered a simple solution, the *obvious* resolution to my melancholy. She suggested that I call Marcelo and find out if he'd like me to return for a few days. After all, the price of the ticket wasn't the issue. The question was *did Marcelo want to see me again*? Something had definitely been started between us and if nothing else, we simply needed to talk.

It was September 10, 1981, and once again there was an Argentine entrance stamp on my American passport. Although Marcelo invited me to stay with his family, I stayed with Bobe Flora. Since Zeide Simon had passed away, she appreciated having company. Besides, Bobe Flora was used to having granddaughters stay with her in Buenos Aires. She told me stories of when Gisela and Monica came up from Bahia Blanca. And then it was Marielita's turn and Susanita's turn when they traveled to the capital. She was thrilled to have me. Mami would have been shocked to know that Bobe Flora was extremely lenient on her house rules. I actually didn't *have* house rules. I came and went as I pleased. Marcelo was welcome to come over at any time. We only had a week and Bobe Flora knew that something was brewing. She was a smart cookie!

Although we had *Carte blanch* with regards to our comings and goings, we had limited funds. Marcelo was adamant that I shouldn't pay for our outings and since his economic status was rather pitiful, we rarely splurged on our dates. We went dancing a few times and I gained admiration, albeit undeserved, by knowing all the words to the more popular songs. American music was back in fashion. Argentine artists who raged against the current state of affairs were stifled by the government's censorships; several outspoken musicians were living in exile, fearful to return.

We went to see Fame, which had been out in American theaters for quite some time - I had already seen it twice; I was surprised the government allowed this form of entertainment. The movie had subtitles, which meant some of the more poignant dialogue was lost in the translation (maybe the government censors couldn't follow along?). I ended up whispering my interpretations, much to the chagrin of the people seated next to us.

On another occasion, while we perused the vast array of shops on Calle Florida, a Minnie Mouse coffee mug enticingly placed on a display shelf caught my attention. My name, MIRTA, was printed across the width of the cup. Growing up in a time where personalized items were the hottest trend, I was hard pressed to find anything engraved, embroidered or printed with *my* unique name in the San Fernando Valley. I insisted that we enter the shop; that coffee mug was coming home with me to America! As I went to pick up the cup, I inadvertently let out a squeal of delight; for placed next to my MIRTA Minnie Mouse mug, was a *MARCELO* Mickey Mouse mug! What were the odds of that happening…Mirta *and* Marcelo? We picked up both mugs and headed to the cash register. In the process of handling our purchase, the clerk looked at us and asked, "Are you two brother and sister? You look so much alike!" I began to giggle and explain when suddenly, Marcelo turned me around and shut me up with a big, sloppy kiss. He turned to the clerk and said, "Yeah…she's my sister." We laughed so hard; we almost dropped our newly bought treasures as we left the store and the dumbfounded clerk behind.

The following day we headed out to Palermo Park for a picnic. Dani and Julian came along for the outing. It was lovely and magical and romantic. After lunch, we rented a paddleboat and we cruised around the lake while Marcelo sang some Argentine rock ballad. I made a mental note to write this moment down so that I could tell Bonnie when I got home! It started to rain and we were drenched. Julian and Dani were ready to head back to the Reisenfeld's house, but Marcelo had other plans for us. Apparently, we were expected at the his house for dinner. In a moment's time, I went through a myriad of emotions. First I was dismayed. I was soaking wet and looked a mess! Then, I was nervous. I was going to meet his family! That was a big deal in Argentine culture. Then I was furious! Why didn't he warn me or give me time to go home and change? Then I was thrilled! *He wants me to meet his family!* Oh my!

We headed to his parents' home on Rivadavia and Medrano. As we were going up the elevator to the seventh floor, he just grinned at me and told me not to fuss. We were welcomed into the apartment with a lovely aroma of delicious food. His parents came out of the kitchen and gave us a kiss hello. His sister, Victoria and brother, Dario came from their rooms down the hall. Introductions were made but it was extremely awkward until Marcelo blurted out, "I'm starving."

We washed up for dinner and immediately sat down to the table. Dario was just about thirteen years old and the family clown. He sensed the tension in the room and so he asked, "Ma, why are we sitting in the dining room instead of eating in the kitchen?"

"Well, I thought it would be more comfortable for us here, since it is so cramped in the kitchen," Ana answered her son with a stern look. Her expression said, "Don't make a scene and embarrass your brother." But Dario had other ideas.

"So, why are we using the fancy china and expensive silverware? Why is everyone dressed up?"

I busied myself with the food on my plate. I saw Marcelo smiling at me through the corner of my eye. Marcelo's father chimed in and said, "Once in a while, it is nice to use the finer things, don't you agree Mirta? However," he stopped to glare at his younger son, "there's no need to be so formal with our names. Let's begin by breaking the ice a little. My given name is Jacobo, but everyone calls me Bito. My wife is Anita."

Marcelo's parents were charming hosts and they asked me to make myself comfortable in their home. They began asking questions about my family in Argentina and my life in America. They told me a little about themselves. By the time the meal was over, I thought the Marcelo's parents were very accomplished, well informed, cultured people. Dario and Vicki made jokes and teased Marcelo, but he didn't seem to mind. I apologized for our soggy appearance and for not bringing anything, such as candies or flowers, but explained that I wasn't forewarned about the dinner plans.

Vicki laughed and said, "That's so typical of him. I don't know what you see in my brother any how!"

Dario began laughing hysterically, so much so that Bito had to ask him to leave the table. Marcelo told his parents that we had plans for the rest of the evening and so, just as quickly as we arrived, we were on our way. As we were walking down the street, I asked him why he invited me to his home so soon into our relationship. Marcelo admitted that his family was curious to meet me since he had been acting rather strangely ever since he had met this *Yanqui.*

We walked quietly for several blocks when I finally asked him where we were going. He sheepishly replied, "We're going to meet my friends." He was just full of surprises today. Luckily, I had a chance to fix myself up a little while at his home. I borrowed Vicki's blow dryer and applied some fresh makeup, so I felt somewhat presentable.

We walked into Frankie's Café and found the guys at their usual table. Marcelo walked us over and greeted everyone. He turned to me and said, "This is my *novia.*" I almost died from the shock. *Novia*! He introduced me as his girlfriend! I hadn't realized that we had made it official!

I wasn't given much time to enjoy that moment, because Marcelo was busy introducing each friend. As he went around the table, he called out, "That is *el Sapo,* that's *el Gordo*, Gabriel, you know him, then *el Turco*, *el Coco,* and on he went. Each guy had a nickname that was more or less slightly derogatory. No one went by his given name, they were simply known as "fathead" or "frog face."

Warily, I looked at Marcelo and said, "So, what's your nickname?"

Suddenly the room was full of laughter, snorts and snickers. "What? You didn't tell her what we call you?" one of the boys shouted out.

"You better run *Yanqui*, 'cause he bites!" shouted another.

"Well, what is it?" I asked.

Marcelo turned to me and grinned, "*Caníbal.* They call me cannibal."

On September 18th, there was another exit stamp in my passport, but there was a little more to this particular departure. Acknowledging that it would be a long-distance relationship, Marcelo and I found ourselves at the beginning of something special.

A Boy Next Door

I began the fall Semester at CSUN in September with as much enthusiasm as I could muster. Mami had put a vase of flowers on the kitchen table with a card that read, "Good Luck at School, With Love, The Argentina Family" (you know, just in case I forgot that I had hundreds of people in South America wishing me luck!). Paula insisted that we join Hillel and try to become more active on campus. She of course, was on the lookout for young men! I was a lost cause. I had no interest, but I tagged along and even though I wasn't intentionally looking for anyone, I found myself in the midst of several potential candidates. I thought it was ironic that all through high school I was pining to have boyfriend to no avail. Then I meet someone who perfectly meets my parents' requirements, Argentine, Jewish, college student, *but he lives in another hemisphere*. Now, with my head in the clouds and my heart in another continent, suddenly boys were starting to take notice of me. Life had a strange sense of humor. John Lennon said it best when he sang; "Life is what happens to you when you're busy making other plans."

Mami insisted that I attend the upcoming *Hebraica* dance. It was an obsession with my mother that I meet someone through the Hebraica network. Although I had met an Argentine Jewish boy, it was not good enough- Marcelo was thousands of miles away. I decided that attending the dance would be easier than dealing with the guilt and the lectures that would certainly follow.

Seated at my table was a group of people I hadn't met before. One of the young men, Horacio, was speaking to another girl at the table. It was apparent that he had just recently arrived from Argentina. Great! Here we go again...Which country is better? Where do you prefer living? But the conversation was *actually interesting*. Horacio had left Argentina at an early age and went to Israel on something called *Plan Tapuz*. He had even traveled throughout Europe, an experience of which I was envious. He obviously was not your typical kid newly arrived from *Arr-hen-tina*. We began talking and sharing traveling experiences. Horacio was shocked at my lack of knowledge regarding Israel's history. I conceded that it was shameful, and suggested that maybe he could help me with my studies.

"Great," he said, "I'll come by to your house and we can talk about it over a coffee, what do you think?

I agreed and told him that I'd look forward to it. He asked where I lived and dared me not to say, "In the Valley," like everyone else did. The San Fernando Valley was bigger than some provinces in Argentina. Laughingly, I responded, "I live in Canoga Park…*in the Valley*!"

He rolled his eyes and groaning, asked, "Where in Canoga Park? I live there too."

"Off of Winnetka and Roscoe, do you know it?"

"*I* live off of Winnetka and Roscoe!" Horacio laughed.

"You're kidding? I live on Penfield Avenue. Where do you live?" I asked curiously.

"I live on Penfield Avenue!! I can't believe it!"

We exchanged addresses and as it turned out, he practically lived next door. He had been there for several months. I couldn't believe that there was an *Arr-hen-tina* family living down the block and my mother wasn't aware of it! Horacio introduced me to his friends and I introduced him to *La Familia*. The mothers in the Hebraica network were all a-buzz with this new addition to the *mench* pool.

Paula and I began to feel more at home with our Hillel chapter after several events with the other students. We did some charity work as a group, participated in religious observances and attended social events. Paula had her eye on a particular boy, Danny, but she always wanted me to tag along…just in case. I met Danny's roommate, Steven, when the boys invited us out dancing one evening. Steven was of Italian descent and was fascinated to find out that I was from Argentina; it turned out that our cultures had many things in common. He said that his parents were driving him crazy to marry an Italian Jewish girl but he was not having any luck finding one. Steven grinned at me and said; "Maybe they wouldn't mind an Argentine-practically the same food, right?"

I smiled back but groaned internally. Steven was a very good-looking guy-a nice Jewish boy, a College student to boot. Not your typical Valley stoner. He was everything that I could fall for, except *I had already fallen for Marcelo.* I spent the majority of the evening talking about this guy in Argentina. Steven realized that I was not interested and he gave up his pursuit. *E la vita*, as they say in Italy!

The kids at Hillel, and pretty much everyone else suddenly had an interest in all things Argentina, ever since the Broadway musical *Evita* started touring the country. I had actually gone to see the musical with a friend. I could have sworn that one of the scenes was shot right on the street where Bobe Flora and Zeide Simon used to live, right on Corrientes and Pasteur. People were ignorant however and they took the play and famous or rather the infamous Evita on face value. Glamour magazine wrote an article about the impact of women such as Evita, stating that her sophistication and elegance coupled with her humanity and ambition made her one of the most significant women of our time. When I read the article, I was infuriated. Evita, her husband, Argentine president, Juan Peron, and the political party known as the *Peronistas* were frequent topics of conversation in our community in America. The Argentina Family only spoke about them in hushed tones and only in certain company for even after all the years that had past; the *Peronistas* were still a formidable party.

I didn't feel the need to speak in hushed tones and grabbed paper and pen and wrote a letter to the magazine. I wanted their editors to hear another side of the story. I signed the letter with my full name, including my city and state. Mami was not convinced that it was a good idea. She was afraid that someone might read it and be offended and that somehow, I might cause trouble for The Argentina Family. But I insisted, after all, I was an American citizen and I had a right to voice my opinion.

I was thrilled to see that my letter was actually published in a subsequent edition. I was proud of myself and reminded my mother that this was what living in America was all about. A few days later, I received a phone call from a girl named Miriam. She was a twenty-three year old Argentine immigrant. She read the letter in the magazine and seeing my name, called the Information Operator; they gave her my phone number. Miriam said she wanted to call and thank me. She was tired of seeing Evita portrayed as a diva and a saint and she was thrilled to see someone have the courage to set the matter straight.

Miriam gave me her phone number and address and suggested we meet for lunch one day. After convincing Mami that it was not some military set-up to kidnap me, Miriam and

I arranged a get-together. We had a lovely lunch at her house however Miriam didn't cook any of it - she couldn't even boil water. It was her Japanese housemate. She and Andy lived together in a small three-bedroom house in Canoga Park, very close to my home. They both worked and attend Pierce College, which is where they met and decided to be housemates. Andy was a riot and kept us in stitches; Miriam acknowledged that it was his sense of humor, even more than his cooking skills that she appreciated. My new friend told me that she had left Argentina two years prior after her family suffered tremendously during the "Dirty War." She didn't go into details and I was admittedly grateful not to hear them. I had heard about the torture; it was still going on. She didn't mention her family again in the months that followed.

My life was a fairy tale compared to what she had experienced. I was at a loss; what could I contribute to this friendship except for idle gossip and stories of my transcontinental romance. Nevertheless, Miriam was interested in my tales and like an older sister gave me advice about boyfriends and the like. Most of the time, we'd stay home and eat a fabulous dinner prepared by Andy and then, we'd watch old scary movies presented by Elvira, a campy T.V. personality. I had warned Miriam that I didn't like scary movies and she laughed at me. She said that these old films were so silly that no one could possibly be frightened. Trying to save face, I wouldn't admit that Vincent Price terrified me.

Other than watching old movies and talking about boys, Miriam taught me how to knit. More to the point, she taught me how to knit a sweater for Marcelo. Bobe Flora had taught me how to knit years ago, but I never learned how to put anything together other than a very long scarf. So, we'd watch Elvira and knit together and Miriam would laugh hysterically at the sexy, vampire character (when she was not laughing at me!) I did manage to produce a sweater for Marcelo. Of course, it wasn't as if he lived next door and I could take measurements. So what if the sleeves were not as long as they should have been and the shoulders were slightly narrow? Quite possibly, my creation better suited one of Elvira's zombies, but I was proud of my accomplishment and no one, not even Vincent Price, could have persuaded me otherwise.

Surprises

Marcelo's letters arrived on a weekly basis; sometimes individually, other times, in bunches. I'd read them again and again; storing my treasures in a recycled box of stationery and then moving up to extra-large May Company gift boxes. Besides keeping the postal service busy, I would call on Sunday afternoons and it was always nice to hear him pick up the receiver on the first ring. It meant that he was waiting by the phone, anxious to talk with me. Marcelo surprised me once by calling via CB radio. His friend, *El Gordo*, Gabriel had a connection with a guy living in Antarctica who had a connection with some other guy. When I answered the call, it took a few minutes to realize what was going on and I actually was a little startled. It wasn't every day that a girl got a phone call from her guy via free citizens band radio.

In our conversations and letters, I told him about school and about my activities. He didn't mind so much when I told him about going to the movies with the girls, but when I started talking about Horacio and the gang or the Hillel activities, he made it very clear that it made him uneasy. I would counter by saying I felt the same way when hearing about his social activities. It was silly to think we would stay home and keep to ourselves. The distance and time that separated us was an ongoing battle. We both had to fight against loneliness, jealousies and uncertainty.

Mami had finally met Marcelo on one of her trips to see The Argentina Family. She brought Marcelo the sweater I knitted, along with a letter and some Milky Way chocolates for Dario. Marcelo had been invited to Tía Lela's house for afternoon tea and he showed up dressed to the nines and with a bouquet of flowers. Imagine my shock when Marcelo wrote that my mother's first response after meeting him was, "You are too short! You are too young and you don't have any money!" Thankfully, he said something witty and charmed her right off her feet. Tía Lela too! By the time they had finished off the last *sandwiche de miga* and ricotta *knish*, Marcelo reassured me, he had both of the sisters wrapped around his little finger.

After regaining my composer, I continued reading Marcelo's letter. He was planning a get-together for his friends for the end of the school year. He explained who was invited, what was on the menu and how they were all going to get to the *quinta*. Everyone was coming with guitars, bathing suits and an assortment of soccer equipment, or rather, *futbol* equipment. He was very excited about it and he wished I could be there with him and meet his new friends. When I completed the letter, I knew I had to call Marcelo right away – I had come up with a plan. After the initial "Hello, how are you" and telling him how mortified I was about the affair with my mom, I explained that as much as I would love to go to his *asado*, it was impossible for me to get away. I fibbed and made up some excuse about a last minute assignment that needed to be completed during winter break. It was sweet to hear his disappointment, but we had known similar disappointments as we had missed sharing several happy events in the course of our relationship.

The following day, I called and spoke with Anita, his mother. Together, we schemed and planned on how best to surprise Marcelo. We organized all the details behind the scenes; Vicki would pick me up from the airport, I would stay with them for my short visit and I would most certainly *not* inform The Argentina Family in order to save precious time.

On the day of my trip, I was busy in my room gathering last minute items to place in my Pan Am flight bag. Mami came to the door and asked, "Mirtita, are you taking a *saquito*?"

Looking up from my bag, I answered, "No Ma. It's going to be 100 degrees in Buenos Aires and it's so humid there. I won't need a sweater."

"But, for the plane Mirtita; you might get cold *mamita*."

"Ma, if I get cold, I'll ask for a blanket. Don't worry. OK?"

Mami sort of grinned and walked away. I kept on with my last minute packing.

Papi came and knocked on the door. "Mirtita," he said sheepishly, "Mami sent me to tell you that you should take a *saquito*." He looked down at his shoes because he didn't want me to see him smiling.

I huffed and said, "Papi, its summer in Buenos Aires. It's hot and humid. I have my purse and this flight bag and I don't want to *schlep* around a sweater that I won't need. OK?"

"OK," he said and he shuffled back to the kitchen.

Five minutes later, Papi came back to my room. "Mirtita, Mami wants me to say that if you don't take a *saquito*, I'm not going to drive you to the airport."

"Pa! You have got to be kidding me!" I couldn't believe my ears. He was not usually so easily swayed by Mami. What was going on?

All this nonsense about a *saquito* was making me nervous and I was already anxious enough. I had to get down to LAX and stand in line with the other "Stand-By" passengers and hope that they would have room on the plane. It was the holiday season. The planes were packed. There was a good chance I wouldn't get on my flight and that would, of course, ruin my surprise. I didn't have time for family drama. I crossed the small hallway, knocked and opened Dani's door. "Pa and Mami won't take me to the airport. I need you to drive me over right now." I closed the door without waiting for a reply.

Dani just recently began driving. She was 16 ½ years old; the ink on her driver's license was still wet for heaven's sake! She had never driven anywhere near Los Angeles or the international airport. But, like a trouper, she grabbed her purse and I grabbed my suitcase and off we went.

Dani managed the 405 freeway traffic *and* my mood swings with great flair and soon, we were at the Pan Am gate, my ticket in hand. I was finally ready to go although it was with a heavy heart. I wasn't thrilled at my behavior with my parents, after all my mother was simply trying to take care of me. I should have taken the stupid sweater and stuffed it in my flight bag. I was feeling pretty immature and ashamed of myself when suddenly, I heard Papi's familiar whistle. Dani and I simultaneously turned around to see our parents coming up to greet us. Papi said that they didn't want me flying to Argentina without saying goodbye and with sore feelings. I gave them both a hug and apologized for my part of the drama. Unexpectedly, Mami brought forward a gift bag that she was holding behind her back. In the bag was…the *saquito*. "Just in case you changed your mind," she said sheepishly.

I hesitated for a moment but replied, "Sorry Ma. I didn't change my mind." Kissing them both goodbye one last time, I crossed through the gate and walked down to *my* 747 that was whisking me away on another adventure.

Vicki was true to her word and was waiting for me at Ezeiza when I arrived. After going through customs, we jumped on a bus and headed back to the apartment. Marcelo had no idea of my surprise; he had no reason to suspect anything. I had called him the Sunday before and wished him luck with his party. I was getting antsy and my heart was jumping out of my chest.

When we arrived, Vicki rang the bell so that Anita could buzz us into the building. I could hardly breathe I was so excited. We reached the seventh floor and Vicki had me wait in the elevator. She went to their apartment and rang the doorbell. Marcelo opened the door and like a grouchy brother growled, "Where is your key?"

"I rang because I need you to help me with something. It's in the elevator and I can't bring it in by myself." Vicki answered with a sassy tone.

I heard them walking down the hall; Marcelo was complaining and Vicki told him to "Just shut up." It seemed like hours instead of seconds, but suddenly he was standing right in front of me. Vicki and I shouted "Surprise!"

Marcelo took a few steps backwards and bumped into the wall. He was pale and couldn't talk. I dropped my purse and my bag and ran to him. Vicki and I helped him back into the apartment. It was truly over ten minutes before his color returned to normal and he could speak. After we greeted each other properly, he said, "I just couldn't understand it. In my brain, I knew that you were home, in America, but my eyes were telling me that you were here, in *my home*-in *our elevator*. It was just overwhelming."

I was glad he finally said *something*, because I was beginning to have my doubts about the whole trip. Maybe I shouldn't have come. Maybe I should have listened to Horacio who teased me about Marcelo having a secret girlfriend. Maybe he didn't want me at this party. But all doubts were washed away as soon as Marcelo had time to assimilate all the information and he gave me his typical bear hug, crushing my ribs and taking my breath away.

After all the excitement of my arrival subsided, the memory of my departure-the *Saquito* Affair, as it would be referred to in the future - plagued my conscience. I told Marcelo about the ridiculous episode and after his laughter died down, he insisted that I call home and clear the air. Mami picked up the phone right away; we apologized to each other and the ordeal was placed behind us. I heard Papi call out in the background. He picked up the line from his office when Mami hung up. Now with some privacy, Papi told me that he was proud of how I handled "the situation." He said that when I convinced Dani to take me to the airport, he inwardly was jumping up and down saying, "Yes! Yes! Yes!" I was completely taken aback. I wasn't sure what he was taking about and asked him to repeat what he said.

"Mirtita, it wasn't *about the saquito.* Mami, although I don't think she realized it at the time, was grasping at straws. Her little girl was suddenly running from her arms across the world to the arms of her young man. Don't you see? Mami wants to hold on to you, her precious little girl. Don't get me wrong! I don't want to let you go either, but when you put your foot down over whether or not you should take that ridiculous sweater, you stood up for yourself; a young lady-not a little girl."

I just stood there, holding the phone and not knowing what to say. Foolishly, I started crying; Marcelo took the receiver from my hand and finished the call. Taking a breath, I calmed down and told Marcelo what had been said. As usual, the emotional level was on overdrive; we were becoming acquainted with the sensation. We were just beginning to take into account the emotional affect our relationship would have on our parents and families.

Trying to readjust and change the level of stress in the room, I opened up my little suitcase and started passing out gifts. This time, I hadn't come empty handed. Probably the most popular item was the bottle of Charlie perfume I brought for Anita. She had mentioned how popular the scent was this season, but the price was exorbitant as it was practically considered a black market item. Of course, I brought gifts for the others and I was thrilled that they were accepted with genuine appreciation. Having a *Yanqui* around was not so bad after all!

Marcelo's *asado* was a great success. Everyone had a wonderful time; there was plenty of food, music and sunshine. Of course, Marcelo's friends were surprised to see me. Those I hadn't met before had heard about our whirlwind romance and were quite taken in by the story. It all sounded extraordinary. They asked a million questions about my life back home. They asked what are plans were for the future. Marcelo and I shrugged our shoulders and sort of smiled. Who knew? We were both very young and in school. We lived on two different continents and were living in fantasyland, always on our best behavior not wanting to waste a precious second on an argument. The girls in the group all said things like, "How romantic!" when in reality they thought we were both insane. I realized that for the first time in my life, I didn't care what people thought. I didn't care that The Argentina Family didn't know I was in town. I didn't care that his friends thought we were crazy or worse, in denial. We didn't have time to worry about such things. The days slipped by and soon it was time for me to go.

The Family Tree

In January 1982, I turned twenty and began another semester at CSUN. I was working at a preschool and setting aside a few dollars, always thinking of the next little trip. It was also during this period of time, with my coming of age and the advent of the newly unleashed World Wide Web, that the genealogy bug bit me. I don't know if growing up apart from The Argentina Family helped or hindered my enthusiasm for my new hobby. Had I grown up alongside my grandparents and other relatives, would I have grown tired of the "old stories" and therefore not have had an interest in my roots? On the other hand, was it because I *didn't* have the opportunities to hear the stories that I felt the strong urge to connect with them? Either way, the subject became more than a hobby, it became my passion. It was as if suddenly, someone switched on the play button and all I could hear was the cry of my ancestors, "Don't forget us; our struggles, our achievements."

Although we didn't have a personal computer at home, I had access to the Internet through the school library. I started looking up genealogy sites but found, that while there was quite a bit of information regarding immigrants that arrived to Ellis Island; it was not as easy when passengers immigrated elsewhere. I knew from speaking with Papi, my genealogy partner-in-crime, that the Trupp family lived in the province of La Pampa, They had settled in the colony of Narcisse Levin of Bernasconi. I looked up the town on the Internet, but couldn't find a page or link to contact. Finally, in the equivalent to our Yellow Pages, I was able to find a phone number for the "Santa Rosa Tourist Center" located on *Avenida San Martin.* Santa Rosa was the capital of the province; I figured that the tourist center was a good place to start. The following day, I woke up earlier than usual because I wanted to call the Center and I knew that they were five hours ahead of our Pacific Standard Time. I missed dialed a few times, partially because I was not fully awake but mostly because there were so many digits to dial: First, the international code, then the country code, the state/province code, the local area code and finally, the actual phone number. Was I calling Mars or Argentina? I eventually was able to place the call and heard the woman on the other line:

"*Hola? Buenas...*"

I was a little taken aback by her less than professional greeting. She basically answered a business phone line with, "Hi, 'afternoon." But since I was eager to get on with my quest, I quickly got on with the task at hand.

"Hi, my name is Mirta Trupp and I'm calling from Los Angeles."

"*Los Ángeles*...which *Los Ángeles?*"

Why did I assume she knew which Los Angeles? I quickly added, "California…Los Angeles, California, you know, in the United States?"

"Yeah, yeah, you're kidding, right? Who is this? *Manola*?"

"No, I'm not kidding. I got your number off the Internet. I have some questions and I thought you could point me in the right direction."

"You got our number off the what? Listen, *nena*, I don't understand what you are talking about."

Nena? She doesn't even know who I am and she is calling me *nena* (girlie)? Again, I disregarded her lack of professionalism and added, "The Internet, the World Wide Web…you know *the computer*?"

"O.K. *nena*, this *is* a joke! I'm going to hang up."

"No!" I shouted out in frustration. "Look, I'm calling long distance. I want to know if you can help me locate a historical society or a public records office."

"So, you *really* are calling from California, as in *Hollywood, California*? This in incredible! Oh, this must be costing you a fortune! Yes, there is the Civil Registry here in town. They are just down the block from us on Avenida San Martin."

"Great! Can you give me their phone number? Do you know if they have access to the Internet?"

"*Nenita*, this is a small town in a provincial area. No one has a computer here; we barely have working phones! Let me give you their number and tell them you spoke with Liliana, or they won't believe you!"

I jotted down the phone number, thanked her for her time and wished her a good afternoon. She replied, "*Chau nena, un beso*! ('Bye girlie, kisses)

I was now on a roll, so I didn't hesitate in placing my next call. Who knew how long the phone gods in Argentina would continue functioning? Hearing the phone ringing, I became so nervous, my stomach began to cramp. Where was my mother's *Hepatalgina*? Ring, ring, ring, click…

"*Hola, Registro Civil. Buenas tardes...*"

"Hello, I'm calling from Los Angeles, California in the United States. My name is Mirta Trupp."

"What? Who is this?"

I repeated my introduction, "My name is Mirta. I just spoke with Liliana in the Tourist Center. She gave me your phone number. With whom am I speaking?"

"This is Angel. You say you spoke with Lili? How did you get her number if you are calling from the United States?"

"I found it on the Internet…*on the computer*," I corrected myself. "I hope it is ok to call your office."

"The computer, *eh*? Sure, sure, it's ok, but what exactly are you calling for?"

"Well, this might sound a little strange to you, but I'm looking for records of my great grandparents and other relatives. They lived in Bernasconi in the early 1900's. I'm not sure of the dates. I was hoping you had records of the early Jewish settlers.

"The early 1900's!" Angel exclaimed. "That is going to be pretty difficult to research. You know, *we* don't have a computer here. Everything is stored in file cabinets, or in this case they would be in storage. Why are you looking for these records anyway?" he said, suddenly sounding a bit incredulous.

"I'm researching my family tree."

"Why don't you just ask your family, *pibita*? (kiddo) You know, these days, people don't like strangers asking questions."

I was aware of the fact that Argentines were dubious about "genealogical research" especially after living through years of military dictatorships, so I wasn't put off by his questions. I simply gave him a truthful answer. "I live in the United States; I have grown up away from the family. My parents were Argentine, but my grandparents and their families were Russian. They would have come to the area through the Jewish Colonization Association. I want to be able to tell my future children about their history."

"*Nena*, this kind of research will take a lot of time and we are very busy here. I'd have to ask my boss for extra time. She might not like the idea. Give me your information and I'll see what I can do."

I gave Angel my name, phone number and address and the names of my relatives. When I hung up the phone, I couldn't help but feel a little disillusioned. I didn't hold out too much hope, even if this nice man spoke to me as if I was a friend from down the street. Why would he go to so much trouble for a complete stranger, thousands of miles away?

Several weeks later, very early one morning, I received an unexpected phone call. Jumping out of bed and struggling to clear my sleepy brain, I stumbled as I picked up the receiver. With a frog in my throat, I managed to croak, "Hello?"

"*Hola pibita*! *Qué tal*? It is your friend, Angel!"

My friend Angel? *Oh*! My friend *Angel*! "*Hola Angel*! How are you? I was going to call you next week." I said, now fully awake.

"Well, I couldn't wait!" he exclaimed. "I was too excited for you! I went through many boxes of papers and found a treasure chest full of your family's documents. I have birth certificates and death certificates and marriage certificates! You name it, I found it!"

"Angel! I can't believe it! That's wonderful! And your boss…she let you put your other assignments aside while you did all this research?"

"No, no, we have been busy here, believe it or not, in our little town. I did this research after work. My friends in the office helped me. I made copies and mailed everything to you. I hope you get the package soon!"

"Angel! I don't know what to say!" I was overwhelmed with gratitude and excitement. "Can I send you a check for all your work? How much will all this cost, your time, the copies and the shipment of the package?"

"No, *nena*, I am your friend! There is no charge! It was exciting for us and we were happy to do it for you. Besides, the early Jewish colonists were well known here in La Pampa. Their contributions to the community were legendary. It was an honor to help you-really. I hope you will tell you future children about us. Tell them about your great grandparents and how they lived in the *La Pampa* with the *gauchos, eh? Besos y suerte nena! Chau*!" (Kisses and good luck, girlie, bye)

"*Chau* Angel and thank you!" I placed the receiver down and just stared at the phone. I was in shock! What a display of generosity. I was so wrapped up in my gratitude to this man that I almost forgot about the treasure he had found for me! I couldn't wait to share the news with Papi! Oh! And didn't I have something exciting to tell Marcelo on our next phone call?

A few weeks later the package from Santa Rosa finally arrived. I couldn't open it up fast enough, but once I managed to stop my hands from trembling, I sat down and slowly read each document, line by line, word for word. Angel was right. These documents were a treasure. The names and dates they supplied created a picture in my mind of my family long gone.

I was overwhelmed once again by the generosity exhibited by Angel and his friends. How could I ever repay him? He said it was an offering of friendship, but I knew that I had to do something to show my appreciation. And then suddenly, I knew exactly what I was going to do. Sitting down with pen and paper, I carefully dialed the number for "my friend Lili" at the Santa Rosa Tourist Center.

"*Hola? Buenas.*"

"Hi Liliana, this is Mirta calling from Los Angeles again."

"Mirta! *Como te va*? What are you doing calling me?

"I need your help again! The people at the Civil Registry were so kind to me. I want to send them a gift. Tell me; is there a flower shop or a bakery nearby?"

"Well, yes of course. We have the *Bombonería Santa Rosa* down the block on *Avenida San Martin*. They have the best chocolates in the world!"

I laughed and asked, "Lili is everything on *Avenida San Martin*?"

My new friend reminded me that the town was fairly small and of course, San Martin was their national hero. I immediately reassured her that I thought it charming and very convenient to have everything located on one main street; I added that many of our streets carried that name of our own national hero, Washington. Lili chuckled at my acknowledgement, passed on the need information and wished me luck. I quickly dialed the number and prepared myself for the conversation I knew was coming.

"*Hola, Bombonería Santa Rosa*"

"Hello, my name is Mirta. Lili gave me your number. I'd like to send a gift to the people at the Civil Registry. Would it be possible for you to deliver for me?"

"Sure, of course. Why don't you stop in and choose from our selection of chocolates?"

"No, I'm sorry, I'm calling long distance. I can't come in. Can't we do this by phone?"

"Well, I don't know…how are you planning to pay for this?"

"I was hoping to pay by credit card."

"What? OK, this is a joke, right? Who is this? Is this Manola? Look *nena*; stop using that phony *norteña* accent, *eh*?"

"No, no, this is not Manola. I'm calling from Los Angeles, California…" I told the shopkeeper the whole story about Angel and all the work he and his friends did for me. Thankfully, she finally believed me. She understood that I was indebted to these folks and wanted to send them a nice gift.

"Look *pibita*, it is Easter, *no*? Why don't you send them a nice basket of chocolates? How much would you like to spend?"

I had already thought about this question and figured I'd spend about $100.00, considering all the time and expense that they went to on my account. When I mentioned my budget, the shopkeeper shrieked.

"No! Are you crazy? That is a fortune! It is unheard of! Even if I wanted to, I don't have enough chocolate to charge you $100 American dollars!" After a short debate, she agreed on a reduced budget of $35.00. "I promise you that this will be the grandest Easter basket in the history of Santa Rosa, or even Buenos Aires for that matter! Now, as far as the payment…"

"Well, since you are not set up to accept credit cards and you don't want an international money order, I thought I could speak to my cousin in Bahia Blanca. Maybe she could get the payment to you." I suggested, knowing that I'd pay my cousin later at some point.

"Bahia…you have family there? That is fairly close-just a couple of hours away."

I quickly provided a few family names and was immediately rewarded with the shopkeeper's response. Apparently, my relatives were well-known and well liked from the Patagonia to Tierra del Fuego.

"You should have told me who your relatives were in the first place," she exclaimed, "I will prepare the basket immediately and deliver it tomorrow. I'll talk to the florist about adding some nice flowers. Don't worry about the bill. I'm sure your cousin will take care of it once you speak with her. Tell her you spoke with Juanita."

After thanking my new friend, I quickly placed another call to Bahia Blanca. In between her shrieks of laughter, Monica agreed to help me pay the shopkeeper, but not before letting me know she thought I was *just a tad* eccentric. I knew everyone thought I went overboard, but in the end, I got my treasure chest of documents and managed to have a beautiful gift basket delivered to Angel and his buddies at the Civil Registry on *Avenida San Martin* in Santa Rosa.

The postman rang our doorbell about a week later. He had a special delivery from La Pampa, Argentina. I signed for the package and hurriedly tore open the wrapping. It was a book and there was note attached.

My dear Miss Trupp,

Allow me to present this memorial keepsake of the founding colonists of Narcisse Levin in La Pampa. Your friend Liliana contacted us here at the Congregation Israelita of Bernasconi and informed us of your research. It is with great pleasure that we provide you this book and wish you the best of luck with your investigations.

I quickly skimmed through the book and found that it was written in Spanish and Yiddish. One chapter was dedicated to listing the names of the founding colonists. Even through my blurred vision caused by the onset of tears, I found my paternal great grandfathers names listed among the pioneers. I felt as if I were dreaming. I closed my eyes and said a prayer of thanks to all of those people who helped me in this quest. I wasn't done yet, but with these recent discoveries, I felt closer to my history, closer to those voices that cried out not to be forgotten.

I took a moment to consider this irresistible need of mine to connect with these family members, now long gone. Where did the desire stem from? Was it some sort of instinctive or universal yearning to connect, to *remain* connected?

Sometimes I felt something close to desperation when I thought of The Argentina Family and the distance between us. Soon, I wouldn't be able to travel back and forth with my Pan Am discount. Could "the ties that bind" be stretched across two continents without constant physical contact? Would the day come when my beloved cousins would say, "Whatever happened to Mirtita?" just like my grandparents asked about *Meier*, and *Avrum* and *Berele*…cousins who stayed behind in the old country?

Maybe the fervent desire to document the family's past stemmed from my desperation of remaining part of the family's future. The book I held in my hand contained the story of my *antepasados*, my ancestors. It was up to me, I supposed, to play an active role in my family's future. I made one last phone call the following morning. I called Lili.

"*Hola? Buenas*"

"Lili, this is Mirta. I just called to thank you for everything you did for me. I got the book yesterday. It's another treasure to be added to my collection and maybe more importantly, it will serve as the roots to my ever-growing, living family tree."

"Mirta, you have to come and visit us one day. The entire street already knows about you! The people at the Civil Registry received your gift and were overwhelmed by your generosity. Everyone is talking about the crazy *Yanqui* from

California! I can almost promise you, if you come, you will find a statue in the park on *Avenida San Martin* with your name on it!"

I giggled along with my new friend. "OK Lili, I'll try to make it out there one day! *Besos! Chau!*"

Caught In-Between

I scheduled my next trip for Spring break. I had less than two weeks to go and come back and get ready for school again. I left on April 1, 1982 and arrived in Buenos Aires on April 2nd, the day Argentina decided to attack England by "invading" the *Malvinas* –otherwise known as the Falkland Islands. It was obviously the only real topic of conversation during my week's stay. People were in an uproar, although not everyone was on the same side. Some thought the action was long overdue ever since Great Britain had colonized the island off Argentina's shores. Others criticized the government for attacking such a powerful country with a national militia that had never been truly tested. Marcelo and his friends had all completed their military service, but their various classes were placed on call. They were told that they might be needed as replacement troops.

The military regime was calling it a reoccupation of its own land, but Great Britain was calling it an invasion of British territory. Some Argentines saw this act as the latest ploy set up by their own government, trying desperately to distract a dissatisfied nation.

Although outrageously dangerous, there were those in the overwrought populous that braved possible retaliation and formed groups to denounce the regime. Without a doubt, one of the more outspoken among these groups was *Las*

Madres de Plaza de Mayo (The Mothers of Plaza de Mayo). Since 1976, men and women had been abducted by agents of the government; their grief stricken mothers began demonstrating on the Plaza de Mayo, directly in front of the presidential palace, the *Casa Rosada.* The women decried the disappearance of their sons and daughters, demanding justice for some 30,000 people who could not speak for themselves.

It all seemed surreal to me; far beyond anything I known or dealt with throughout my sheltered, quiet life. What with the economic upheaval, the war and the tyrannical regime, I simply wanted Marcelo out of the country and out of danger. Yet, on April 10th, just a few days later, I returned to America with nothing resolved and a great sense of helplessness.

The flight stopped in Rio de Janeiro for the usual layover. I had been through this airport countless times, but as we were disembarking, it was quite noticeable that they had been doing some rearranging. The terminals had been redistributed; signs and cones were set up to direct traffic. A very attractive young man stood sandwiched in between two competing airlines courteously greeting the confused passengers. "*Olá*, My name is Ricardo. Welcome to *Brasil!*" The young man smiled at each one of us, checked our tickets and directed passengers to various gates or luggage retrieval areas. He noticed my passport had several visas for Brazilian entry and commented on my short stay in Argentina. I responded without thinking and said that I just went to visit my boyfriend and was going home. Ricardo roguishly replied, "Maybe you will try a Brazilian boyfriend next time." Any other time, I might have blushed and felt flattered by his attention, but under the current circumstances, I simply shook my head and walked away.

In May, I went back for another quick visit to celebrate Marcelo's birthday. The Falklands War was raging on and Marcelo was still on-call. Needless to say, we were all on edge and it was understandably disconcerting. The United States was caught in between the dispute; on one side was their longtime ally and on the other, fellow cosigners of the Monroe Doctrine- a document that declared that the Americas would stick together against foreign invaders. With this dismal mood affecting all, Marcelo's 21st birthday was a welcomed opportunity to change our focus; even it was to be short lived.

Marcelo thought it would be nice to have our grandmothers' meet, so Anita prepared a lovely afternoon tea and the four matriarchs were invited to attend. When Bobe Golda arrived, Marcelo put his arm around his grandmother, faced me and asked, "She is a *sheine meidelach*, *eh* Bobe?" Bobe Golda looked at me and gave him a weak smile. "Yes, yes, of course she is a beautiful girl." Marcelo gave each of us a quick peck on the cheek and went into the kitchen looking to pilfer some sweet *kugel.* I was left alone with Bobe Golda. She was a sweet and charming lady, but I couldn't help think that when she looked at me, she didn't see a *sheine meidelach*; she saw the girl who was going to steal away her beloved grandson.

Thankfully, Bobe Beatriz, Bito's mother, rang the doorbell and Marcelo came running out of the kitchen to greet her. My grandmothers followed soon after. Sitting around the coffee table, Marcelo and I nervously tried to make small talk, trying to find common ground for the four matriarchs to discuss. Our concerns were put to rest as the women soon were trying to outshine the other with tales about their gorgeous and brilliant grandchildren. Bobe Beatriz and Bobe Golda began sharing stories about Marcelo, each one trying to outdo the other with anecdotes of athleticism, scholastic accomplishments and *mench*-like qualities. Each sentence started similarly, "Do you remember when Marcelito…?"

It was very endearing actually, but I grew a little anxious worrying about what my grandmothers would be able to share. After all, they had very little to do with my upbringing. I had seen them sporadically throughout the years and even then, they had to share me with the rest of The Argentina Family. While lost in my silent reverie, I didn't realize that Bobe Flora had been speaking about me. Bobe

Carmen, not to be outdone, interrupted her *macheteineste* with her own stories. I listened as my grandmothers listed a glowing outline of my triumphs and qualities.

I giggled and begged them to stop. "Bobe Carmen, Bobe Flora, *enough*! It's embarrassing!"

"Why is it embarrassing, Mirtita? We are proud of you and we want Golda and Beatriz to know what a beautiful and accomplished *meidelach* you are." Bobe Flora gloated like a proud peacock.

"I am a little surprised you know so much!" I suddenly became teary eyed.

Why was I so moved, I wondered? "All these years…we were not together… it's not the same as with Marcelo and his family."

"C*ucale,* what is this *narrishkeit*?" Bobe Carmen said as she put her arm around my shoulder. "What nonsense are you talking about? Maybe we were not with you every day, but we were with you in spirit. Your mama and papa were always so proud of you and Danielita."

Bobe Flora jumped in, "All those letters crossing thc continents back and forth. What do you think we wrote about?" Chuckling and throwing up her hands as if in resignation she continued, "The *kinderlach*, of course! Of course we *know* your stories. We are your family! It doesn't matter if you live here in Buenos Aires or in *Norte America* or even Odessa for that matter. I was only three years old when I came to this country. Our families, *Alav ha shalom,* watched us sail away, knowing that they would never see us again, but my mama wrote long letters to Russia; she had twelve children to *kvell* about! The point is that family *is* family, no matter where you are, no matter where you go; you go with our love and God's blessings. That is why you mama always adds a little card or a little something from the family."

"You know about that?"

"*Bubbeleh*, of course we do! It is her way of keeping us in your thoughts, to keep us present in your lives. We all have our little ways of doing such things."

The four grandmothers nodded in agreement and continued with their stories; however since the conversation had taken an emotional turn, they began sharing their *tsures*, their tales of woe, recalling years of struggles and all sorts of disorders. Rather abruptly, the topic switched from gall bladder issues and liver ailments to dietary rituals and the grandmothers began comparing recipes. Someone said something about adding a *bisel tsuker* to the dough when making *varenekes.* Apparently adding a little sugar was an outrage and immediately revealed a *Poylish* upbringing. *Oy vey!* This opened the proverbial can of worms.

Do you make *lokshen kugel* or potato *kugel*?

Does your family like sweet gefilte or savory?

How do you make your *matzo brie* - onions or no onions?

Luckily, Anita changed the subject with her discovery of a new dress shop on Corrientes and Callao and the afternoon's "Meet and Greet" came to a satisfactory conclusion. Marcelo and I were showered with kisses and blessings-"*Kinderlach, A leben ahf dir!*" (Children, you should live and be well)

On May 23rd, I was on my way back home again. Running through the airport in Rio, Ricardo who had greeted me just a few days before on May 14th welcomed me again with his gorgeous smile and romantic accent, saying, "Your boyfriend is a lucky man."

I was not in the mood to play a flirting game, so I gave him half a smile and said, "Can't talk now…need to catch my connecting flight."

Frequent Flyer

Although Marcelo had previously toyed with the idea of making aliyah to Israel, moving to the United States had never been a goal. With our ongoing long-distance relationship however; thoughts of visiting California began to make more sense. Marcelo and I left conversations regarding long-term commitments on the back burner because we couldn't see how to resolve several issues, educational and economical restraints being important concerns. We tried to focus on the next hurdle: just getting Marcelo to California. He began setting aside his earnings to purchase a round-trip ticket.

In June 1982, The Falklands War had come to an end after the loss of over 900 lives and a diplomatic visit from the Pope and his "Pope Mobil." In addition, with great relief and some trepidation, the country began witnessing the deterioration of the military regime. There was talk of a transitional government which would eventually hold the first presidential elections in over twenty-five years. Of course, the military had to be assured that they would not be held accountable for the Dirty War, or rather the "anti-guerilla campaign," as they referred to their reign of totalitarianism.

Marcelo and I began to have some hope; things looked like they were finally progressing when suddenly; Bito suffered a debilitating heart attack. The money Marcelo had been saving was put towards paying medical bills. He was needed at home and we were back at square one, both of us in school, with no money and thousands of miles apart.

Reviewing the turn of events, I reflected on our circumstances and the roller coaster ride Marcelo and I began the day we met. I began thinking seriously about our future. What did I want out of life? I had been raised to think that being a wife and a mother should be my main goals. What use was a college degree if I was going to stay home with my family? It suddenly occurred to me that I should quit school and get a job. But what kind of job could I get with only a high school diploma? I knew that I'd need something more substantial to quickly get into the "real world" and start making money. I had seen ads on T.V. for a medical assistance program. I thought I would be very happy in that sort of field. I liked the idea of helping people. I liked the idea of the accelerated program even better! A local, vocational college was offering a two-year course in an accelerated program for students showing proficiency and having the required grade point average. In six months, I could have a certificate and find a job. I could even hope to make one thousand dollars a month! That seemed like a fortune! I carefully planned to present my idea to my parents. I had to word it *just so.*

We sat down around our white Formica table with the yellow pleather chairs while Mami sipped her *mate* and Papi tried to look stern yet democratic. I presented my case and explained what I could do with a certificate as a medical assistant. I told them about the tuition but explained that the school offered a payment plan. Mami and Papi were happy to know that I'd have some kind of "title" and some sort of income *to help my future husband.* All in all, they accepted the idea fairly well. They did however have one area of concern. Mami hesitated slightly, but then firmly stated, "Mirtita, you mustn't tell The Argentina Family about your studies."

Seeing my confusion, Papi stated, "A young lady from a good Jewish family does not work as a nurse in Argentina."

"I'm going to be a medical assistant, not a nurse. A nurse is a higher position," I explained again. "Anyway, what is wrong with being a nurse?"

"A young lady from a good family shouldn't *see* certain things, Mirtita. You might have to work with *male* patients, something that I would certainly not like, I might add. Maybe you could work with a lady doctor who treats lady problems," Papi suggested.

Taking a sip of *mate* as if to fortify herself for the discussion, Mami added, "Mirtita, a nurse in Argentina is just a step above a maid. At least, that's how it was in my day. They didn't go to school and get a certificate. The Argentina

Family will not understand. We will have to break it to them gently and in person, so that they will be proud of your accomplishments, like we are."

And so it came to be that I started my certificate program. I enjoyed my courses and appreciated the fast paced. Each week, new topics were introduced and every Friday, there was an exam. Every month, there was a final exam, which allowed the student to proceed to the next module. It was intense and I did well under pressure. I met a new friend, an Armenian girl named Sona. She was the only daughter in a family with three sons. She too was raised to believe that her husband would be the main breadwinner and that her "little medical assistant certificate" would give her something to do before the babies came. Sona was engaged to be married. Her fiancé, a well-off jeweler from "the old country," didn't want his future wife to be a medical assistant, but he knew better than to argue with Sona. I was glad that she was able to convince him. Sona and I led the class with our exam scores and our work in the practical labs was always of the highest caliber. Our teachers were impressed with us and nicknamed us the "A Team." The letter "A" was not only for our grades, but also for Armenia and Argentina. A little cheesy, but we enjoyed the acclaim.

Since I was well known and liked in the program, I felt comfortable speaking to Mrs. O'Reilly, the director of the school, regarding my frequent traveling to Argentina. I explained how and why I traveled so often and asked if the strict attendance rules could be relaxed in my situation. Mrs. O'Reilly was inspired by my story, calling it a modern day "Romeo and Juliet." Being a true romantic, she said that she would be more than happy to help us in our endeavor to be together, however, there was one stipulation. I had to continue passing my exams with no less than 100%. A lesser grade would not allow excuse my absences. For my upcoming trip, Mrs. O'Reilly agreed to change my exam schedule. I would take my Friday test on Thursday morning and be back in school on Tuesday. I was up for the challenge.

On Thursday, August 4, 1982, I set off for an extended weekend with Marcelo and his family. Papi picked me up from school and drove me straight to LAX. I had a small bag and no luggage to dispatch, so it should have been an easy process however; we did run into a small setback. According to the Pan Am ticketing agent, the plane was full. Papi's friend informed us that an entourage of government aides was flying to Argentina. In order to avoid being bumped off the flight, I was upgraded to First Class, with seating *in the secluded upper deck!*

I had flown First Class before, but as I climbed up the spiral staircase to the upper level, I felt like a movie star. The flight attendants, now no longer called stewardesses, *treated* me like a movie star! They didn't know or care if my father worked in the Fleet Service or if he was a pilot of a 747 Intercontinental. My ticket allowed me access to the upper echelons of traveling. I enjoyed every minute of it, from the luxurious seats to the delectable meals. The seats were not only leather, but also much larger, as were the windows allowing for spectacular views. The ceiling was covered in black velvet and had tiny points of fiber optic lights. It looked like a high-end discothèque. There were only a handful of passengers on the deck and we were pampered every inch of the way. The man seated next to me struck up a conversation asking if it was business or pleasure that inspired such a long trip to South America.

"I'm on my way to visit my boyfriend," I responded.

With a raised eyebrow, he said, "It must be difficult to have a long distance relationship."

I giggled and explained, "I visit him frequently, actually as often as I can get off of school." I realized how improbable the whole thing sounded. I must have come across as a spoiled, rich girl, the daughter of someone important. I added quickly, "My father works for the airlines. We have traveling privileges."

"Ah well, that explains it. I wish you good luck! It sounds like a modern day romance in the making."

"Thanks! We need it, especially with the current political situation," I replied.

"Well, that's why I'm on my way to Argentina myself. I am on staff with the Secretary of State. We are working with the Argentine government to see if we can't mend some bridges now that the Falklands War has ended."

"I am honored to be speaking with you then. I never met anyone that worked for the US government. I'm very proud to be an American."

"That is very nice to hear. I'm proud myself. There is no other country like ours!"

And with that, our conversation came to an end as we were served dessert-a scrumptious slice of cheesecake and a lovely Champagne cocktail. Following dessert, the lights in the cabin were lowered so that they glimmered like the stars outside our window. It looked almost magical and I soon fell asleep to the hum of the jet engines.

The Grill and the Beautiful Flower

The next morning, Friday, August 5, 1982, we arrived in Buenos Aires. I thanked the attendants for a lovely flight and wished my traveling companion good luck with his duties in Argentina. Grabbing my Pan Am flight bag and my little carry-on suitcase, I glided down the spiral staircase and out the First Class door. Feeling very confident and heady, I practically floated over to Customs area. There was a small line ahead of me, but I didn't mind. I assumed that I'd be cleared rather quickly since I had very little baggage. Marcelo would be waiting for me on the other side of the familiar glass partition.

I heard some quarrelling up ahead in the line and I tried to look over the other passengers to see what the matter was. I saw a pudgy man in a three-piece, pin stripe suit arguing with an elderly gentleman. The passenger finally produced a document that satisfied Mr. Pin Stripes, as I had dubbed him instantly, and the line began moving again. I had my passport ready and was beginning to get fidgety. I was so anxious to see Marcelo! Finally it was my turn, but rather than turning my passport over to the Customs agent, Mr. Pin Stripes practically grabbed it out of my hand. He turned the pages back and forth, examining each entry and exit stamp carefully.

He turned to me and said, "I will need you to come with me, *señorita.*"

I looked around and the other passengers were looking at me curiously. One lady was shaking her head, as if saying, "What a shame." Another passenger glanced at me and then quickly turned away. Mr. Pin Stripes had two soldiers with him. They couldn't have been more than twenty, but they each had a rifle, or some sort of gun. What did I know about guns? I looked at the Customs agent and asked him, "Do I need to go with him?"

He pursed his lips and grimly said, "Yes miss. I'm afraid that you will have to go with this gentleman."

I picked up my two little bags and almost defiantly walked passed Mr. Pin Stripes as he pointed out a hallway. He quickly stepped ahead of me while the two soldiers followed behind. My brain was going a mile a minute. Where was I being taken? Why was I singled out? The first thing that popped into my mind was how the Argentina militia had taken prisoner a beloved cousin. She was held against her will, tortured and abused because they felt she had some knowledge of some college-aged revolutionaries. This happened only a few years ago. *What did they want with me?*

The stocky man in his fine suit stopped abruptly in front of an office. He opened the door and asked me to step inside. I was so riled that as I walked past him, I blurted, "I demand to know why you are holding me and I insist on calling the American Embassy to lodge a complaint."

Pin Stripes grinned and said, "You are not in the position to demand anything miss. And you may not call the United States Embassy. Sit down, please." He offered me a chair and he sat opposite of me across a long metal table. The soldiers were instructed to stand by the door, their rifles held up high across their chests. Pin Stripes flipped through my passport once again.

"Señorita Mirta Ines Trupp? *Trupp*? Is that a German name?"

"No, my grandfather was a Russian immigrant," I replied hesitantly.

"Russian, you say? When did you grandparents immigrate to Argentina?

"I'm not sure, but they were small children...possibly in the early 1900's." I said, recalling my father's tales.

"Ah, so they were not truly Russian. Would you not admit that they were actuality- *Jewish*?" He accused, practically sneering at me.

"Of course I will *admit* they were Jewish. We *are* Jewish. That doesn't mean that they were not Russian. They were born there, for heaven's sake. They were Russian citizens."

"Ah." And he made a few notes on a sheet of paper. "Miss Trupp, it says here that *you* were born in Argentina," pointing to my passport. "Why do you travel as an American citizen when you return to your mother country? Where is your *Cedula*? Where are your Argentine documents?"

"I was only 11 months old when my parents immigrated to the United States. I didn't have any Argentine documents at the time however; I'm an American citizen now," I said, raising my chin up in the air.

"Why did your parents leave Argentina? What were they running away from?"

"My parents weren't *running away* from anything. Again, I really must insist that you allow me a phone call to the Embassy. You have no right to grill me like this."

"Miss Trupp, you may not call the Embassy and we will keep you here until you answer my questions. "Why do you travel so often to Argentina? And why do you come for such short amounts of time? It is rather unlikely that you would travel thousands of miles, endure a 20-hour flight and then return to the United States so quickly. What is your business here?"

"I usually come to visit my family. But, today, I have come to visit my boyfriend."

"A wealthy American…" he scoffed and made a few notes.

"We are not wealthy," I replied trying to keep my tears at bay. I was angry and scared and *frustrated* at my lack of power. "My father works for Pan American Airlines. We have traveling privileges."

"He must be very important or have connections for you to travel in First Class," he said waiving my ticket stub in front of my face.

"My father is a "simple workingman," I used Papi's favorite line. "He works in the Fleet Service. He loads baggage and services the plane."

"This seems highly unlikely. In Argentina, a *simple workingman* in *Fleet Service*, as you say, would not be able to have such traveling privileges. He must have some other kind of clandestine arrangement."

"My father is an upstanding American citizen. *In America*, a simple workingman does have certain privileges that probably don't exist here. *That's* probably why my parents left this country." I knew that I shouldn't antagonize the man; I took a deep breath and tried to calm myself. "Please, just tell me why I am here. What do you want?"

Suddenly, he pulled out a file from his briefcase, slammed it down on the table and slid it across to me. "You will read this and sign it."

"I'm not signing anything without representation from the American Embassy. Look, people are expecting me.

They are going to question my whereabouts. I want to make a phone call," I insisted.

"Miss Trupp, I repeat, no one is going to know where you are until you read this document and sign it. This country has recently been at war with England. The United States mistakenly sided with our enemy. We are aware of people traveling in and out of the country for covert activities. You are suspiciously traveling back and forth, without proper Argentine documentation, unashamedly denouncing your Argentine nationality, I might add," now bellowing as he flicked my passport across the tabletop.

I was becoming more and more distraught by the moment. Marcelo would believe that I was detained in Rio, possibly being bumped off the plane. It hadn't happened before, but we had spoken about the possibility of it since I traveled on a "stand by" condition. If I didn't clear Customs soon, it was likely that he'd go home to await my phone call. My parents would probably think I was stuck in Rio as well. It would be hours before anyone realized that I was not delayed in Rio and then, *would it be too late*? My mind was racing through the images I had seen on television; stories we have heard about from family and friends. People disappeared; they were tortured and some were never heard from again. Was I in danger or was I over reacting? Yet the reality was that this man was holding me in a room against my will. I was locked in and guarded by armed soldiers. In just a few seconds, my mind raced through all these thoughts and I began to thumb through the tome of *legaleeze*. "I can't read this. My reading comprehension is not at this level," I regretfully admitted to Pin Stripes.

"How is it that your parents did not educate you in your mother tongue? Were they so ashamed?"

"My parents taught me to speak Spanish and to read and write, but I have been educated in America. I can read a letter or maybe even a newspaper article in Spanish, but this is legal terminology and written in an academic style. I can probably understand every other word. I'm not going to sign something that I don't understand."

Pin Stripes nodded and got up to speak to one of the soldiers, who immediately saluted, turned and exited the room. A few minutes later, he returned with another man. Although not in military uniform, the man wore a sweater vest that reeked of cigarette smoke; his tie was loose and slightly astray. His overall disheveled appearance did nothing to calm my nerves.

Pin Stripes turned to me and said, "Miss Trupp, allow me the pleasure of introducing you to Mr. Romero. He is our …our official interpreter and as such, he will explain the document to you and you will sign it."

Mr. Romero glanced at the file and began reading the first paragraph. He turned to me and began to speak, slowly and deliberately. He looked as if he were in pain as he thought of each word. The problem was that he was trying to translate and not interpret the document. His translations were nonsense, almost to the point of gibberish. I was in such an altered state that I practically shouted at him to stop. I grabbed the notebook I forced myself to try to make sense of the text. I actually tried to implement some tools I had learned back in my Power Reading class, so that I could pull out key words and skim over the fancy lingo that was confusing the issue. After about ten minutes, I heard the men huffing and sighing, the soldiers shuffling their feet. Although I couldn't have cared less for their discomfort, I was acutely aware that I needed to get out of there. I believed that the contents of the document were stripping me of my rights as an Argentine citizen. I tried to find words that insinuated my guilt in some radical activity, but not finding any; I picked up the pen and signed my name. I prayed that I didn't just sign away my life by admitting guilt of espionage.

The "interpreter" took his leave and Pin Stripes turned to me and offered me his hand. "Thank you Miss Trupp. I hope you have a pleasant stay in Argentina." He stamped my passport and returned it to me. "Maybe you will marry your young man and return to our beautiful country."

I grabbed my passport but didn't take his hand. I didn't want to touch him and I certainly did not want to thank him. He had purposely scared me out of my wits. He could have easily made the entire scenario a lot less stressful, but he chose to use his power over me and practically terrified me into submission. Pin Stripes left the room but I was still in there with the two soldiers. I looked at them apprehensively. "May I leave now?" I asked not hiding my disdain.

One of them turned to me and said, "We have a couple of questions for you," he winked at his companion.

I stood up and my chair screeched against the wooden floor. I heard myself gulp and asked, "What do you want?"

The other soldier smiled bashfully and blurted out all in one breath, "We want to know if it's true what they say about the goings on in Malibu. Are their wild parties on the beach? Do the police wear shorts and ride bikes? Are the girls all blond? Have you been to Disneyland? What about Hollywood?"

I glared at them both took a deep breath and practically shouted, "Can I *go*?"

They both shrugged their shoulders and stepped aside from the door. I was in such a state that I began shouting obscenities as I raced up and down the hallway. I couldn't find my way out. One of the soldiers came to escort me. We walked down a different hallway until finally; I could see the glass wall that separated the customs area from the waiting area. The soldier talked briefly with the customs guard; I barely acknowledged him. I walked through the glass sliding doors and was amazed to see Marcelo was pacing back and forth. I ran to him and as we embraced, I began shouting through my tears, "People have no rights in this God-forsaken place! This is an insane asylum! The country is full of…."

Marcelo slapped his hand over my mouth and he told me to wait until we were outside. He grabbed my overnight bag and we walked quickly out of the airport. While we were waiting for the bus, he asked me to quietly explain what had happened. I was still very angry and shaken up, but I explained the ordeal. As we boarded, he whispered that I needed to stop raving; the other passengers had noticed my outburst and he wanted to avoid any further attention.

When we finally arrived at his apartment, I called home and informed my parents. Papi called the Argentine Embassy in Los Angeles right away. Later that evening, he called us with an update on his findings. All in all, I had been lucky. As it turned out, I was right about the content of the document; I had signed away my rights as an Argentine citizen. The clerk had tried to explain to my father about a new law; Article 7, Code 21.795. It all sounded like gibberish and at that given moment, I couldn't have cared less.

Because we only had that short weekend, I had to quickly put aside my flustered emotions if I wanted to enjoy my time in Buenos Aires. It was, after all, the first anniversary of our first date! Not even bothering to unpack as I was leaving in three days, I was ready to head out and share some quality time with Marcelo. As usual, we left the apartment building and just began walking. At some point, we jumped on a bus that took us downtown. I had a present for Marcelo in my purse and my fingers were just itching to reach in and grab the gift box, but I wanted to wait for the right time. As we passed each intimate café or quaint little plaza, I thought this would be a nice place to stop, but we kept walking.

Quite abruptly, Marcelo came to a stop in front of a jewelry store. Winking at me, he said, "Want to go in?" What girl wouldn't want to go in a jewelry store with her boyfriend? But in the span of second, I was bombarded with thoughts like, "What are we looking for in the jewelry store? Is he thinking of buying me a gift? Could it be a ring? *Is he thinking of buying me an engagement ring?*" Oh my!

Holding hands, we went inside the store, yet Marcelo hadn't said a word. He cocked his head to the side indicating a showcase of bracelets and then we stood in front of a case full of charms. He pointed at a necklace and then stopped in front of rings. A salesman came over to us and asked if we needed help. I didn't say a word because I still wasn't sure what was going on. Marcelo perused the ring selection and seemed to have zeroed in on one that he liked. He asked the salesman to pull it out of the case. It was a lovely little gold ring. The setting of the stone made it appear as if it was a flower. I tried to act nonchalant and snuck a peek at the tiny price tag. As usual, I couldn't make out the cost, because I got so easily confused seeing so many zeros. A pair of shoes could cost 1,000,000.00 pesos. This ring was well over that, but I couldn't do the math fast enough to know what that would translate into American dollars.

Marcelo held the ring and turned to me, "A beautiful flower for *my* beautiful flower. Do you like it?"

"Yes, of course I like it! But can you afford it?" I whispered.

"Don't worry about that. If you like it, we'll take it." And he handed the ring back to man so he could write up the sale. As we left the store, Marcelo pointed to the small plaza across the street. We walked over and sat down on a park bench facing the playground. He took the ring out of the box and held it out. "It is pretty, no?"

I gulped and replied, "Yes, it's beautiful. But…" I didn't know how to ask my next question. It could be an extremely awkward situation if I said the wrong thing.

"Which finger should I put it on?" I asked, figuring that would solve the issue of it was an engagement ring or not.

"Oh, I don't care about that- whichever one you like!" He said smiling, completely unaware of any repercussions.

I figured that a blunt approach was warranted here; hadn't we both been completely open and honest with each other from the beginning? "Marcelo, here's the thing…Um…see…*in America-* I think a ring might mean something different than in Argentina." I hoped that he would understand my meaning and help me out. But he didn't, so I continued. "Well, if I place the ring on my left hand, *in America*, well, it would be considered an engagement ring. Is that where you want me to wear this ring?"

Marcelo looked at me funny for a moment before answering. "I don't know. What do you think?"

"Are you asking me if you think we should get engaged?"

"Yes, what do you think? If yes, then maybe we need to buy another ring. You know, people today don't usually buy engagement rings. It's just not in the budget of most young Argentine couples. This ring was just to mark our first year of meeting each other. It's just a piece of cut glass there in the center of the flower. I wish I could afford the real thing, but it does have nice sparkle to it, *no*?"

I let out the breath I was holding and said, "Yes, it does have a nice sparkle. And maybe we should just let it be to mark our first year together. We have a lot of issues to resolve before we become engaged, right?"

Marcelo shrugged his shoulders. "Yes, I suppose so, but nothing that we can't overcome. We love each other, right?"

"Yes! Yes, we do. Oh! I almost forgot! I have a present for you too!"

I reached into my purse and pulled out my gift. Marcelo removed the paper and lifted the small box top. He pulled out an I.D. bracelet, a thick silver chain with his name engraved on main link.

"Do you like it?" I asked.

"Yes, I like it very much, but this most of cost a fortune!" He said repeating my earlier sentiments.

"Oh, don't worry, it's silver-plated. I couldn't afford the *real thing* either! Turn it over. I had something else engraved on the inside. Something unique to us, a little bit me and a little bit you."

He flipped over the link and read out loud, "I *amo* you-August 5, 1982."

Before we shared an anniversary kiss, he said, "I *amo* you *también*."

The Embassy

When I returned in October for another short visit, Marcelo informed me that a tea party had been arranged by his neighbor and English tutor, Mary. Although he was studying the language at school, Marcelo began taking private lessons with this delightful lady shortly after we began "dating." During his lessons, Marcelo revealed one of his main objectives for learning the English language. He explained about meeting "this *Yanqui*," our uncanny union, the trips back and forth, the letters that crossed the continents and Mary, being a romantic at heart, couldn't help but be charmed by the whole scenario. When Marcelo informed her of my arrival, Mary invited us to "take afternoon tea" accompanied of course, by her British husband Johnny.

Walking into their apartment was like walking into a parlor in an English cottage. The décor was classic Britannica and Johnny exemplified the look of the landed gentry. Thankfully, Marcelo had warned me about Johnny's habit of stealthily introducing a "spot of libation" into his Earl Grey. I wasn't taken aback when Johnny's charming British accent was slurred ever so slightly by the time the afternoon engagement was over. Our hostess reminded me a little bit of Mary Poppins, but her sugary sweetness was counteracted by her humor and cleverness. She was an avid novel reader and we compared notes on the many great classics we both had enjoyed. The couple attended monthly meetings of a local British poets' society and Marcelo and I were invited to attend the next gathering. We accepted, Marcelo slightly out of a sense of duty and I, out of sheer delight.

When we meet the group of authors and poets, we quickly realized that our story preceded our introduction. Mary, it seems, had elaborated on our already unusual tale and we had become the stuff of legends.

"Why, they are two star-crossed lovers!" exclaimed one of the attendees. "Just like Catherine and Heathcliff."

"Just like Jane Eyre and Mr. Rochester!" another member added.

Marcelo looked perplexed and said, "Who?"

Mary patted his arm maternally and said, "Like Romeo and Juliet."

I giggled in delight to the references of the legendary couples. Marcelo shuffled his feet back and forth and said, "We are not *that* melodramatic."

Apparently, the poets' society disagreed with his assessment. Before returning back home to California, Mary invited us back up to her apartment for tea. We enjoyed our visit and right before we said our goodbyes, Mary presented us with a poem that she and her friends composed. They were so moved by our story, Mary explained, that they felt the need to put pen to paper. They were certain that our love story would come to a happy ending. It was a lovely gesture and we were truly moved by their skill and thoughtfulness. We however, were not quite so certain of a happy ending. With so many obstacles, it would be a difficult journey. My October visit had come to an end and I boarded yet another plane back home.

A significant component was lacking in our relationship: Marcelo had yet to come to America. Albeit resolute in his attempts to obtain a visa, he failed each and every time. Marcelo's uncle accompanied him to the American Embassy and offered his personal assurances, showing financial records and bank statements, proving that his nephew had no reason to immigrate to the United States. He was willing to vouch for Marcelo's return to Argentina. It was not acceptable; they were turned away.

It was early in November when through one of his letters I heard the Embassy's decision. I had lost my patience. True to form, I thought that I could handle the situation better myself, so I called Marcelo and asked if I could come down for a long weekend. After all, Thanksgiving was coming up and I had a few days off. This time, I did call The Argentina Family and told them I was coming. It was not worth the guilt and stress of trying to keep my trip a secret. I arrived in Buenos Aires on November 25, 1982. Marcelo picked me up at the airport and thankfully; there were no issues with Customs. We went straight to the American Embassy, because as was normally our case, there was no time to lose!

Driving down the familiar cobble stone streets of Buenos Aires in an over packed city bus; quintessential Argentine sights and sounds overwhelmed all of my senses. The careless bus driver abruptly turned a corner and I was practically tossed out of my seat. As I adjusted my clothing and sat myself upright, I saw the American flag, *my* flag, flying proudly in front of the embassy. Albeit a corny emotion, there was no denying the lump in my throat when I saw the building that belonged to *me*. I entered the embassy with an overwhelming sense of patriotism and satisfaction. I felt like I was home. Marcelo and I walked in, by-passed the line of Argentine applicants and walked straight up to a window labeled "American Citizens."

"Good afternoon, how may I help you?" The young man asked politely.

"Hi," I said reaching across the counter to shake his hand. My name is Mirta Trupp and I am an American citizen. I'd like to speak to someone about getting a Tourist Visa for my friend." I replied in my most *Don't-Rain-On-My-Parade* tone.

The young man looked me up and down and asked me for my passport. I handed it over and smiled. "Is there anyone in particular I should speak with? Can we begin the paperwork?"

"I'm very sorry Miss Trupp, but your friend has been here before I believe and has been declined." The young man looked over my shoulder and shook his head at Marcelo.

"Look, this is not such a big deal. He only wants to come for a few weeks' vacation."

"Again, I'm sorry to say that there is nothing I can do for you at this time."

Marcelo looked at me as if to say, "I told you so." That look was all I needed to prompt me into overdrive.

"Is there someone else I can talk to? May I speak to the Consul?"

"Miss Trupp, I'm sure you realize that this is a holiday weekend. We are short of staff and the Consul is on vacation."

"I'm sorry, but there must be someone left in charge. I really would like to speak to whoever is *in charge*," I said very nearly girding myself for battle.

With great dramatic effort, the young man sighed and lifted his arm to reach for the phone. He whispered something into the receiver and then asked us to wait in the reception area. Marcelo and I sat down and I tried not to look too smug. *Now* we were getting somewhere. A few minutes passed and young woman came to the counter. We were waved up to meet her.

"Hello. My name is Mirta Trupp. Thank you for taking the time to meet with us. I am here to find out about getting a Tourist Visa for my friend here," I blurted out all in one breath.

"I'm sorry Miss Trupp, but we are not issuing visas at this time."

And I had thought I was getting somewhere. "I don't understand. His family is willing to vouch for him. What is the problem Miss…?"

"Elizabeth Danvers and I am truly sorry for…Excuse me, what did you say your name was?"

"My name is Mirta Trupp. Is there a problem?" My first thought was "Here we go again!" Could this have anything to do with the airport fiasco?

"Miss *Trupp*? I'm sorry, but…what school did you go to?"

"Uh, excuse me? What school? Do you mean which university?"

"No, no. Which junior high school did you go to?"

"I went to Sutter Junior High in California. I'm sorry Miss Danvers, what is this all about?" *Miss Danvers*? Where had I heard that name before?

"This is unbelievable, but *I know you* Miss Trupp. I think we met years ago at Sutter, actually, in Mrs. Michaels' Girls Glee Club. I was the student teacher in your class. You sat in the Alto section. Do you still sing? I remember how you enjoyed it."

"*Miss Danvers*? I can't believe it! This is incredible!" I turned to Marcelo and saw his puzzlement. He had understood most of the conversation, but it was *so incredible* that he doubted his interpretation.

"Miss Danvers," I said leaning over the counter, "Please… you really have to help us. Is there anywhere we could talk?"

She smiled and with a wave of her hand, showed us the way to her office. We walked past the young man who first attended us and I had to try very hard to wipe the smile off my face. Once seated in her office, I told Miss Danvers our entire story. All about Pan Am, the trips back and forth. She reacted as everyone else always reacted. *How romantic! Just like a modern day Romeo and Juliet!*

"Miss Danvers, as you see, our only intention is to spend some time together and for Marcelo to visit my home. He can only stay a few weeks. He'll come back after that and we will go back to our routine. His whole family is here. He is going to college…

"Miss Trupp, let me be perfectly frank. There are no special strings I can pull for you. We are not issuing Tourists Visas at this time however..." Miss Danvers took a deep breath and continued, "We can issue a Fiancé Visa - *if* that is something you are interested in."

"Fiancé Visa?" Both of us asked at the same time. "What is that?"

"Fiancé Visa or *Visa de Novios*...It means that you, sir, would be traveling to the United States as the engaged partner of Miss Trupp. You will be eligible for a work visa, but Miss Trupp, your parents will have to sign an affidavit indicating that your young man will not become a burden to the United States government. The stipulation requires that you marry within three months or he must return to Argentina."

"Miss Danvers, there has to be another way! We had no intention of marrying at this point. It's just a vacation in California, for heaven's sake."

"I'm sorry Miss Trupp, *Mirta*. There is no other way at this time. If you meet the requirements of the program, it is a legitimate option to consider." Miss Danvers handed me an application and stood up.

Marcelo and I shook her hand and thanked her for her time and consideration. She walked up back to the reception area and I turned to give her a hug. "It was truly extraordinary meeting you here Miss Danvers, after so many years and so far from home!"

"Mirta, it was lovely seeing you again. I wish you the best of luck. You two have an incredible story. I'm honored to have a small part in it!"

In shock, we barely spoke all the way home. Upon arriving at the apartment, Marcelo and I decided to talk with his parents and see how they felt about the issue. Anita and Bito did not think too long and hard on the subject. Considering the dire situation in Argentina, it wasn't a bad idea to look at all the options. Young people across the country were leaving, seeking out stability and security in other lands. In the end, they gave us their full support.

When I called my parents and informed them of the turn of events, it was completely different story. Papi was adamant that I come home and concentrate on completing my certificate program. He suggested that Marcelo stay in Buenos Aires and concentrate on his career as well. By the tone of his voice, I knew there was no convincing him otherwise, at least not on the phone thousands of miles apart.

A Ticket to Ride

I left Buenos Aires with a heavy heart. We had not made definitive plans, but we did promise ourselves that we'd think about all the repercussions. When I got on that plane and they closed the doors, I knew in my heart, that I had made my decision. I wanted to be with Marcelo. Needless to say, when I got back home, the main topic was the Fiancé Visa. Mami and Papi couldn't come to an agreement between themselves, let alone with me.

"Mirtita, do you understand what this would mean if you allow Marcelito come here with this visa?" Papi asked. "If he stays, you have to get *married.* Are you ready to get married?"

"No, we are not ready! Everything is happening out of sync! We just wanted to be in the same country *at the same time* for a couple of weeks! We were not planning on getting married, but..."

"But if you do get married just so that you can be together and it doesn't work out, you *have to get a divorce*! This is not a game!"

"Papi, I understand. But, I'm tired of going back and forth. If he can't come here, then I'll go there!"

"What?" Mami piped in. "What are you talking about? You would go to live to Argentina after all we have been through?

"Mami, I could live with Bobe Flora and find a job. It would just be temporary, of course. I saw lots of jobs advertised in the *Buenos Aires Herald* for Americans. Marcelo can study and finish school and then, we could revisit the subject of marriage."

"Ruben, I do not think this is a good idea. I do not think Mirtita should have to go to live in Argentina. This truly *is* madness!"

By this time, both Mami and I were in tears. The whole situation was out of control. Papi caved in. "Mirtita, if this is what you want, then go ahead and tell Marcelito to come. We will help in any way we can. We just want what is best for you."

"Papi that's just it, we don't know what is best for us. All we know is that we *just need time*."

A few weeks later, I was back on a Pan Am flight. It was December 24, 1982. I was lucky to get on the flight with all the last minute holiday travelers. The first thing that hit me when I stepped off the plane in Buenos Aires was the heat and humidity; next, came the realization that this could be the last time I had to travel to Argentina to see Marcelo. Since we decided to apply for the Fiancé Visa, Marcelo would be doing the traveling, *not me*.

Arriving in Buenos Aires on December 25th was an interesting experience. Most of the population was out of the city because of the insufferable heat. The grand majority of the remaining population was celebrating Christmas Day. Marcelo and I spent a lazy afternoon in the apartment, trying to keep cool and enjoying each other's company. Vicki accused us of being *dos viejitos* (two old people) but we didn't venture out until late in the evening when at last, a cool breeze alleviated the lethargic mood.

We walked block after block, commenting on how quiet the streets were except for the rustling of movie leaflets and political flyers promoting Raul Alfonsin as a presidential candidate. Naturally, shops were closed and the traffic was fairly light. When we happened upon an open cafe, we decided to pop in to share a slice of pizza. There was an elderly man, sitting alone under a barely-there string of Christmas lights and ceiling fan with a single, lonely blade. A waiter came out from the kitchen to greet us. He also was an older man, with a full head of gray hair and a weathered face. He cheerfully said, "*Feliz Navidad*" and told us to sit anywhere we liked. Choosing a table by the window, Marcelo and I sat down facing each other and held hands across the table. The old waiter came to take our order and asked, "What can I get you two love birds on this fine Christmas evening?"

Marcelo smiled at the term "love birds" and I blushed under his gaze. "Just a slice of pizza and two sodas please," he replied.

When the waiter returned with our order, he lingered and looked deliberately at the both of us. Marcelo and I just smiled back at the old man, thinking maybe he was lonely and missing his family. He suddenly blurted out, "You two are very old souls."

Marcelo looked at him curiously and said, "Excuse me?"

"Yes," the old man said, "It's a good match," and with that, he walked away.

Although it was a peculiar interchange between complete strangers, somehow it seemed to fit right in with all the other bizarre occurrences we experienced in our transcontinental romance. We spent the next two weeks talking and planning, organizing and yes, even arguing. We gave ourselves the luxury to argue, secure in the knowledge that we would have time to make up and move on.

Although originally Marcelo refused to accept any money from my parents, he came to admit that under his current circumstances, there was no other way. While there was quite a bit of speculation about Argentina's future, his friends urged him to accept the money for the ticket, to get out of Argentina and not to look back. I was grateful for their help because I had been hearing about Argentina's recovery for the last 20-odd years. When had there *not* been speculation about Argentina's future? I understood that

Marcelo and his friends were anxious to see what Raul Alfonsin, the presidential candidate for the *Radicales, (*the equivalent to America's Democratic Party) would be able to accomplish. If elected, Alfonsin would inherit a platter full of problems, the biggest nightmare being the financial collapse. In addition to the economic depression, Alfonsin promised to hold the militia accountable for their crimes against the people of Argentina. His stance on Human Rights and his disdain for the *Peronista* party was inspirational. Yet it was almost too good to be true, and many young people, jaded after years of disillusionment, continued with their plans of immigrating.

Marcelo's friends were adamant that he accept my parents offer; the plane fare was his proverbial ticket to ride. The only opposition came from Hernán, a friend with another proposal. Instead of flying, he suggested that they travel by train across South America, Central America and finally, reach the United States. Hernán had a girlfriend in Mexico and he was eager to implement his dream of crossing the Pan American Highway. Marcelo immediately took to the idea. It was reminiscent of his adventures in Bolivia when he traveled there as young boy.

I was not as eager, to say the least. "Are you insane?" I shrieked at both of them. "Don't you realize that most of

Central America is in the middle of guerilla warfare-and what about Brazil? You are willing to risk *your life?*"

Poor Marcelo didn't have much of a chance. His parents weren't too thrilled with the train idea either. Hernán would have to make the trip on his own. We found out much later that Hernán did implement his plan and began traveling across the continent. When he reached Peru however, the military police "politely" asked him to return to his country and find other modes of transportation to Mexico.

Marcelo purchased his ticket and I visited The Argentina Family saying my goodbyes with a heavy heart, feeling the strain of the distance that would soon be between us. Marcelo and I celebrated a bittersweet New Year's Eve with his family and friends. When I left on January 6th, one day short of my 21st birthday, I knew that I'd see Marcelo again in less than two weeks; our parting was full of excitement and anticipation. But inwardly I knew myself to be a coward. I was glad that I wouldn't have to be in the airport when he had to say *his* goodbyes.

Hit the Ground Running

It was a dream! *It had to be a dream* I was driving in LAX to pick up Marcelo. What a glorious day! The moment finally arrived; January 20, 1983, the day I would drive Marcelo home on the 405 and point out the San Bernardino Mountains. I'd show him *my* mountain. I point out the Hollywood Sign and the freeway exits to the famous California coast. I'd have the radio turned on, the windows turned down and the cool Santa Monica air would come breezing through as we drove down the Ventura Highway. I had a picture in my mind; it was the classic Southern California T.V. commercial.

When he finally cleared Customs, I spied him sauntering down the now-familiar escalator, wearing a new pair of Wranglers, a blue-jean jacket and his guitar case strapped across his chest. He had one suitcase, and only $50.00 in his wallet, but across his face, was the biggest smile I had ever seen. What a moment for us! I hoped he felt the "welcome home" within my hugs and kisses.

Mami, Papi and Daniela were waiting anxiously at home. Mami prepared a lovely meal. We were all on our best behavior and most importantly; we were all avoiding the subject of the Fiancé Visa. The subject *Mami* wanted to speak of was work. Poor Marcelo hadn't even had the chance to unpack and Mami unleashed her surprise. If Marcelo was up for it, she had a job waiting for him. Unbeknownst to Papi or me for that matter, Mami had been accessing the "Argentina network," asking friends and family for work for "Mirtita's *novio*." The Saban family had a locksmith business and they were looking for help. Marcelo hadn't even had a chance to unpack; the effects of jet lag were just settling in, but of course he accepted the offer. The sooner he paid back my parents, the happier he'd be.

Marcelo settled down in Papi's office, the spare room. He was just one door down the hall from me, but with Papi's hawk eyes glaring down upon us, we might as well have been on separate continents once again. And with Dani, Marcelo and I sharing one bathroom, it was almost like having a messy brother living down the hall, rather than an amorous suitor. We did manage to spend some time together and we visited the typical California tourist sites. I also slowly began introducing him to my family and friends.

Jorge and Armando gave their brotherly approval, but not before they supplied Marcelo with childhood stories and familial anecdotes, such as the time when ten-year-old Mando had to improvise while babysitting his toddler cousin. I feigned embarrassment when Mando animatedly described how he had to swap my dirty diaper for a pair of his tidy-whities. When Marcelo and Horacio first met, I admit, I was a little worried. Horacio had been ruthless with his constant teasing about our long distance "love affair" and Marcelo had been green with jealousy regarding our close-knit friendship. I should not have wasted one moment of worry about the two of them. They immediately became great friends and I became the third wheel!

Although initially Marcelo had accept the job with Cesar Saban, he eventually branched out on his own and found work in the electronics field. It was just another stepping stone that allowed him to taste the possibilities that this country had to offer. In fact, it was pleasant surprise to see how naturally he adapted. An easygoing guy to begin with, Marcelo just seemed to go with the flow; learning a new language and getting accustomed to all things American. I would tease him and say that he must have been a *Yanqui* in a past life, but with all kidding aside, it was a relief to see him taking things in stride and progressing each and every day.

The sense of normalcy that we craved continued to evade us. Although we were finally living in the same country, we were awkwardly living under the same roof with my family. We were thrown into a domestic routine before having the chance to experience a genuine courtship. When returning from an evening out, Marcelo would play act-pretending that he was dropping me off after a date. He'd jokingly say, "I'll call you tomorrow, ok love?" Yeah, right…our conversations were usually more like, "Can you hurry up? I need to get into the bathroom and don't forget to throw your dirty socks in the clothes hamper!"

Time was ticking by and in a blink of an eye, our three months were up; there was no getting around the subject of Marcelo's visa. Papi had taken his bright red marker and circled the date on the calendar. When we finally all sat down in the kitchen to discuss the issue, my face was as white as the Formica on the kitchen table. Papi laid down the law; either get married or go home. He had nothing against Marcelo, he made that clear, but he thought the whole idea was a mess from the beginning. Marcelo admitted to my parents that we were not ready to get married. We were not financially able to take on that responsibility and more importantly we were not emotionally ready.

"Fine, fine, then there's no problem," my father granted, "We will call the airlines and schedule your flight back home."

That's when I jumped in. "Papi, you left Argentina to make something of yourself in this country. Marcelo is just getting started; *we* are just getting started. If he goes back, then I will have to go back with him."

With Papi clenching his jaw tight and my tears flowing freely now beyond any hope of restraint, Marcelo calmly began speaking. "I have been discussing the matter with our friends. We can get married, a civil ceremony with everything done properly and meet the requirements of the Fiancé Visa."

"What are you talking about? If you get married, then you get married! That's all I'm asking you do," Papi rumbled.

"What? No! Ruben, we need time to plan the wedding!" Mami cried. "Aren't we going to give Mirtita a wedding *como la gente*?" (a decent or acceptable wedding)

"Wait a moment Lina." Marcelo interjected. "As we said, we are not *ready* to get married. Mirta wants her traditional wedding. I want to make sure that we have enough money to live on. This is what I'm proposing: I will continue to work and set aside money. Mirta will do the same, but we will continue to live here, as we are. As far as the law goes, by having the civil marriage we are following the rules with honest intentions; but we will not live as husband and wife until we get married in a temple."

"Marcelito, this is insanity! I've never heard of such a thing. I do not agree with anything you are saying. You are going to get married and go to sleep alone in my office? *Why*?"

"I want to start off on the right foot; I want to have a stable job and have a nice apartment. We just need a little more time; the civil ceremony will buy us some time to prepare for our future. Look, Mirta and I have been sacrificing since we met each other. A little more won't hurt us."

"Mirtita, you will be a *wife* when you sign those papers," Mami said softly, holding back her own flood of tears.

"Ma, I can't be a wife if I am not *a bride* first. I won't feel like a bride until Marcelo and I are standing under the *chuppah,* just like you did with Papi, just like all the others before me in The Argentina Family."

We were officially married on April 15, 1983 in front of a Justice of the Peace in a seedy part of downtown Los Angeles. It was all above board and neatly accomplished, and yet, as we left the office and walked to our car, not one word was spoken between us. It was not until we were on the freeway and heading back home, that I began to cry. Marcelo reached over and grabbed my hand.

"This day never happened. We will not remember it as our anniversary. It was just a day of legalities, just like in Argentina. People get married *por civil,* through the Civil Registry and then if they want to, they have their religious ceremony. We won't be married until I see you in your wedding dress and we walk up to the *chuppah* together."

And that is exactly what occurred. We were legally married, but when we went home that evening Marcelo went to his room and I went to my mine. A few months later,

Marcelo invited me to a dinner date. I was told to dress up, but I wasn't told where we were going. Heading south on the 405, I tried to imagine where he was taking me, but quickly gave up realizing that it would be impossible to guess. We eventually found ourselves in downtown Los Angeles in front of the Top of Five building. Marcelo and I had visited the luxury towers before, but only to peruse the city's skyline from the famous rotating bar. When he escorted me to the main restaurant, I couldn't help but think that this was way out of our league.

Seated amongst the other elegant diners, we splurged on a lavish meal. The waiter came to clear the dishes and to offer us treats from a tempting dessert tray. With a clean table and the waiter off to collect our crème bruleé, Marcelo took the opportunity to remove a small velvet box out of his coat pocket. I was blushing ferociously and I thought my heart would burst out of my chest. We hadn't discussed engagement rings, at least not since our anniversary when Marcelo ingenuously purchased the flower ring. Considering our financial circumstances, I thought we'd have to bypass the tradition all together.

As Marcelo opened the box and asked me with a huge grin on his face, "Will you marry me?" the waiter reappeared. There was an audible gasp as our fellow diners realized that the waiter had interrupted a romantic yet, very public, scene.

The mortified waiter quickly retreated and Marcelo laughed. The diners tried not to look as he slipped the ring on my finger and sealed the deal with a kiss. It was a beautiful ring, also shaped in the form of a flower but with a lovely diamond in the center, instead of a piece of cut glass. I was curious to know when Marcelo had the time to go looking for the unusual ring. Apparently, my good friend Sona and her jeweler fiancé were more than happy to help him with his selection. I felt giddy with the romance of the proposal and the extravagance of the evening.

We worked hard and soon, our savings account began to show the fruits of our labor. My parents offered to pay for our dream wedding and the four of us contemplated on returning to Argentina for the event. There were numerous enticements to having the wedding in Buenos Aires. We would be surrounded by The Argentina Family, which now of course, included all of Marcelo's relatives and our friends. The money exchange was ideal and weighed heavily on the "pro" side of the debate. Considering we were talking about a colossal Argentine wedding, complete with *sandwichitos de lomo* as a "snack" around three o'clock a.m. and the *cafecitos con media lunas* as a parting breakfast treat, the difference between the dollar and weak peso was very tempting. However, the idea was soon shut down when relatives began playing devil's advocate. The current economic situation was again (*still?*)

very unstable; no merchant would honor estimates or down payments. Even with a signed contract, on the day of the wedding they might demand further compensation. *Not honor a contract?* Papi immediately informed us that he could not and would not pay for the wedding in Argentina. So, our plans had to change. Marcelo and I would purchase the plane tickets for his parents and siblings to attend our wedding in America.

We were not affiliated with a temple but after attending our friends' wedding, Marcelo and I agreed that we liked the synagogue and decided to find out if they would cater to nonmembers. We set up an appointment to discuss our situation with the rabbi. The elderly man was very kind and he listened patiently as we explained our long distance, whirlwind courtship and more to the point, our current marital status. At the conclusion of my monologue, Marcelo and I prepared ourselves for his response.

"Why, this is like a modern day Romeo and Juliet, but with a happy ending!" he said merrily with his soft, German accent.

"Yes, Rabbi, that's what everyone says," I giggled girlishly.

"But if you are married, my dear, why are you not actually living as a married couple?"

"Rabbi, I don't know if I can explain this. Our courtship was unique; our time together was rushed. We had to deal with the distance and what it would mean to our families if one of us moved away. We had to deal with economic obstacles, delays due to health reasons, and immigration regulations. We had to focus on everything except for the one thing that was most important, our relationship. We took a chance; went on our gut feelings. Maybe deep down, we knew things would work out, but we *just couldn't be rushed.*"

"But my dear, *you are* married!"

"Rabbi, I want the wedding of my dreams. I want family and friends celebrating with us. And more importantly, I want the *chuppah*, the prayers and the vows of my religion."

"Are you an observant family, my dear?"

"No Rabbi, I wouldn't say that either of our families are observant, but I am trying to learn as much as I can, and on our wedding day, I want us to be surrounded by our traditions so that we can start off on the right foot. That's what we both want. Actually, I think that was our bond from the beginning. We saw in each other a partner that shared the same culture, the same heritage and the same goals."

"Very well my dear. I think you explained it very nicely. Now, let us set the date!" He opened his calendar and started making notes. He picked one date and then mumbled something about it being during *Pesach*, then circling another set of dates he turned to us, "Since *you are already married*, and I promise that I won't mention it again, but in the wedding ceremony you see – I will not be able to say "By the powers vested in me by the State of California" etc. I will only say, "By the laws of Moses and the people of Israel…"

Marcelo and I looked at each other and smiled. "Rabbi, *that's* exactly what this wedding is about."

The Culmination and the Beginning

With a lot of hard work and dedication, Marcelo and I saved enough money to rent and furnish our first apartment and to bring his parents and siblings to California for the wedding. On April 7, 1984, we were, *once and for all,* married surround by loving family and friends. My two grandmothers, who were able to make the long journey, represented The Argentina Family. They led the procession and regally walked down the aisle accompanied by my cousin Fabian. Our wedding party made up of dear friends and treasured cousins, included Marcelo as a groomsman, Valeria as a bridesmaid and Mando's youngest daughter as the flower girl. Soon, Marcelo and I stood underneath the *chuppah* with our parents and siblings at our side. The *chazan* chanted from the *ketubah* (marriage contract) and the rabbi began to speak. I had no way of knowing that the next few phrases would stick with me throughout my life.

"As you came up to this *bimah*," he said, "you ascended to stand together under the *chuppah*, the symbol of your new home. Your ascent to the pulpit is symbolic of the spirit with which you enter into your married life. You see, marriage, in order to be successful, must be kept on a higher level. There will be times of trouble; *we all* have times of sorrow and pain. But allow yourselves to create a spiritual plateau so that nothing can *interfere* with what brought you together. Take strength from your love, let it guide you and when you find yourself burdened with outside negativity, allow yourself to ascend once more to this singular moment where you pledged your love."

Marcelo and I overwhelmed by the affection and the sense of tradition emanating within the walls of the sanctuary. We seemed to float through the prayers, pledges and blessings. The ceremony was over in a blink of an eye and when Marcelo's heel shattered the glass, a resounding "Mazal Tov" brought us back to reality.

The reception was held high up in the hills overlooking the San Fernando Valley. My mother had hired Attila, a Ukrainian videographer she encountered one night at a reception held at The Odessa restaurant. During the wedding ceremony, Attila was stationed subtly behind flowers or columns, so his presence went unnoticed. During the reception however, people paused and smiled as if he was the photographer, the advent of videotape being a rarity amongst the majority of guests. Fabian marched in front of a group of posing revelers and laughed, "This is not a photo. Talk! Move around!" Attila, who apparently had a video camera shoved into his hands with no professional instruction as soon as he stepped off the place from *Novy Buk*, videotaped the entire event- no editing, no special effects-unless of course, the tilting of the camera from one side to another counted as special effects. Still, Mami earned points for being one of the first *Arr-hen-tinas* to have her daughter's wedding captured on tape for time immemorial.

Another one of my mother's innovations pertained to the wedding party and our procession into the main reception room. Once the guests had been seated, the wedding party was announced. Two by two, we entered the salon to the sounds of…"*Open a new window, open a new door*!" Dani had participated in her high school production of *Auntie Mame* and Mami thought by using this inspirational tune; she was inconspicuously given a nod to her younger daughter and allowing Danielita a moment in the spotlight. I didn't mind; I was floating in seventh heaven and wouldn't have minded if it were *Mrs. Lewis* from Hazeltine Avenue belting out the anthem.

We shared the evening with all the incredibly special people that made up our family in America. All my *tíos* and *tías* and assorted cousins were in attendance. Half of the *Hebraica* club was there as well and Mami was delighted that she could reciprocate in kind. We had been attending their weddings and baby showers for years and finally today, Mami was their proud hostess. The Israelis were included in the festivities, as was my friend, Dodie Friedman and her mother. Mr. Olafson attended as well and I couldn't have been happier or more honored.

My parents gave us an incredible send off. And if it wasn't the wedding of the decade according to the Hollywood gossip papers, it certainly made a big impression amongst the Argentina crowd in the San Fernando Valley. It was quite a coup to contract The Latin Connection as the entertainment for the evening. The band was known to play in only the best social events throughout the Spanish speaking community, especially in *la colectividad* (the Jewish community). Their musical repertoire ranged from *tangos* and *milongas*, to *freilachs* and *nigguns* and back to salsas, sambas and meringues! My thoughts rambled back to the days when I wished for a sociologist's report on my *meshugana* family. What would the good doctor say about our dancing routines? When they played *Heveinu Shalom Alecheim*, our steps seemed instinctively to sway with some *cumbia* flair. When they played *Cuando El Amor Llega Así*, without missing a beat, we ended up in *hora* formation. There was no escaping the final analysis; it was in our blood!

Marcelo and I danced each and every dance throughout the evening and when it was time to leave the hall, our good friend Horacio drove us to the Sheraton International Hotel in a borrowed white Cadillac, appropriately decorated with a barrage of bridal paraphernalia. With my last Pan American ticket, we honeymooned in Argentina, sharing our happiness with the *bobes* and *zeides*, *tíos*, *tías*, *primos* and all of our friends. We were showered with love and blessings and good wishes, a glorious way to end one chapter of our lives as we began another.

Almost two years later, we announced my pregnancy right before midnight on New Year's Eve, 1986. With glasses filled with champagne, everyone began offering toasts for prosperity and good health in the year to come. Of course, the traditional toast, "*Para los presentes y ausentes*" was offered up with teary eyes and melancholy. Marcelo, sensed the shift in the mood, raised his glass high and declared, "Next year, there will be one more of us!" It took a moment for everyone to react when suddenly our parents and siblings surrounded us. There were shouts of "Mazal Tov!" and tears of joy.

When the family began discussing the possibilities of needing a *mohel* to conduct a *bris* (circumcision), I grew a little anxious, but I didn't bolt. Something finally had clicked into place for me. Maybe it was a case of hormones working overtime or some maternal instinct prompting me to act. I knew that I'd be able to nourish and nurture my child, but I didn't feel prepared in the least to take care of this baby's spiritual needs. Due to a lack of knowledge, I had spent years challenging or worse, stifling my true heritage, but now I sensed the need to be *connected*. I was ready to embrace the gift that my ancestors willed to me. How could I turn my back on such a legacy? A legacy upheld by people who gave up their homes and their families, and sometimes, *their lives* in order to secure freedom and prosperity for future generations.

The acknowledgment that I was light years away from being "observant" didn't deter my enthusiasm. It became clear to me that the spiritual journey should be personal-meaningful to each unique individual. Even though Judaism was meant to be experienced as a community, each person had their own link to God. I recalled my experiences in the temple watching the men wrap themselves up in their *tallitot*. I thought it was odd at that time, but I realized now what a magical place they created. Underneath the protective covering of a prayer shawl, a person could shut out the world and commune with their soul and with their Creator. When performing acts of *tzedakah*, a person could achieve a sense of connection as well. These were things that *I* could do. I could perform acts of charity and kindness. I could study my history and learn the prayers. I could sing the music of my people and in doing so, touch not only my soul, but reach out to others as well. *I* could make Judaism meaningful and relevant to me and hopefully, to my future family.

With this new goal in mind, I prepared to receive our first child. Mami and Anita announced that they were going to host a baby shower in our honor. The party was to be held at our home away from home, Two Guys from Italy. Sixty-five women were invited, all close family and friends from the tightly knitted cluster of immigrants. Vicki was elected to be my chauffer for the day and I gratefully accepted the offer. The two grandmothers-to-be conspired with their eager accomplice to delay my arrival so that I would make a proper entrance, *Arr-hen-tina* style- I was over an hour late! I fought against my innate urge to point out the obvious social blunder; I thought it beyond rude to be late to my own party!

I was quickly won over by the warm greetings, the delicious food and the array of gifts piled high and charmingly decorated. The chatter and chaos produced by a room full of *Arr-hen-tina* women was overwhelming, but in truth, I was touched by everyone's kindness and generosity. Mami and Anita had outdone themselves thinking of every detail, however it wasn't until the waiters brought in dessert that *I lost it.* The inscription on the cake threw me over the emotional edge. How could I have forgotten? We were surrounded by their love. The cake read, "Welcome Baby, We Love You, The Argentina Family."

Family…the word conjured up a myriad of emotions. I had family seemingly all over the world: America, Argentina, Israel, Russia, and who knew where else. Whether we saw each other every day, once a year, or once in a lifetime, we were connected, we formed a link. My grandmothers told me that whatever we would go, we would go with their love and God's blessings.

I had to accept these blessings and let go of the struggle; my family, with all their *meshugas,* with all the shouting and laughter, drama and commotion, was what made me, **me.** Complicated, unique, caring, headstrong, *Arr-hen-tina*, American, Jewish…*loved.*

Photo Album

December 8, 1962; Admitted into the United States

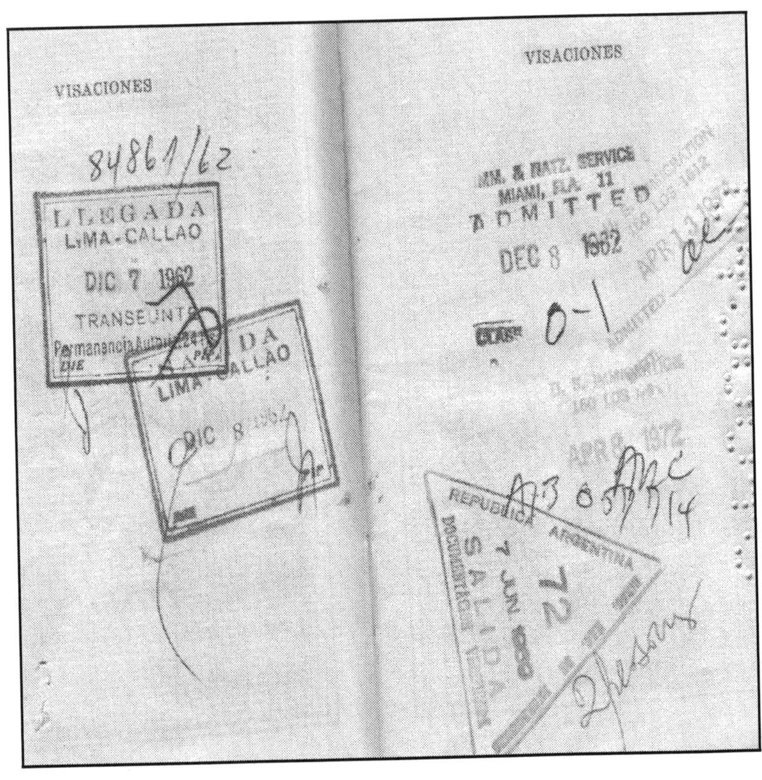

Arriving at Ezeiza International Airport; March 18, 1972

I took this picture while we waiting for our "Stand-By" status.

PAN AM; Buenos Aires, Argentina

We arrived *criollo* style.

Five passports before the age of twenty-two.

During my detainment at Ezeiza International Airport,
I was stripped of my Argentine citizenship.

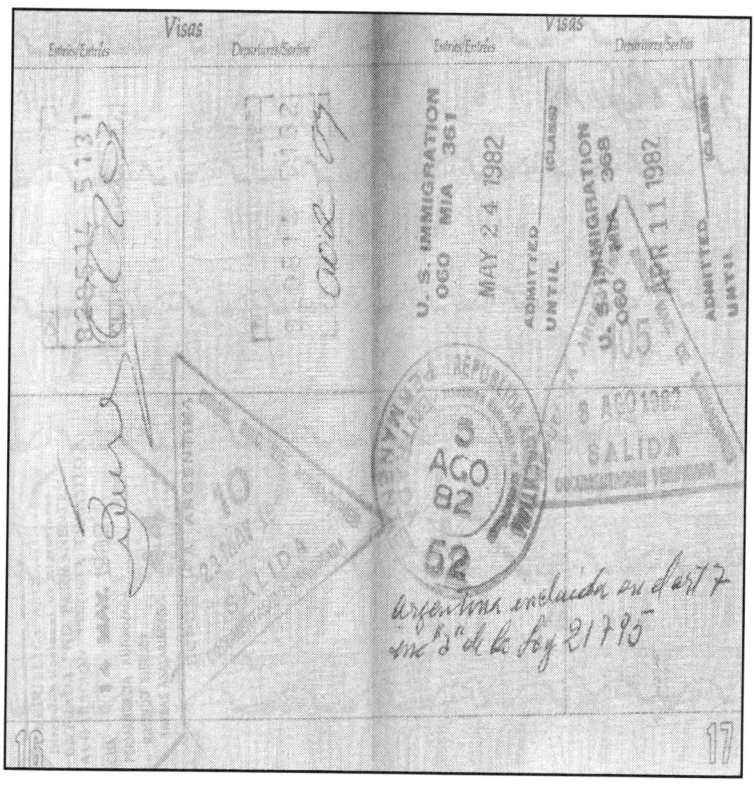

The hand written statement was included on a following trip attesting to the fact that I *was* Argentine, per article 7, line item "3" of law 21.795. - Go figure.

A sample of the letters I received from Marcelo.

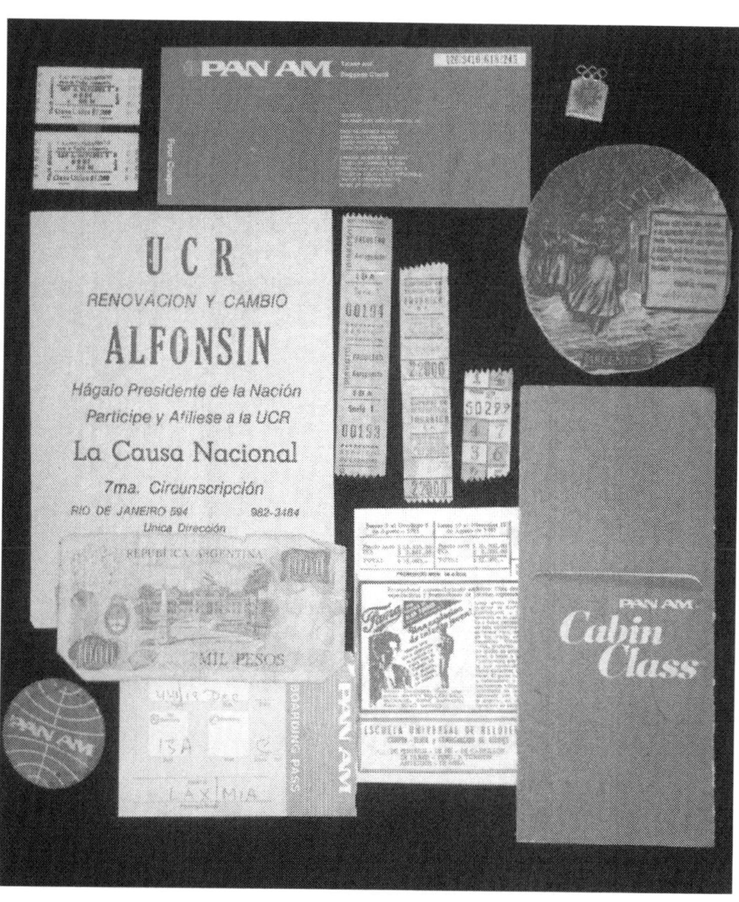
PAN AM
UCR
RENOVACION Y CAMBIO
ALFONSIN
Hágalo Presidente de la Nación
Participe y Afiliese a la UCR
La Causa Nacional
7ma. Circunscripción
RIO DE JANEIRO 594
982-3484
Unica Dirección
REPUBLICA ARGENTINA
MIL PESOS
BOARDING PASS
PAN AM
PAN AM
Cabin Class

Faustino's *Canasta de Moisés*; 30 years later.

Our Chuppah

We were presented with this cake at our baby shower.

It was sent With Love, the Argentina Family.

Para los presentes y los ausentes, and for those yet to come.

Made in the USA
Lexington, KY
05 August 2012